The Finest Judges
Money Can Buy

OTHER BOOKS BY CHARLES ASHMAN

Angela
The People vs. Angela Davis
Kissinger: The Adventures of Super-Kraut

The Finest Judges Money Can Buy
And Other Forms of Judicial Pollution

by Charles R. Ashman

Nash Publishing, Los Angeles

Library of Congress Catalog Card Number: 73-83520
International Standard Book Number: 0-8402-1316-6

Published simultaneously in the United States and Canada
by Nash Publishing Corporation, 9255 Sunset Boulevard,
Los Angeles, California 90069

Printed in the United States of America

First Printing

*This book is dedicated to those judges
who have resisted the temptations of corruption,
avoided political influence
and consistently remained above moral compromise
in fact and in appearance.
Congratulations . . . to both of you.*

ACKNOWLEDGMENTS

This book would never have been were it not for the cooperation of court clerks, law librarians, and bar associations in the numerous jurisdictions noted. To Victor, Sandra, Linda and Susan, whose combined talents achieved monumental research and investigation, many thanks. Finally, I must thank a courageous publisher determined to allow the truth to reach the public.

As in all other things, printed or otherwise, Pamela and Shireen are directly responsible for our achievements.

Contents

Prologue *3*

Judge John B. Tally *3*

Chapter One: Black-Robed Mafia *11*

Justice Mitchell D. Schweitzer *12*
Judge Edward J. DeSaulnier *21*
Judge Vincent R. Brogna *21*
Judge Ralph DeVita *24*
Judge Anthony Guiliano *27*
Judge James DelMauro *29*
Judge John N. Stice *31*
Judge Raulston Schoolfield *34*

Chapter Two: The High Cost of Justice *41*

Judge Martin T. Manton *42*
Judge J. Warren Davis *48*
Judge Albert W. Johnson *53*
Judge Robert W. Archibald *57*

Justice Nelson S. Corn   *59*

Justice Earl Welch   *59*

Justice Napoleon Bonaparte Johnson   *59*

Justice Wayne W. Bayless   *64*

Justice Joseph P. Pfingst   *65*

Almost-Justice Seymour R. Thaler   *67*

Chapter Three: Bargains   *75*

Judge Halsted L. Ritter   *77*

Judge Glenn J. Sharpe   *79*

Judge J. Cedric Conover   *80*

Judge William M. A. Romans   *81*

Judge Maynard B. Clinkscales   *82*

Judge Stanley J. Polack   *83*

Magistrate Alfred F. Orsini   *84*

Magistrate Mark Rudich   *85*

Judge Louis W. Kizas   *91*

Judge James E. Murphy   *94*

Justice Michael M. D'Auria   *95*

Judge Henderson Graham   *97*

Judge Frank O. Alonzo   *101*

Judge John Lodwick, Jr.   *104*

Justice Aaron G. Windheim   *107*

Justice Robert Maidman   *107*

Chapter Four: The Sensuous Judge   *111*

Judge Edward A. Haggerty, Sr.   *112*

Judge Floyd S. Sarisohn   *115*

Judge John D. Hasler   *120*

Judge J. Allen O'Conner   *123*

Judge James H. Edgar   *125*
Magistrate James Lee Blodgett   *125*

Chapter Five: Court Jesters   *127*

Judge John Pickering   *128*
Judge James H. Peck   *131*
Judge Harold L. Louderback   *133*
Judge David Copland   *134*
Judge Loren H. Hullinger, Jr.   *135*
Judge Howard W. McLaughlin   *137*
Judge J. Miles Pound   *138*

Chapter Six: The Corrupters   *141*

Judge Frank R. Franko   *142*
Magistrate Martin L. Pagliughi   *145*
Judge C. Woodrow Laughlin   *149*
Judge Charles Swayne   *152*
Judge Louis L. Friedman   *154*
Judge Edwin L. Jenkins   *157*
Magistrate E. David Keiser   *160*
Judge L. D. Tallent   *162*
Judge Melvin H. Osterman   *163*
Judge Benjamin H. Schor   *170*

Chapter Seven: Current Bench Warmers   *173*

Judge Stephen S. Chandler   *174*
Judge Malcolm V. O'Hara   *176*
Judge Ernest J. Somers   *180*
Judge Neville Tucker   *181*
Judge Bernard Klieger   *182*

Judge Ross J. DiLorenzo   *184*
Judge William F. Suglia   *186*
Judge Bernard B. Glickfield   *187*
Judge Leland W. Geiler   *189*

Chapter Eight: The Chicago Three   *193*

Justice Roy J. Solfisburg   *195*
Justice Ray I. Klingbiel   *195*
Judge Otto Kerner   *200*

Chapter Nine: Article I, Section III   *207*

Justice Samuel Chase   *208*
Justice Abe Fortas   *211*
Justice William O. Douglas   *220*

**Chapter Ten: Playing Musical Judges—
The Selection of Our Judiciary**   *225*

Epilogue: Where Do We Go From Here?   *251*

Affidavit of Verification   *265*

**Appendix I: A Quick Reference
Guide to the Finest Judges Money Can Buy**   *269*

Appendix II: Canons of Judicial Ethics   *279*

**Appendix III: Articles of Impeachment
of Sir Francis Bacon, Lord Chancellor**   *297*

**Appendix IV: Retirement
and Removal of State Judges**   *303*

The Finest Judges
Money Can Buy

Prologue

I usually accept bribes from both sides so that tainted money can never influence my decision.

          —Sir Francis Bacon
          Lord Chancellor of England

American justice is choking on judicial pollution. The following cases are documented proof that it is no longer a question of occasional corruption, but a decided pattern of conflicts of interest, chronic bribery, profound abuse of office, loathsome nepotism, infamous sexual perversions and pernicious payoffs. The American public can no longer retain an attitude of vacant apathy as incorrigible corruption destroys the effectiveness of our system of justice. So what else is new!

There are many in life whose expertise and integrity we take for granted. At least we don't risk challenging them while they are doing their thing. The doctor in surgery, the lawyer in court, the TV repairman and the mother all escape stern scrutiny either because we are brainwashed as to their superiority or embarrassed to ask a question.

But one group in our society epitomizes the mysticism of superiority. The courtroom is his dominion. Our lives and property are his jurisdiction. We robe him in black and announce his arrival in medieval French incantations. He is physically elevated amidst ceremonial architecture further to enhance his exalted status in life. He presides. He listens. He sleeps. He administers. He punishes instantly for any minor deviation from the protocol of his sanctimonious court or any insult to his person, and he assumes an imperial air when he sentences. No one in our society, including the president, exercises equal summary power or more censorial prerogatives.

Unfortunately, we have never taken the trouble to establish an effective way to select judges. First, we have never been able to agree whether the public is intelligent enough to sift through political promises and elect qualified men and women to judge us, or whether other officials we've elected should be given the right to appoint the proprietors of justice. Second, even among those who have agreed whether elected or appointed judges are better, the methods of selection vary.

No judge is outrageously corrupt by himself. For every judge that money can buy there must be buyers and brokers. Most of the judicial corrupters are relatives of judges, practicing lawyers or their predatory intermediaries. All the bribes paid or tendered in any one year could undoubtedly eliminate much of the poverty that breeds the crimes that outrage America. And the cost of exposing and trying corrupt judges compounds society's debt.

In this country we believe, or at least claim to believe, in equality before the law. But those who have the money or the contacts, or both, exert a judicial pressure that eliminates equality and promotes a double standard of justice. For there are those who stand before the bar relying only on their lawyers and their hopes. And there are those whose cases are more clandestinely and hurriedly resolved by a fix.

In 1924 the American Bar Association promulgated the Canons of Judicial Ethics. Those appointed by Chief Justice William Howard Taft preambled their juridic decree by declaring that "ethical standards tend to become habits of life" and set forth a "reminder for judges indicating what the public has a right to expect from them." The judicial canons were merely the codification of moral guidelines that date back at least to Deuteronomy: "Thou shalt not respect persons, neither take a gift; for a gift doth blind the eyes of the wise, and pervert the words of the righteous." Unfortunately, since loading, the canons have fired mostly blanks.

We can no longer dismiss cases of corruption on the bench as isolated indiscretions. There are too many, too often. This book describes over seventy classic examples of judicial pollution. Unfortunately, for each case discussed there is a handful we have not included, and for each handful not included there are scores yet undiscovered.

Witness the dignified New England judge who paid the fine for a defendant appearing before him and then took him home for a sexual encounter—a peccadillo which the judge admitted. And, of course, there was the Louisiana judge who presided at the Kennedy-Shaw conspiracy trial. The jurist was later arrested for pimping, showing pornographic films, gambling and the rest. Scandal shattered the quiet life of the people of Oklahoma a few years ago when the majority of their own supreme court was convicted of having shamelessly wholesaled justice for years.

5

Recently, a former governor who had been appointed to the second highest appellate court in the nation was convicted and disgraced in Illinois. Judge Kerner had been the pinnacle of integrity, or at least he had appeared to be.

This past year one of New York's most distinguished statesmen climaxed his career of public service by his election to that state's supreme court. Weeks before he was to be sworn in, Justice-elect Seymour R. Thaler was indicted for "fencing" stolen United States Treasury bills worth a few hundred thousand dollars. Thus, the citizens of New York were denied the unique experience of Thaler's judicial pronouncements.

The black-robed Mafia is an even more mercenary intrusion in American justice than its Sicilian counterpart. Among the finest judges money can buy are those who have peddled justice for payoffs and yielded to pressure from organized crime and other "benevolent fraternities." One of the most common offenses among judges who enforce laws one day and ignore laws the next, is income tax evasion. Their defenses are novel. In one case, the judge claimed he was so busy trying cases that he simply forgot to pay his taxes for five years.

Scandalous corruption seems to be contagious among judges in certain states. Several members of the Oklahoma Supreme Court were charged with bribery, income tax evasion and conspiracy to bribe each other. And similar patterns may be noted in New York, New Jersey and Illinois.

Certainly the most shocking aspect of "the finest judges money can buy" is the casual reaction of the public and our state and federal officials to judicial corruption. It seems as if there is a reluctance to punish any judge for fear that the public will not lose its respect for all judges. Thus the punishment is directed at the community at large in the form of such mild disciplinary action against the guilty, that numerous judges found guilty of serious offenses continue to sit in judgment of us all.

There has recently been a rash of cases involving jurists accused of abusing criminal bond procedures for their bail-bondsmen friends. In no less than fifteen states, investigations have revealed violations of state bonding practices which enable the bondsmen, in effect, to determine if an accused criminal should be released. On June 11, 1973 the California Judicial Qualification Commission recommended only censure of two Los Angeles County judges who issued numerous blank, presigned release forms to close friends who happen to be bondsmen.

A seventeen-page report urged the California Supreme Court to "severely and publicly censure" Superior Judge Leopoldo Sanchez, and merely "censure" Municipal Judge Antonio E. Chavez.

Judge Sanchez remained on full salary but was not allowed to sit on the bench while his case was under study. And now, if the Supreme Court follows the Commission's recommendation, the effect will be that Sanchez received a six-months paid holiday as a result of the censure. In the meantime, he is back on the bench.

The Commission's investigation proved that a Los Angeles bondsman named Joey Barnum had used, and sold to other bondsmen, hundreds of blank forms signed by his friend, Judge Sanchez. The Judicial Commission decided that "what Judge Sanchez did appears to be the result of incredibly bad judgment and his inability to say 'no' to his friend, Joey Barnum."

One California lawyer reacted by promising that the next

time he has a case in front of Judge Sanchez he will offer a novel defense. He will argue that his client "just could not say 'no' to his friend and that is why he robbed the bank."

On occasion, judges have even been charged with crimes resulting in death. At the turn of the century, one of Alabama's more popular circuit judges, John B. Tally, conspired with his family to murder a neighbor who was having an affair with the judge's sister-in-law. The judge and his brother-in-law gunned down the offender and utilized the then modern railroad and telegraph to cover their tracks. The Supreme Court of Alabama, in a confusing decision, ruled that the popular Scottsboro jurist had not neglected his judicial duties by participating in the murder plot. Nevertheless, they found him guilty of aiding and abetting and removed him from the bench.

Politicians have attempted to impeach members of the Supreme Court of the United States. On only one occasion were they successful, but there have been resignations and lingering doubts. Some people are still devoted to impeaching Justice William O. Douglas.

And then there are those judges named in this book who are still sitting in judgment of others. This is so despite the judges' administrative and judicial problems.

Somewhere there is a former defendant whose right to freedom may have been abused by one of these judges now revealed to be a criminal himself. After talking with the finest judges money *cannot* buy and the lawyers who appear before them, we believe there is an answer.

Sir Francis Bacon authored much of the philosophy of temperate justice when he dominated the English Renaissance as the most gifted and eloquent of that nation's judges. He was revered as infallible while serving as Attorney General and Lord Chancellor of England. His ethical utterings are

8

preserved in legal textbooks, and his words are chiseled on the cornerstones of palaces of justice throughout the world.

Unfortunately, the chiseling did not stop there. Three years after he attained the highest judicial position in England, Sir Francis Bacon—philosopher, scientist and jurist *extraordinaire*—was impeached. The House of Commons determined he had accepted at least twenty-eight bribes. His defense was novel. Bacon claimed he took bribes from both sides, and so never allowed dirty money to influence his decisions. Parliament wasn't impressed, and he was sentenced to the Tower of London.

King James, in a moment of melancholy, pardoned him, but Bacon never returned to Parliament and was not allowed "within the verge of the court." Five years later he caught a cold while experimenting in refrigeration. He was stuffing a goose with snow. He died, but his humiliation and corruption live on.

Chapter One
Black-Robed Mafia

"We got judges on the payroll that can straighten it out—one, two, three."

—TOMMY GAMINDORRA
Joseph Colombo family

Those who claim there is no Mafia in this country are either disastrously ignorant or members in good standing. Organized crime cannot function without "organized justice."

In 1972 a trio of judges from New York and Massachusetts was implicated in a Senate crime investigation. All were accused of bribery. One was disbarred, one resigned and one is still sitting.

A federal investigation recently resulted in a score of indictments of New Jersey officials. Mayors, councilmen and judges were charged with bribery, conspiracy and tax evasion.

One judge went to prison, and another returned to a city job, off the bench, where he has again been indicted.

In the Midwest a trial judge was repeatedly lenient in

sentencing members of a particular burglary ring and then was charged with being the ringleader himself.

To lead their nefarious double lives, the black-robed Mafia abuses court personnel and compromises innocent colleagues. And how many more members are still to be discovered?

JUSTICE MITCHELL D. SCHWEITZER (NEW YORK)

In twenty-six years as a judge, Mitchell D. Schweitzer, at the age of sixty-six, had set records for the swift disposition of cases. Because of his efficiency and seniority, he was regarded as one of the most influential judges in the state of New York.

He was first elected to the bench in 1944 as a judge of New York City's municipal court. Ten years later, with the support of both the Democratic and Liberal parties, he was elected to the Court of General Sessions, which was later merged with the New York State Supreme Court.

Judges are theoretically supposed to rotate assignments. But in practice those with the most seniority are usually allowed to pick their own spots. Justice Schweitzer favored Division 30, where defendants who plead guilty are sentenced and where lawyers are assigned to represent indigents at the state's expense.

Some defense lawyers regarded Schweitzer's courtroom as a circus. "The judge shouts," one said, "and he snorts and he puffs and he cajoles frightened lawyers and their clients into copping pleas [pleading guilty] to save time. I dread every time I have to appear before him. But I must admit it is entertaining."

Another lawyer recalled being summoned to the bench by Justice Schweitzer and being angrily but quietly warned to have his client plead guilty or face the consequences. "He wrote a number on a piece of paper," the lawyer said. "The number was what my client was going to get if he insisted on being a wise guy and put the state to the expense of a trial that the judge felt would prove him guilty anyhow." But the lawyer refused and the trial was held. True to Justice Schweitzer's prediction, the accused was convicted and sentenced to the written number of years.

On another occasion, Schweitzer surprised his former Columbia Law School classmate New York District Attorney Frank Hogan, by ignoring objections made by the DA's office to the revocation and suspension of sentences imposed on a man who had been arrested sixteen times between 1947 and 1964 and convicted of three felonies.

The judge's conduct ceased to be "entertaining" in the fall of 1969 when an investigation of Schweitzer and several other city judges was started by U.S. Attorney Robert M. Morgenthau. A separate inquiry was started later by the New York State Joint Legislative Committee on Crime. No charges were ever brought.

But in the course of investigations by the U.S. Senate Permanent Investigations Subcommittee and the Joint Legislative Committee on Crime into the use of Speaker of the House of Representatives John McCormack's office by Nathan P. Voloshen, Justice Schweitzer's name began making the headlines. He was described by one witness as "the best judge money can buy."

Voloshen, a seventy-one-year-old "politician-lawyer," was accused of fixing criminal cases with prison and parole officials for income tax evaders and Mafia members. He had obtained access to the office of the Speaker of the House in Washington, D.C., through McCormack's chief aide, Dr. Martin Sweig. Voloshen blatantly operated his judicial brokerage firm right there on Capitol Hill.

Dr. Irving Helpert, a Dayton, Ohio, urologist, helped expose Voloshen and his associates. Helpert was accused of income tax evasion and gave Voloshen $300,000 to fix the case. Voloshen promised to mail him a receipt and keep him informed of progress. Helpert never heard from him again and was convicted, fined $15,000 and given a suspended jail sentence.

Another case involved Georgette Saffian, a French widow accused in New York of forgery and perjury in connection with an inheritance. She sent $5,000 to Voloshen through a friend, and her case was suddenly assigned to Justice Schweitzer's court. Then Mrs. Saffian started getting calls from Voloshen asking for more money. At one time he demanded $20,000, warning that if she didn't pay, she would get a long jail term. Disgusted and frightened, she went to the authorities instead.

Life magazine's inquiries uncovered literally dozens of fixed cases, near fixes and just plain shakedowns emanating from Voloshen's power base in his "congressional office." Voloshen offered the *Life* writer $50,000 to drop the story. But the now-defunct *Life* ran the article and suggested prosecution.

Voloshen was indicted January 13, 1970. Pleading guilty to conspiracy to defraud federal agencies, he was fined and given a suspended jail sentence on November 24, 1970.

Voloshen and Justice Schweitzer frequently saw each other socially. Schweitzer admitted to a long and close friendship dating back eight to ten years. But he told investigators he had no knowledge or suspicion of Voloshen's involvements and had seen no reason not to associate with him. In fact, he continued seeing Voloshen even after the indictment.

There is nothing illegal about a judge's meeting privately with a man under indictment. However, Canon 4 of the Canons of Judicial Ethics says, "A judge's official conduct should be free from impropriety and the appearance of impropriety; he should avoid infractions of law and his personal behavior, not only upon the bench and in the performance of judicial duties but also in his everyday life, should be beyond reproach."

Canon 17 says in part, "A judge should not permit private interviews, arguments or communications designed to influence his judicial action, where interests to be affected thereby are not represented before him except where provision is made by law for ex parte [with one side only] application." Canon 13 says in part that a judge "should not suffer his conduct to justify the impression that any person can influence him unduly or enjoy his favor." During the three months after Voloshen was formally accused, Schweitzer met with him privately at least five times.

On at least two other occasions, Justice Schweitzer and Voloshen met, ex parte (without the prosecution's being present), with the lawyers to discuss the cases of clients who later came before the justice and won releases from prison.

One of these meetings was held at the Orangerie Restaurant in Manhattan with a lawyer named Harry Blumenthal. Blumenthal was then representing Manuel Bello, a gangster linked by federal investigators to the Mafia. Bello was serving fifteen to thirty months in prison for trying to dispose of $100,000 in stolen securities.

Voloshen had unsuccessfully tried to influence New York Corrections Commissioner Russell G. Oswald about Bello's parole chances. Then Justice Schweitzer, who had sentenced Bello, ordered a hearing and allowed him to withdraw his guilty plea and then permitted him to plead guilty again, to the same charge. This time Schweitzer sentenced him to a shorter term which made him eligible for immediate release. Bello walked out of the courtroom a free man. Voloshen prospered.

Schweitzer tried to justify his action by contending that Bello had been suffering from heart trouble and that all legal motions for a rehearing had been properly made. But the judge's critics were given more ammunition.

Schweitzer and Voloshen's second meeting with a prisoner's counsel, a lawyer named Stanley Reiben, was held at the Pier 52 Restaurant. Reiben at the time represented Raymond Freda, who had pleaded guilty June 21, 1966, to unlawful entry, third-degree assault and carrying a dangerous weapon.

Freda had been sentenced by Justice Schweitzer to one year for unlawful entry and ten months each for the other two counts, to be served consecutively. At the time of the sentencing, Freda was already in federal prison serving a five-year term. In August 1968 he was released from the federal penitentiary at Lewisburg, Pennsylvania, and turned over to New York State to serve the local sentences. After serving the one year for unlawful entry, Freda moved, through Reiben, for resentencing on the two remaining counts.

On April 11, 1969, the case appeared on Justice Schweitzer's calendar; he ordered a stay on Freda's commitment until May twelfth and had him released on $1,200 bail. On May 21, 1969, Justice Schweitzer ruled that the consecutive sentences he himself had imposed were "improper" and revoked them, enabling Freda to remain free.

Another bizarre case involving Justice Schweitzer concerned Robert Friede. Friede was arrested on February 7, 1966, while sitting in his car. Police asked him for his driver's license; when he opened his wallet, two packets of heroin fell out. The police searched the car and discovered the body of Celeste Crenshaw in the trunk. She had died from a narcotics injection that Friede admitted having given her.

In court Friede said he didn't mean to kill Miss Crenshaw and pleaded guilty to second-degree manslaughter, possession of narcotics and violation of probation. Second-degree manslaughter is punishable by up to fifteen years, but Friede had a previous felony conviction and therefore faced a sentence of up to thirty years.

On April 15, 1966, Justice Schweitzer gave Friede a suspended sentence on the manslaughter and narcotics charges, but ordered a prison term of two and a half to five years for his violation of probation.

But Schweitzer's sentencing of Friede didn't end his involvement in the case. The next year the judge met privately with William Jaffe, a prominent lawyer who was also Friede's stepfather, to discuss the young addict's case. In his chauffeured Rolls Royce, Jaffe drove from New York at the invitation of the judge to the Schweitzer home in Scarsdale. They talked for more than an hour.

Friede's lawyers then wrote to Parole Commissioner Oswald, claiming Justice Schweitzer felt that, all things considered, Robert Friede represented a good risk for parole as soon as he became eligible. Friede was paroled on November 13, 1967, and is now living in the state of Washington.

Justice Schweitzer always enjoyed the luxurious life. He was well-known at New York's most expensive restaurants and clubs. One of his many wealthy friends was Louis Seeman, president of an umbrella manufacturing company in

Manhattan. The company maintained an apartment at the Drake Hotel, since 1965, at an annual rental of more than $10,000.

Justice Schweitzer used the apartment often, entertaining his friends there and paying for drinks and dinner by signing Mr. Seeman's name. The hotel confirmed the authorization. It appeared Seeman had never had any legal matter before Justice Schweitzer. But when Seeman was called before the grand jury and questioned about his friendship with the judge, he refused to testify on the grounds of possible self-incrimination.

In January 1971, the New York Court on the Judiciary was convened for the purpose of determining whether charges of official misconduct should be brought against Justice Schweitzer. Among other evidence, the court was to receive a report on an investigation being conducted by the Senate Permanent Investigations Subcommittee.

The investigation had grown partly out of testimony given by a secret hooded witness who had appeared before that subcommittee in 1970 during hearings on underworld influence in legitimate business. The witness, an admitted stock manipulator, was later identified as Michael Raymond. He testified that he had been told by Tommy Gamindorra, a lieutenant in the Joseph Colombo "family," that he didn't have to worry if he was ever arrested in Brooklyn. Gamindorra said, "We got judges on the payroll that can straighten it out—one, two, three."

Raymond accused Justice Schweitzer on July 20, 1971. The judge refused to make any comment. Later Schweitzer's son said, "My father's record speaks for itself."

It certainly did. It spoke so loud and so clear that on July twenty-eighth Schweitzer asked to be relieved of his duties pending the outcome of the investigation. Of course, he continued to draw his salary of $39,100 per year in the meantime. (He also continued to draw a comparable amount on his investments.)

Raymond testified that he was indicted in 1955 for grand larceny in a stock manipulation case, as a result of complaints filed by his two partners. He said that he paid $25,000 to Justice Schweitzer to give him a light jail sentence.

According to Raymond, the contact was made through a man named Stanley Polly, who was "well connected with organized crime." The night before Raymond was to be sentenced by Schweitzer, he and Polly drove to a hotel in the Bronx where Justice Schweitzer was spending the evening. Raymond stayed in the car and Polly ". . . met Schweitzer in the lobby in my [Raymond's] plain view." When Polly returned, he informed Raymond that everything was taken care of. The next morning Raymond was given a suspended sentence.

Raymond also said he paid another $25,000 to Polly to arrange for Schweitzer to give him "a hook into the New York City Probation Department." This second bribe was made in December 1961, after Raymond had pleaded guilty in Massachusetts to fraud charges resulting from the sale of Canadian oil leases and had been placed on probation in New York.

Being placed on probation wasn't good enough, since under the supervision of a probation officer Raymond couldn't continue his illegal securities operations. "I might as well be in jail," he said. So Raymond and Polly again made a trip to see Justice Schweitzer, taking $25,000 with them as a token of their appreciation. Polly went inside the house and returned in thirty minutes, announcing that "the probation department in New York would be no problem."

Raymond testified he "was assigned to a probation officer

and that was the end of it. He never knew whether I had a job or not, and I think he would have been happy if I never came to see him."

In the course of his testimony before the Senate subcommittee, Raymond described a twenty-year record of deals involving underworld characters and apparently legitimate businesses. He told the committee that he had begun cooperating with the Justice Department and other federal authorities in 1963 to help expose frauds involving stolen securities, forged traveler's checks and other swindles. He said he had made "many millions of dollars" over the years, including the years he worked for the Justice Department.

He recounted having dealt during his career with associates of Jimmy Hoffa and of Meyer Lansky, financial boss of organized crime in the United States and recently extradited from Israel. Raymond said his career had convinced him that "there has been substantial infiltration of the banking, brokerage, insurance and other financial communities by many persons who are directly or indirectly connected with organized crime."

Raymond himself was indicted at least a half a dozen times, fined, given suspended sentences and short terms in jail. Still, he continued to operate. He had only to put up with increased overhead in the form of higher judicial bribes.

After Raymond testified to twice buying Schweitzer, Michael Molese, a prisoner in the Men's House of Detention in New York, wrote a letter to U.S. Senator John McClellan. Molese wanted to testify that he had bribed Schweitzer's secretary with $15,000 in an attempt to avoid a conviction for arson, burglary and grand larceny. He said he had been double-crossed when his case was transferred to another judge, who convicted him.

When the Court on the Judiciary issued formal charges

against Justice Schweitzer in September 1971, additional problems involving a number of money-lending transactions were brought to light. The judge had borrowed $100,000 from the Royal National Bank at low interest rates and then lent it to taxicab companies, real estate operators and loan companies at very high rates.

On December 23, 1971, Justice Schweitzer announced he was retiring from the bench as of January 24, 1972, the day the Court on the Judiciary was to have begun removal hearings on the charges against him. He said he was "most reluctant to do this" while the charges against him remained unresolved. However, he said his doctor had warned him that stress and strain might result in a complete mental and physical breakdown. Therefore, his ill health left him with "no alternative."

JUDGE EDWARD J. DeSAULNIER AND JUDGE VINCENT R. BROGNA (MASSACHUSETTS)

Judges Edward J. DeSaulnier and Vincent R. Brogna, of the Middlesex Superior Court, were also named by Michael Raymond during the hearings investigating the conduct of New York's Justice Schweitzer. Judge Brogna had presided at Raymond's trial for stock fraud in Massachusetts in 1962. Brogna suspended Raymond's three-year sentence and transferred his probation to New York, where Schweitzer took over.

Judge DeSaulnier became one of the nation's youngest

trial judges on January 8, 1959, at the age of thirty-seven. He had served four terms in the Massachusetts house and two in the state senate as a Republican. After he broke with his party and backed an opposition bill to increase the number of judges in the superior court, he was appointed to the bench by Governor Foster Furgolo.

Judge Brogna, fifty-four, was appointed to the court in 1960, also by Furgolo whom he had served as a special counsel. Brogna's father, who died in 1960, was also a superior-court judge.

Raymond testified that it cost him over $100,000 to have his Massachusetts sentence suspended and his probation transferred under the state's "Mayflower clause," which permits Massachusetts defendants to have their probations transferred to the states in which they live.

He said that $65,000 had gone to Charles and Nathan Baker, bail bondsmen who paid Judge DeSaulnier to "make arrangements with Judge Brogna."

Both judges denied any wrongdoing. DeSaulnier said, "The accusation is preposterous. I will rely on my record as a judge. I welcome any and all investigations, and I think it's a tragedy that somebody's reputation can be maligned by someone who is anonymous." (Raymond, at that time, had not been identified by the subcommittee due to his need for protection.)

The Supreme Judicial Court of Massachusetts took up DeSaulnier's challenge. Although the court had no power to remove a judge from office, it ordered, "as a matter of judicial administration," that Judge DeSaulnier not hear cases until further notice. Three days later DeSaulnier resigned.

Neither judge could be tried on criminal charges since the six-year statute of limitations had already run, and judges in Massachusetts can only be removed by the legislature. But the supreme court did have the power of censure and disbarment, and it instituted hearings for that purpose.

On January 11, 1972, the Massachusetts Supreme Court censured Judge DeSaulnier. The court found he was unfit to continue either as a judge or as a lawyer. In its thirty-eight-page ruling, the court said its inquiry showed that Judge DeSaulnier and Charles Baker "conspired to influence the ultimate disposition of Raymond's cases for a consideration to be paid," and that "Judge DeSaulnier received or expected to receive some form of consideration or benefit either directly or indirectly from one or both of the Baker brothers." He was disbarred by default when he failed to appear for his hearing.

No direct evidence was produced that Judge Brogna received anything of value from DeSaulnier or Baker. Yet he was censured. The court said it acted because of a news conference the judge held on July 28, 1971, when he identified himself as the one who had handled Raymond's cases and released the record of proceedings. The state supreme court ruled that the news conference was "of highly questionable propriety."

Governor Sargent demanded Brogna's resignation. The judge refused. He said, "My refusal is not grounded in arrogance or defiance, but rather because I share that sentiment which your excellency expressed, to the effect that the confidence of the people is fundamental to the court's function." He claimed that his resignation at that time would be construed as a tacit admission of judicial misconduct, which would have diminished public confidence . . . and, so he sits.

JUDGE RALPH DeVITA (NEW JERSEY)

During the past few years New Jersey has been the scene of intensive federal investigation of organized crime and official corruption. A score of public figures, including mayors, city officials and others were found to have fallen together with a Mafia-controlled illegal gambling syndicate. That same broad investigation led to the case against Union County Judge Ralph DeVita.

Governor Richard Hughes had to overcome considerable opposition to appoint Judge DeVita to a position of public trust. State Attorney General Arthur Sills advised the governor not to appoint DeVita as First Assistant County Prosecutor of Union County. Despite such advice, DeVita was appointed in 1956.

Subsequent to his appointment, his boss, Union County Prosecutor Leo Kaplowitz, had sought to have DeVita removed as first assistant because of his alleged ties to organized crime.

In 1966, when DeVita was being considered as an appointee to the post of Union County District Judge, Sills again warned the governor of the prospective judge's suspected mob ties. The warning was continued in a secret report by the state police, which investigates all judicial nominees of the governor. Hughes was unmoved. He said he could not reject a nominee put forth by the Democratic party in Union County unless the state police had more concrete evidence against him. In true New Jersey fashion, the state senate approved the nomination.

The repeated warnings about Judge DeVita's mob ties proved to be well-founded. On December 2, 1969, the judge was summarily suspended from the bench on charges of bribery in a case involving organized crime. It was the first time a judge in New Jersey had ever been suspended before any hearing had been held.

On December ninth the judge appeared with his lawyer before the New Jersey Supreme Court to show cause why he should not be indefinitely suspended without pay, pending the outcome of a special administrative proceeding to be conducted by Superior Court Judge James J. Guiliano. But the court suspended DeVita as a judge and as a practicing lawyer. He was indicted by a grand jury on December 10, 1969, on charges of attempting to bribe and obstructing justice. He faced a possible maximum penalty of six years in jail and a heavy fine.

The charges involved an attempted bribe to quash an indictment against Nicholas Guida, Jr., and David Tenney, who were arrested together in Somerset County by a Bridgewater police sergeant on September 27, 1968. Guida and Tenney were facing charges of bookmaking, attempting to bribe the arresting officer and possession of burglary tools. They were scheduled to be tried in January 1970. Guida, a million-dollar-a-year bookie, primarily handled bets made on sporting events in the Elizabeth, New Jersey, area, where illegal gambling was controlled by Louis (Fat Louis) Larasso, a member of the Mafia family headed by Simone Rizzo (Sam the Plumber) DeCavalcante. When Guida was picked up, he had $21,000 in betting slips in his sock. He also was found with a battery-powered electric drill with which he would make holes in pay telephones. He would then insert a metal bar that would return all coins used to make his "business" calls. Guida had been arrested twice for bookmaking in 1954 and once in 1960, receiving suspended sentences. Both Guida and Tenney were subsequently found guilty.

Judge DeVita and the prosecutor in the Guida-Tenney case, Michael Imbriani, were former colleagues, both having been assistant prosecutors at the same time. According to Imbriani, on November 17, 1969, Judge DeVita met Imbriani for drinks at the Winfield Scott Hotel in Elizabeth. During the automobile ride from the courthouse to the hotel, the judge initiated a conversation about the pending case. He told the prosecutor that the indictment against the two men "has got to be killed" and that if it were, "there are ten big ones [$10,000] in it for you." DeVita also told Imbriani that the bribe money was coming from "people high in the Democratic party." Imbriani made no definite response to the offer.

That afternoon Imbriani reported the bribe offer to the Chief Justice of the Supreme Court of New Jersey and the state police. On November twenty-fifth a telephone conversation between the two men was arranged, monitored by the police and later introduced as evidence at Judge DeVita's trial.

On December first, the state police went to DeVita's chambers in Elizabeth and served him with an arrest warrant. They also took a search warrant and discovered a copy of the indictment against Guida and Tenney in the judge's desk drawer. Since the case was not assigned to him, he had no official reason to possess such a copy.

At his trial in April 1970, Judge DeVita took the stand in his own defense and categorically denied the charges. Twenty prominent New Jersey lawyers and businessmen appeared as character witnesses for the defense.

On April 15, 1970, after twenty-seven hours of deliberation, the jury returned a verdict of guilty of obstructing justice, but not of bribery.

On April twenty-eighth Judge DeVita resigned. He was sentenced to one to two years in prison. DeVita's lawyer had begged for a suspended sentence for him rather than a jail term. DeVita claimed he had learned his life would be in danger the moment he stepped inside the gates of prison. He had both prosecuted and passed sentence on men then serving time.

Just before being sentenced, DeVita told the court, "I don't have anyone to blame but myself. I have lost my self-respect, my license to practice law, my judgeship."

JUDGE ANTHONY GUILIANO (NEW JERSEY)

The federal investigation of corruption in New Jersey was climaxed with the indictment of Newark Mayor Hugh J. Addonizio and fourteen other city officials, together with five others identified as Mafia members or contacts. They included Anthony (Tony Boy) Boiardo and his father Ruggiero (Richie The Boot) Boiardo. Both were identified as members of the Mafia family of Gerardo (Jerry) Catena. Anthony Boiardo was also listed as a salesman for an electric company holding lucrative city contracts. Among the corrupt practices charged was that a quarter of a million dollars had changed hands in payoff monies as part of a conspiracy to obtain contracts and evade taxes. Municipal Court Judge Anthony Guiliano, one of the Republican party's top vote-getters in the area, was also indicted.

Judge Guiliano graduated from New York University Law School in 1920 and became active in politics while practicing law. He was elected to the New Jersey Assembly in 1927 on the Republican ticket and later in that year was named assistant U.S. attorney. In the 1930s and 1940s he main-

27

tained a private law practice in Newark, and in 1948 made an unsuccessful bid for Congress. Four years later he was appointed a city magistrate, but resigned in 1955 to become Essex County clerk. In 1960 he served as county registrar.

In 1962 Judge Guiliano easily defeated seven opponents for an at-large seat on the Newark City Council, and was reelected in 1966. Mayor Addonizio appointed him to the municipal court bench in 1968 at the age of seventy.

The judge's brother, James Guiliano, was the judge assigned to conduct disciplinary proceedings against Judge DeVita. His cousin, also named Anthony Guiliano, was a member of the city council at the time the indictments were issued.

Judge Guiliano's official conduct was called into question as a result of the grand jury's inquiry into payoffs made to city officials in exchange for the awarding of city contracts. He was accused of sharing in the cash payments but denied that there was any truth to the accusation.

Mayor Addonizio said that his corporation counsel, Philip W. Gordon, had admitted to him that he had taken cash payments and shared them with another official. Gordon substantiated the statement in testimony before the grand jury. When he emerged from the jury room, he told Guiliano, "I testified that I got four thousand and I gave you one."

The judge, after identifying himself as the official to whom Gordon was referring, said, "I don't know what the hell he said that for." In response to questions by newsmen, he said the only possible reason he could find for Gordon's accusation was an ill feeling that went back to 1966 when Guiliano, then a member of the city council, ran for council president and Gordon refused to support his candidacy. "I guess I'm just going to have to ride this out," Guiliano remarked "A man is innocent until proven guilty, but this is a hell of a lot of pressure."

Gordon, who resigned his post immediately after his brief appearance before the grand jury, refused to comment on either the judge's or the mayor's statements. When asked by a reporter if he would give an interview to lay his version before the public, he exclaimed, "You must be crazy to ask that question! I have no comment to make."

Immediately after the indictment against Judge Guiliano was made public, he was suspended from the bench by the state supreme court pending disposition of the case against him. He never stood trial. In the early morning of February 4, 1970, the judge suffered a heart attack and died. Since then, Mayor Addonizio has faced his own problems— but that's another book, on "The Finest Mayors Money Can Buy."

JUDGE JAMES DelMAURO (NEW JERSEY)

Another New Jersey jurist accused by federal investigators in the penetrating investigation of Newark government was Chief Municipal Court Judge James DelMauro. DelMauro's income tax returns came to the attention of federal officials because he failed to declare fees for performing wedding ceremonies. The judge appeared, on December 3, 1969, before a grand jury inquiring into organized crime in New Jersey and refused to answer any questions on the grounds of self-incrimination.

The Supreme Court of New Jersey ordered a special investigation to determine whether the judge's conduct warranted disciplinary action. As a result of that investigation, on January 25, 1971, the court suspended DelMauro from the practice of law for one year. It said the reason he was not disbarred permanently was that this appeared to be the first time he had stolen wedding fees. (One wonders whether defendants who were not judges were always afforded the same moderate treatment.)

Although DelMauro was never himself indicted, his name figured prominently in the cases of others. In late December 1969 an Essex County grand jury indicted Herminio Nieves, official liaison between City Hall and the Puerto Rican community, and Andres Soto, a Spanish-language interpreter in municipal court, on charges of having demanded and accepted money from persons for whom they had interceded in criminal cases. The two were charged with conspiracy to violate a state law that forbids public officers from demanding or taking payment for any service in a criminal case.

Nieves and Soto had obtained $350 from Dora Cruz to get bail reduced for Angelo Morales, who later was sentenced by the superior court to a prison term of two to four years for possession of narcotics. Separate counts were found against the two officials for accepting unlawful fees in cases heard before Judge DelMauro.

Nieves was accused of having received $250 from Eulalio De Leone to influence the outcome of the case (in which the judge later gave De Leone a suspended sentence of three months and fined him only $52 for receiving stolen goods). Soto was charged with having received $700 from De Leone to influence the outcome of another case against him in which Judge DelMauro imposed a suspended sentence of three months for breaking and entering.

In the course of other grand jury investigations, it was disclosed that DelMauro, before being appointed to the bench in 1964, represented Anthony (Gyp) DeCarlo, a New Jersey Mafia leader under indictment for extortion. A close associate of the notorious Mayor Addonizio, DelMauro publicly admitted knowing Anthony (Tony Boy) Boiardo, the Mafia figure involved with Judge Guiliano.

Although DelMauro resigned from the bench and was suspended from the practice of law, the public has by no means finished paying for his "services." Having served for twenty-three years with the Newark Housing Authority before assuming the bench, he requested reinstatement to his $20,000 job as assistant authority director.

Despite a protest from LeRoi Jones on behalf of the Committee for a United Newark and the public objection of soon-to-be-elected mayor Kenneth Gibson, Joseph Sivolella, head of the authority, found that the ex-judge was on a "leave of absence" and could return if he so desired. He said that civil service law compelled reinstatement as long as DelMauro had not been convicted of a criminal charge.

He worked quietly at the Newark Housing Authority until October 3, 1972, when he was indicted by another federal grand jury on charges of income tax evasion.

JUDGE JOHN N. STICE (KANSAS)

Kansas is a quiet state. Midwestern calmness is evident everywhere. The quietude was abruptly invaded in 1957 when the Wichita police discovered that a burglary ring which had evaded arrest for nearly two years included a local judge, a prominent lawyer and a bail bondsman.

The team's action resembled a fixed college football game. The ball went first to the running backs; then a defensive play was made by team member Trail, the lawyer. The referee was another team member, John Stice, judge of the Court of Common Pleas. In the event of a penalty, another team member, the bail bondsman, was called. In addition to abusing his official capacity to aid the criminals, Judge Stice was charged with active personal involvement in some of the jobs.

On the night of November 13, 1956, some of the men burglarized a Standard Food Market in Wichita, taking with them the store's safe. Fearing discovery, they were forced to abandon it a few blocks away and take to hiding. Stice advised them that the police had their descriptions and would be watching for them. Accordingly, Stice, Trail and another drove to the location where the safe had been abandoned, picked it up and took it to Stice's house where all the men got together and divided the contents.

Later that same month, in a meeting at Dett's Transfer Company in Wichita, Judge Stice advised Jimmie Crisler and Pooter Russell that there would be $12,000 in the IGA Food Store in Mulvane. Crisler and Russell each agreed to pay the judge $500 from the proceeds of the burglary. After breaking into the store, they could only find $100 in change in the cash register. Russell immediately called Stice long distance at his home and reported finding no safe in the building.

In December 1956 Judge Stice again advised Crisler and Russell that they would find $12,000 in the safe and cash registers of an IGA Food Store—this time in Pawnee. Thereafter, Crisler, Russell and three others broke into the store and scored $11,000 in currency and coin. They immediately divided the loot, Russell's share being approximately $1,960. On the following Sunday Russell contacted Stice by telephone to arrange a meeting so that the judge could receive his cut of about $750.

After several months of lucrative operations, some of the members started getting sloppy due to overconfidence in their "foolproof" system, and they were caught. Their activities were eventually connected with Judge Stice and Attorney Trail.

On March 19, 1957, disbarment proceedings were brought against both Stice and Trail by the Kansas State Board of Law Examiners. The two were charged with burglary, robbery, conspiracy and receiving stolen property.

Yet they tried still one more scheme. They prepared affidavits containing false information and statements to the effect that both men were completely innocent, and had at least six people (some of whom were in jail) sign them. These affidavits were then introduced as evidence in the disbarment case.

The scheme failed. Instead of resulting in dismissal of the charges against them, it resulted in the addition of a new charge—procuring false affidavits.

At this point Trail had had enough. He voluntarily surrendered his license and on July 26, 1957, was permanently disbarred from the practice of law in Kansas.

Judge Stice, however, was not quite so cooperative. Not until May 16, 1959, was he finally disbarred by the Kansas Supreme Court. He took advantage of every procedure and line of argument imaginable. He even contended that he couldn't be disbarred as a lawyer because the conduct in question had occurred in his capacity as a judge. (Arguments like that may bring back vaudeville!)

John Stice wouldn't give up. He filed a $1,000,000 law suit against the Beacon Newspaper Corporation alleging that the newspaper, when covering the police burglary investigation, had printed articles about him that were libelous, defamatory, malicious and untrue. He claimed the articles falsely implied that as an attorney and judge of the Court of Common Pleas, he was criminal, dishonest, guilty of misconduct, lacking integrity and unfit to serve as a judge. One of the articles stated that the police had named Stice and Trail as the ringleaders of the gang.

The trial court ruled in favor of the newspaper, and Stice then appealed. The Supreme Court of Kansas put the matter to rest, affirming the decision of the lower court and saying that the articles and their accompanying headlines were not an exaggeration of the judge's misconduct.

JUDGE RAULSTON SCHOOLFIELD (TENNESSEE)

Judge Raulston Schoolfield of Chattanooga, Tennessee, was a colorful character on the bench, reminiscent of some of those jurists who made Wild West courtrooms seem more like saloons.

In 1957 Judge Schoolfield, at fifty-one, appeared to be a man of quiet manner, but he was noted for a violent temper. He would fight at the drop of a hat.

As Chattanooga's foremost criminal lawyer before he was elected to the bench, Schoolfield defended a wide range of gamblers and hoodlums. It was said he never had a client he couldn't whip. Some of these men were his close friends. As a trial lawyer he scored victory after victory before juries entranced at the audacity of his slashing attacks on prosecution witnesses.

As a politician, Schoolfield was regarded as an expert manipulator and a forceful campaign orator. In 1954 he was the "avowed racist" candidate for the Democratic gubernatorial nomination against former Governor Gordon Browning and the incumbent Governor Frank G. Clement. Schoolfield received 29,000 votes of a total of 605,000.

He was first elected criminal court judge in 1948 to fill out an unexpired term. In 1950 he won a full eight-year term.

There was never a breath of scandal attached to his name until December 1957 when the Senate Select Committee on Improper Activities in the Labor or Management Field heard evidence of a reported payoff of $20,000 by a Chattanooga local of the International Brotherhood of Teamsters. Much of the testimony centered on the actions of Raulston Schoolfield. It seemed that Judge Schoolfield had dismissed indictments against thirteen teamsters in 1951 and 1953.

A key witness before the committee was Glenn W. Smith, who held two union offices, serving as president of Chattanooga Teamsters Local 515 and president of Joint Council 87, made up of teamster locals in Tennessee. He had also served two prison terms for robbery and larceny.

Smith and twelve others were indicted in the Hamilton County Criminal Court in 1951. They were charged with dynamiting, arson and other acts of violence in connection with teamster organizing.

In June of that year Smith negotiated a loan of $13,500 from the Southern Conference of Teamsters. The money was added to the thin bank account of the Chattanooga local on July second. On that same date Smith and H. L. Boling (secretary-treasurer of the local and also one of the defendants) cashed a draft for $18,500, charging it on the union books to "attorney's fees." Smith refused to tell the committee whether any of the money had gone to the judge, and claimed the Fifth in refusing to answer any questions about the money or who got it.

Raymond Hixon, a deputy state fire marshal, testified that on July eighth Boling had offered to bet him $500 that there would not be a trial. Hixon said, "Then he told me that $18,500 had been passed to quash the indictment."

On March 14, 1952, Judge Schoolfield quashed the indictments.

On March 17, 1952, officers of the local cashed a draft for $1,500 and again charged it to "attorney's fees."

On February 25, 1953, the Tennessee Supreme Court reversed the judge's decision and sent the case back for trial.

The trial began in late June 1953. After the prosecution had completed its case, Judge Schoolfield ordered a directed verdict of not guilty. The prosecutor was stunned. In his research and preparation of the indictments he had relied in part on a similar case in which the judge himself had helped to draw the indictment.

The courthouse was full of rumors of a "fix."

On December 18, 1957, another Senate committee witness testified that he had paid $1,000 to have a case "fixed" in a Tennessee court. The witness was James Spence Galloway, a one-time filling-station operator. Soon after he paid the $1,000, Galloway testified, he received a new trial, pleaded guilty, was sentenced to three years and was paroled—all in Judge Schoolfield's court in Chattanooga.

Galloway had been convicted of concealing stolen property. Judge Schoolfield, on May 24, 1954, overruled a motion for a new trial.

Galloway then went to Raymond Boling, still secretary-treasurer of Teamsters Local 515, "who said he'd see what he could do to help me." Boling talked to Sam C. Jones, a professional bail bondsman, who said "he could get the thing handled for $1,000." Galloway raised the money and turned it over to Jones between June 5 and June 10, 1954.

Jones and Boling together met Mr. Harold Brown, a special prosecutor in the Galloway case (who was at the time of the Schoolfield scandal an Assistant Attorney General of Tennessee), in the courthouse corridor one day. According to Jones, Boling and Brown went off to the side and spoke together for awhile. After a few minutes Mr. Jones handed over the $1,000 to Mr. Brown.

When Brown testified before the committee, he insisted that he had regarded the money only as a legitimate contribution from Sam Jones to Judge Schoolfield's campaign for the gubernatorial nomination. Mr. Jones, however, said he had understood the payment had been made to help Galloway. Boling pleaded the Fifth.

In order to resolve the conflict in the testimony as to whether or not the payment was a campaign contribution, a search was made of Schoolfield's financial reports for the 1954 campaign. The search failed to show that the judge had filed any document reporting a campaign contribution, as required by Tennessee law.

On December 27, 1957, Judge Schoolfield, in an hour-long speech over local radio and television, scathingly denounced the committee witnesses, the committee, the governor, the supreme court, the Chattanooga *Times* and the *New York Times.* In addition to this list of enemies, he said there was "a hidden and secret government devoted to the destruction of all precepts of liberty and freedom heretofore enjoyed by the citizens of this country and to deliver the people of this nation into the hands of an international conspiracy too horrible to think about." He claimed that a "tyrannical central government" aided by "arrogant bureaucrats" wanted to destroy him because of his advocation of state sovereignty.

The judge denied any wrongdoing in the Galloway case, or in the case of the $20,000 bribe allegation. In the case of the campaign contribution, he pleaded that because of fatigue at the end of a grueling campaign, he had forgotten about the filing provisions.

He closed by warning his listeners, "if they are going to bring me crashing to earth, then the shackles and forges being fashioned for me today may well fit your hands and ankles tomorrow."

The authorities in Tennessee were not impressed. Governor Clement initiated a complete investigation into the judge's activities with a report to be made to the Tennessee legislature. Both the state and Chattanooga bar associations recommended that Judge Schoolfield step down from the bench pending completion of the inquiry. He refused. Clement then appointed dapper John J. Hooker, Jr., as a special prosecutor.

On May 3, 1958, Schoolfield held a political rally in his courtroom and announced he would enter the June third primary to seek his party's renomination for criminal court judge. He lost.

On May 6, 1958, the Tennessee House of Representatives, called into special session by the governor, began considering charges of impeachment. Within a few days, it issued a report containing some twenty-five charges of misconduct.

The report also declared that grand juries chosen by Judge Schoolfield had released more accused law violators in two court terms than had been released in that county in the last ten years. (Harold Brown, the special prosecutor in the Galloway case who resigned as assistant attorney general, had once been appointed by the judge as foreman of the county grand jury.)

On May sixteenth the house voted 89 to 7 to impeach on twenty-four charges. The trial began in the senate on June 10, 1958.

Judge Raulston Schoolfield was convicted on July 11, 1958, on three articles of impeachment, and removed from office. The senate failed by three votes to disqualify him from again holding public office in Tennessee. The charges in the three articles on which he was found guilty were distinct from those disclosed in the hearings before the senate subcommittee in 1957.

Judge Schoolfield was convicted of having, in 1950, accepted a gift of a new Pontiac automobile in return for favors he had extended, and was to extend, in his official capacity to some of the donors. The money to buy the car had been solicited and collected by the judge's court officer from defendants and lawyers who practiced before his court.

He was also found guilty of engaging in active politics, using the power of his judicial office to promote the candidacy of political friends and to influence persons in politics to become or not become candidates for public office. He commanded and directed the political actions of known racketeers and met with them at "shady and questionable places" to coerce them to do his "political will." In connection with these activities, he had accepted $2,500 from Joe Frank, a former Chattanooga gambler, to be used in preventing passage of an antigambling bill in the 1949 state legislature.

Finally, the judge was found guilty of using profane and obscene language while acting as judge.

But the matter was not closed with Schoolfield's removal from the bench. The Tennessee and Chattanooga bar associations still had a few jabs to take.

Disbarment proceedings were instituted in August 1959 using the same charges relied upon in the impeachment action. In the course of the proceedings it was further discovered that Schoolfield had on two previous occasions been before the supreme court for disciplinary action in matters in which he had been found guilty.

In the first of these indictments he had impersonated someone else and taken the bar examination for him. The second incident related to his refusal, when a lawyer, to represent two defendants jointly indicted for burglary; for this refusal he was fined for contempt of court.

Raulston Schoolfield was permanently disbarred from the practice of law in the state of Tennessee on January 21, 1960. That year his son, a brilliant student, graduated from Cumberland Law School, and John Hooker, Jr. launched a political career that took him almost to the governor's mansion.

Chapter Two
The High Cost of Justice

"I have no excuse. I was just greedy."
　　　　　　　—NEW YORK SUPREME COURT JUSTICE-ELECT
　　　　　　　SEYMOUR R. THALER—convicted March 23, 1972

The insatiable greed of members of the Supreme Court of Oklahoma brought about one of the most colossal scandals in contemporary American history. The story was suppressed in many communities by those officials who felt that emphasis placed on the barefaced bribery of the justices of the Supreme Court of Oklahoma could undermine the state's entire judicial system. They were right. Oklahoma jurisprudence has not been the same since.

In 1972, one of New York's most honored political leaders was about to climax a distinguished career of public service by ascending to the supreme court of that state. Between the time of his election and the swearing-in ceremonies, he was indicted and later convicted of extensive and expensive felonies.

41

The United States has come a long way in eliminating the double standard of justice that for too many generations prevented blacks, browns and the poor from a fair shake in court. The irony is that while we have appointed more public defenders and sponsored more programs for the poor, we have been derelict in safeguarding communities from those who profit from justice for sale. The real double standard today is between those who appear in court legitimately and those who have bought their verdict before the trial. From 1912 to 1973 the pattern of corruption never varied. It only intensified.

JUDGE MARTIN T. MANTON (FEDERAL-NEW YORK)

Martin T. Manton began his judicial career in 1916 when he was appointed by President Woodrow Wilson as a U.S. district court judge for the Southern District of New York. At thirty-six he was the youngest federal judge in the country. After only eighteen months as a district judge, he was promoted to the Second Circuit Court of Appeals.

By January 1939 Judge Manton had reached a position of such eminence that he was regarded as a tenth justice of the Supreme Court. In the second circuit, encompassing New York, Vermont and Connecticut, he had jurisdiction over the richest industrial and financial complex in the world. During his last ten years on the bench he presided over 2,000 cases and wrote some 650 opinions, a record few judges in the federal judiciary can equal.

Manton earned a reputation as one of the top authorities on patent law in the United States; he was often called upon to advise Congress and to testify before its committees on this complicated branch of the law. His advice on legislation affecting bankruptcy was given serious consideration in both houses of Congress. Rumors spread periodically that President Hoover was considering elevating Manton to the Supreme Court.

Manton's decisions and articles in professional journals were cited as authority by other judges and lawyers alike. He addressed such distinguished groups as the Academy of Political Science and the American Bar Association on a variety of subjects. He was even considered as a possible candidate for mayor of New York. To the nation at large he was a distinguished judicial personality—almost too good to be true.

Manton was equally active in the business world. He was secretly a real estate tycoon and corporate executive who quietly conducted private businesses on a broad and busy scale. His hidden assets consisted of two large hotels, eight apartment houses, fourteen duplexes, 206 acres of undeveloped land on Long Island, a carpet-cleaning establishment, a paper products company and a laundry concern. Then he got reckless.

In the midst of the Depression the judge's financial empire began to crumble, and the extent of his holdings began to unfold before an unbelieving public. When the Bank of the United States filed bankruptcy, bank inspectors discovered that a number of top judges were engaged in extensive private businesses and deeply involved with loans. Among those listed as heavy borrowers was Martin T. Manton.

On February 2, 1931, the *New York Times* reported that the bank's inventory showed Judge Manton borrowed

$39,000 on a personal unsecured loan, in addition to en-
dorsing loans for $70,000 and $69,000. When asked to
comment on the transactions, the judge said, "The note for
the $39,000 was paid on maturity." (This note became due
several days after the bank closed.) "On the other two notes I
was merely an endorser. The note for $70,000 of the Forest
Hills Terrace Corporation, on which I was an endorser, will
be paid when due. This note I understand matures during the
week. The other note, for the Camala Corporation, on which
I was an endorser, will also be paid when it matures."

Also included in the bank's inventory was an additional
unsecured loan to the Forest Hills Terrace Corporation for
$175,000. It was also reported that Judge Manton's name
appeared as co-endorser on two notes totaling $200,000 held
by the closed Chelsea Bank and Trust Company. Manton
explained that these loans were made to two real estate
companies in which he held stock but was not an officer. He
declined to give the names of the companies.

The public apparently believed Manton's shallow explanations that the loans were not for him personally, and he
escaped public censure. People were at that time more reluctant to accept the obvious corruption of a "distinguished"
judge.

Though the disclosures of 1931 showed the large scale of
Manton's private business and financial involvements, it was
not until 1934 that the real consequences were revealed. In
the course of testifying in the bankruptcy proceedings,
Manton disclosed that he had been insolvent since 1931. He
had borrowed on his life insurance policies as a last resort,
but real estate values had dropped so sharply that by February 1931 he found himself in an impossible position. By
1934 the stock of his Forest Hills Terrace Corporation was
absolutely worthless. All the properties owned by his cor-

porations were encumbered with first and second, and often third, mortgages. Many of them were either undergoing foreclosures or were on the brink of it.

Between June 1934 and May 1935 Manton made a remarkable financial recovery. He moved from a net debt position of $730,000 to a net worth of $750,000, a gain of nearly $1,500,000 in less than a year. To explain this accomplishment, he cited a long series of "loans," advance payments on contracts, sales of stock, and bank indebtedness, which amounted to $2,217,924. Of this sum, $184,000 had mysteriously been paid to him in cash. And then everything exploded.

On January 29, 1939, a young Manhattan district attorney named Tom Dewey compiled for the Judiciary Committee of the House of Representatives an itemized list of Judge Manton's corrupt transactions. The list included six cases of criminal acts by the judge and added that additional matters were still under investigation. Manton was charged with hiring fixers, taking bribes and kickbacks, approaching litigants for "loans," engaging in blantantly corrupt bankruptcy practices and a wide variety of other methods of selling his judicial authority. Dewey was beginning to earn the reputation as a crime fighter that would catapult him to a presidential nomination.

The day after the story broke, Manton announced he would issue a statement that would "satisfy the public that there was nothing wrong or immoral" about his judicial conduct. When asked by reporters whether he thought there was anything wrong or immoral about a judge having business interests outside his judicial duties, he said, "I never thought it was wrong or immoral. I know that other judges have such interests."

Instead of issuing the promised statement, on January 30,

1939, Judge Manton tendered his resignation to President Roosevelt, who accepted it instantly. Manton contended that his resignation was motivated solely by his desire to avoid becoming the central figure in a controversy that would weaken public confidence in the administration of justice. He would not admit any wrongdoing despite the documented proof by Dewey. The acceptance of his resignation under fire was to be expected. This, traditionally, has been the practice when a corrupt judge is exposed. Congress does not relish the task of impeachment and even considers it needless exposure as long as the judge conveniently resigns. When asked whether Manton should not be impeached to prevent him from ever again holding an office of honor and trust, Rep. Hatton Sumners, chairman of the House Judiciary Committee, replied, "Why kick at the place where the fellow used to be?"

But the relentless Dewey turned over all the evidence he had collected to a grand jury, and a formidable case against Manton became certain.

The grand jury began returning one indictment after another against Manton and his accomplices. Finally, in April 1939 the government put its entire case together in one indictment, a saga of barefaced bribery and insatiable corruption. It named as defendants, Martin T. Manton, William J. Fallon, Forrest W. Davis, George M. Spector, and John L. Lotsch. U.S. Attorney Cahill assembled reports of eight instances when Manton corrupted his office and charged that he accepted $186,000 in bribes from parties having litigation in the courts over which he presided. The indictment also charged the defendants with obstructing justice and with intent to defraud the United States. It was utterly incredible that Manton's pattern of blatant deceit wasn't discovered sooner.

All four of Manton's colleagues on the circuit court bench (Judges Harrie B. Chase, Augustus N. Hand, Learned B. Hand and Thomas W. Swan) appeared as defense witnesses during his trial. Manton was obviously influential in the inner sanctum of the judicial conference room. His colleagues must have been extremely myopic not to have noticed the strange assortment of questionable characters frequently seen in Manton's company. His go-betweens were constant visitors to his chambers and seemed to have free run of his court.

Manton's trial lasted from May 22 to June 3, 1939. In his charge to the jury, the presiding judge said, "The charge of conspiracy to sell justice, made against a ranking federal judge, is unprecedented in the 150 years of the federal judiciary." Not since Sir Francis Bacon had anything like it occurred.

The jury deliberated only four hours before returning a verdict of guilty. Manton claimed that a judge could not be guilty of obstructing justice in his own court and made a motion for a new trial. The motion was denied, and he was sentenced to two years imprisonment with a fine of $10,000.

When the Supreme Court in February 1940 rejected Manton's appeal to have his case reviewed, he paid his $10,000 fine and began his two-year term at Lewisburg, Pennsylvania, on March 7, 1940. He served one year and seven months and died in 1946 in an aura of unprecedented disgrace. The high cost of justice was affirmed. Twenty-seven years after his death another ranking federal appeals judge, Otto Kerner, would reaffirm the Manton tradition.

JUDGE J. WARREN DAVIS (FEDERAL—NEW JERSEY)

Senior Judge John Warren Davis of the Third Circuit Court of Appeals of the United States, like Judge Manton, presided over a rich industrial area including New Jersey, Delaware and Pennsylvania. Unlike Manton, however, he was neither convicted nor disbarred.

Davis attended Chester Military Academy, Bucknell University, and Crozer Theological Seminary, where he received a Bachelor of Divinity degree in 1899. For three years after graduation he remained at Crozer to teach Sanskrit, Latin and classical Hebrew. Then he entered the ministry and held a pastorate as an ordained Baptist minister in Pedricktown, New Jersey. Finally he turned to the study of law and graduated from the University of Pennsylvania Law School in 1906.

He practiced law in New Salem, New Jersey, and became interested in reform politics. In 1911 he was elected New Jersey state senator. In the senate he helped to secure the passage of a number of bills recommended by then Governor Woodrow Wilson. When Wilson became president in 1913 he appointed Davis U.S. District Attorney for New Jersey. There Davis came to know federal judge Thomas G. Haight. In 1920, when Haight resigned, President Wilson once again rewarded Davis with an appointment to the vacant seat. Judge Davis served as circuit court judge until 1939, when he retired with full salary and benefits.

When Davis became a federal judge, a small group of stockbrokers, bankers, and lawyers discovered he was a stockmarket addict. When the market crashed in 1929, Davis, like Manton, was wiped out.

He conducted most of his dealings with the brokerage firm

of Samuel Ungerleider & Company, whose generosity to Davis is quite baffling. By 1937 Davis owed various banks $85,000, and Ungerleider came to the rescue.

The broker entered into negotiations with the banks that were giving Judge Davis a bad time and arranged a composition of the debts for $37,674.50. In return, Davis signed notes for the amount and assigned as security his life insurance policies whose value, however, was no more than $20,000. To the banks, their officers, lawyers and a growing list of creditors, Davis' situation was soon no longer a secret.

In addition, others had to be involved—either through active conspiracy or unwitting cooperation. Subsequent events during the period of Davis' judicial tenure were just incredible.

Joseph Buffington was senior judge of the Third Circuit Court of Appeals during most of the time Davis was sitting on the bench. Buffington had graduated from Trinity College in Connecticut. A Phi Beta Kappa, he was admitted to the bar in 1875 at the age of twenty. His first federal judicial appointment was made by Benjamin Harrison in 1892. Teddy Roosevelt promoted him to the Third Circuit Court of Appeals in 1906, where he served until 1939. He acted as a federal judge for almost half a century.

He was also president of the Salvation Army and the Carnegie Hero Commission and author of a book, *The Soul of George Washington.*

Judge Buffington had challenged those who would·repeal the prohibition laws, and he had advocated the whipping of criminals.

By the year 1935 Judge Buffington was helpless and senile. He was eighty years old, almost totally deaf, and for all practical purposes blind (he could not read a newspaper). For some reason, Buffington refused to employ a law clerk to

49

look up the law, read briefs, and help write decisions, yet decisions with his signature were regularly handed down from 1935 to 1939. It was revealed that Judge Davis had not only been writing, but selling, the decisions Judge Buffington was signing.

Three cases of outrageous corruption led to the exposure of Judge Davis. The first was the bankruptcy of William Fox, organizer of the Fox Film Corporation. By purchasing other properties, he soon owned a string of over six hundred theaters. He also had purchased personally a set of patents relating to electronic sound.

After the 1929 crash Fox began attempting to enforce these patents through a series of lawsuits. If the patents were judged valid, then his status in the motion picture industry would be restored, not to mention an additional income of $23 million a year. But the decisions were against him. The defeat was financially mortal to Fox and he signed a petition in bankruptcy in May 1936 in the federal district court in New Jersey.

At about the same time, William Fox met Judge Davis. Fox came directly to the point and asked the judge to influence the referee in the bankruptcy case. Judge Davis, also involved in a financial crisis due to the expensive nature of his stock-market habit, accepted substantial bribes from Fox in fifty and one-hundred dollar bills.

A change in Fox's fortunes became visible. Cases he appealed in his bankruptcy proceedings were now won. Five times between 1936 and 1938 the district court held for the trustee in bankruptcy, and each time Fox appealed. All five times the circuit court reversed the decision and held in favor of Fox. All five times the opinions were signed by Buffington and written by Davis.

Morgan Kaufman, Fox's lawyer, knew a good thing when he saw it. After completing the Fox litigation, he acted as counsel and go-between for Judge Davis on behalf of Universal Oil Products Company, the American Safety Table Company and other important companies that were not unwilling to spread a little cash wherever it would promote their corporate interests.

Universal Oil Company, an oil refining business, had begun a patent infringement battle against its powerful competitors, including Standard Oil of New Jersey, the Texas Company, Standard Oil of Indiana and the Root Refining Company.

The appeal was argued in the Third Circuit Court before a bench consisting of Judges Davis, Buffington, and Thompson. At the judges' conference on January 7, 1935, Davis and Thompson were in favor of Universal, while Buffington was for reversal. The next day Buffington assigned the writing of the opinion to Davis. It was important to have an undivided court holding for Universal to reduce the possibility of the Supreme Court's granting certiorari (Latin for to be certified, made more certain). The high court is less likely to reverse a decision unanimously reached below.

Shortly thereafter, Buffington, Davis and Kaufman went on vacation together in Miami, Florida. Both on the way to Florida and on the way back, they stopped to visit Davis' cousin. It was on this vacation that Buffington apparently changed his view of the Universal-Root litigation; when Davis handed down his opinion on June 29, 1935, he spoke for an undivided court.

The third case leading to the exposure of Judge Davis was also a patent infringement suit—involving the Singer Sewing Machine Company. Singer had been charged with infringing a patent on a mechanical clutch connecting a sewing machine to a power shaft. The suit was brought in 1937 in the Eastern District Court of Pennsylvania, and the decision was in favor of Singer.

The complaining company, American Safety Table, was not satisfied. Louis Frankel, president of the company, went to New York, supposedly to discuss the employment of additional counsel. Instead he called upon Murray Becker, an attorney for William Fox. Becker told Frankel how the Fox interests had employed Morgan Kaufman with great success as local counsel in the third circuit for the patent suits and recommended that Frankel also employ him. Kaufman was hired.

On March 9, 1938, a bench consisting of Circuit Court Judges Buffington and Davis, and Albert W. Johnson, a district court judge temporarily assigned, reversed the district court and ruled in favor of American Safety Table Company. Buffington once again signed the opinion written by Davis.

But American got greedy. When a special master was appointed for the purpose of determining damages, American objected to the master's report, claiming the award was too small. While this exception was being considered, the strange relations of Judge Davis, William Fox, and Morgan Kaufman became the subject of a series of official inquiries.

In desperation, Davis retired from the bench on April 5, 1939, with full salary and pension rights. But the judge continued to be under official scrutiny.

A featured series on Davis' suspicious conduct and the strange activities of some of his colleagues appeared in the New York *World-Telegram* in December 1939. Subsequently, both Davis and Fox told stories that changed almost daily.

Finally, Fox made a full confession of his transactions with Davis to the U.S. attorney in New York. As a result of the exposure of their flexible virtue, Judge Davis, Morgan S.

Kaufman and William Fox were indicted by a federal grand jury in Philadelphia, in March 1941, for obstructing justice.

Fox pleaded guilty and became a government witness after making a deal with the U.S. attorney to change his plea if Davis and Kaufman were acquitted. Davis and Kaufman went through two trials, from May 19 to May 29, 1941, and from July 28 to August 21, 1941. Both cases resulted in hung juries, and the indictment was dismissed.

Since Davis was on pension and, therefore, still a member of the federal judiciary, on November 8, 1941, the U.S. attorney general asked Congress to impeach Judge Davis. Within two weeks Davis blocked a move for his impeachment by fully resigning, waiving all pension and retirement rights. But the high cost of justice had been once again underscored.

JUDGE ALBERT W. JOHNSON (FEDERAL)

U.S. District Court Judge Albert W. Johnson served as a federal judge for twenty years beginning in 1925. He was appointed by President Calvin Coolidge over the strenuous objections of his fellow lawyers and the press. Ten years earlier, in the same district, Judge Archibald of the U.S. Commerce Court had been impeached, convicted and removed from his post.

Johnson had received a B.A. degree from Bucknell University in 1896, graduating with highest honors. He accepted a position as a teacher in the public schools and studied law at night on his own. He was admitted to the Pennsylvania bar in

1898. In 1901 he was elected to the Pennsylvania House of Representatives and served one term. In 1912 he was elected Presiding Judge of the Seventeenth Judicial District. Then Johnson returned to the state legislature. Four years later he was appointed to the federal court by President Coolidge. Johnson's oath of office was, fittingly enough, administered by Judge J. Warren Davis. Johnson was state and national president of the Patriotic Order of Sons of America.

Complaints about his conduct on the bench started soon after he took the oath of office. Early in 1931 the Philadelphia *Inquirer* disclosed that Judge Johnson had appointed his son-in-law Carl Schug as trustee in eleven of the first twenty bankruptcy cases filed that year. It was also disclosed that Judge Johnson's sons, Donald and Albert, Jr., had been appointed in bankruptcy cases in other counties. Of the seventy lawyers in the county, the administration of all bankruptcies had gone to only five. A coincidence, no doubt!

Further probing proved that Judge Johnson and his sons owned an exclusive hunting club called the Tea Springs Lodge. The high initiation fee and annual dues were apparently worth the price. Eighty-two percent of the members were appointed by Judge Johnson to lucrative posts as appraisers, receivers, trustees, attorneys for trustees, special masters, or referees in bankruptcy. The lodge's income from dues amounted to $265,000 per year.

A federal grand jury, in 1934, began an inquiry into the "receivership racket" in Pennsylvania. A. R. Jackson, a Williamsport attorney, was indicted for embezzling $174,000 in thirty-seven bankruptcy cases. In sixteen of these cases, Carl Schug, Johnson's son-in-law, was the trustee and Jackson his attorney.

In 1934 Johnson's son Donald, a lawyer, was indicted and charged with misappropriation of funds while serving as trustee in bankruptcy for the Glendale Collieries Company. Because a judge's son was the defendant, Senior Judge of the Third Circuit Court of Appeals Joseph Buffington (remember him?) designated himself a district court judge to hear the case. Not surprisingly, Judge Buffington directed a verdict of not guilty.

In 1936 and again in 1939 federal investigations of Johnson's judicial behavior were conducted. In 1941 Judge Albert L. Watson, who sat on the same court with Judge Johnson, officially complained that Johnson was "hoarding" the bankruptcy business.

Judge Johnson miraculously survived all of this, until 1943 when the United States prosecuted a clothing manufacturer for stealing cloth from the government. The case was tried in Johnson's court. The U.S. attorney had heard rumors that it was very difficult to win a case in Judge Johnson's court when one of his sons was employed by the defendant. But the attorney thought he had a clear-cut case, so he wasn't worried when it became known that the judge's son was associated with the defense. However, as the trial progressed, the prosecution's suspicion was aroused by a number of incidents.

The judge directed the jury to find the defendant innocent of all charges. The jury refused this instruction and found the defendant guilty. Judge Johnson refused to accept this verdict, scolded the jury, and sent it back to the jury room with instructions to bring in a verdict of not guilty. The jury compromised this time and found the defendant guilty on some counts of the indictment and not guilty on others. Then came the sentencing. A local reporter predicted to the government attorneys that the defendant would withdraw his motion for the new trial then pending and throw himself on the mercy of the court, and that Judge Johnson would do no more than impose a nominal fine. And it happened exactly that way. The government lawyers returned to Washington ready to fight.

They informed Congressman Sautoff in Wisconsin of the case, and he discussed it on the floor of the House of Representatives. A few days later the House passed a resolution authorizing an investigation by the House Judiciary Committee.

The investigation was conducted by Representative (later Senator and vice-presidential candidate) Estes Kefauver of Tennessee, who, after lengthy hearings, issued a scathing report. He concluded that Judge Johnson had "notoriously engaged in the barter and sale of his court offices," and that "his decisions, decrees, orders, and rulings commonly were sold for all the traffic would bear." The Bethlehem Steel Company, for example, had paid Judge Johnson $250,000 for a decision in a bankruptcy case where it wanted a priority position over other creditors.

The Kefauver report showed that very few opportunities had escaped Johnson's profound greed. He owned an apartment house where all his court staff were required to live at rents higher than those paid by other tenants for similar quarters. He even required his secretary to begin her day's work by cleaning and dusting his home and preparing his breakfast. The committee's disclosures of Judge Johnson's corruption indicated that it had begun from the moment he reached the bench. It continued without interruption—even during the various investigations by the Department of Justice.

When the report was made public, Judge Johnson promptly resigned, and the committee voted to let the matter drop because the "Senate is engaged in the consideration of so many issues vital to the welfare of the nation."

Two of Johnson's sons, along with two of the other

defendants, were later found guilty of bribery and conspiracy to obstruct justice. Judge Johnson returned to the private practice of law and was elected president of his local bar association.

JUDGE ROBERT W. ARCHIBALD (FEDERAL—NEW YORK)

In 1912 Robert W. Archibald, judge of the United States Commerce Court, and former U.S. district court judge, was impeached and convicted on charges of having used his judicial office and influence for his personal financial profit.

Judge Archibald had accepted a free trip to Europe for himself and his family from a railroad tycoon whose companies then had various matters pending before Archibald's court.

While holding the office of district judge, he accepted and received a large sum of money contributed by various attorneys who practiced in his court. The money had been conveniently raised through the solicitation work of two court officers who had been appointed to their positions by none other than Judge Archibald himself. (One "good" turn deserves another.) Judge Archibald also appointed the Lehigh Valley Railroad Company's general counsel to act as jury commissioner for the judge's district, thus giving the counsel responsibility for selecting prospective jurors who would end up deciding cases involving the railroad. During the whole time the attorney served as jury commissioner, he continued to hold his position of general counsel.

Throughout his career on the bench, Archibald continued

to amass stocks, leaseholds, and various other interests in railroads, coal companies and gold-mining operations through peddling the influence of his position and his actual decisions to companies involved in litigation before his court.

The U.S. Senate ultimately brought thirteen articles against Judge Archibald. The first six related to his conduct while serving on the Commerce Court. Articles seven to twelve charged misconduct as a U.S. district judge. Article thirteen was a blanket count, charging a general course of misconduct which embodied all the various acts alleged in the other articles. The trial resulted in Archibald's conviction by an overwhelming vote. By the judgment of the Senate he was removed from office and disqualified to hold any office of honor, trust or profit under the United States.

The Commerce Court of which Judge Archibald was a member was created by the administration of President Taft to review the orders and decisions of the Interstate Commerce Commission. Increasingly, the commission ruled against the railroads on behalf of the consumers; and just as consistently, the Commerce Court ruled against the commission when the railroads appealed. As a result of this state of affairs and the bias and corruption of such stalwarts as Robert W. Archibald, the Commerce Court, as an institution, became the focus of a bitter political controversy. Teddy Roosevelt, campaigning for the presidency, promised to abolish the court if elected, but the Democratic majority in Congress pre-empted the issue (and the popular appeal) by voting to abolish the court during the campaign.

THE SUPREME COURT OF OKLAHOMA

There are scandals and there are scandals, but corruption took on a new dimension in 1964 when the pillars of justice of the State of Oklahoma began to tremble. It was discovered that a bribery ring involving four justices of the supreme court and a former Oklahoma City mayor and prominent attorney had been in existence for twenty years. A candidate for governor was also implicated. The lawyer-mayor had once served as a special member of the supreme court, and each justice had been a rotating chief justice of the highest court in the state.

The scandal became public on April 8, 1964. A federal grand jury indicted Supreme Court Justices Welch and Corn for income tax evasion. The events leading to the scandal were revealed by the testimony at the trial that followed.

In 1953 the Oklahoma Tax Commission had brought suit against Selected Investments Corporation, charging that it failed to pay state income taxes for 1948 on the income from its trust fund. The Oklahoma County District Court agreed. In 1957 the Oklahoma Supreme Court reversed the decision, saving Selected nearly $200,000 in back taxes and interest and an untold amount of future taxes on its payments to investors. Chief Justice Welch wrote the majority opinion in the 6-2 decision. Justices Johnson, Carlisle and Corn (then Vice Chief Justice) joined him.

In 1958 the Oklahoma Securities Commission ordered a halt to the sale of Selected's stock in Oklahoma. Later that year the federal district court declared the business bankrupt. The value of the certificates held by 7,000 Oklahomans had dropped $11 million.

At the bankruptcy proceedings Hugh A. Carroll, Selected's

founder and president, testified that he had "loaned" $150,000 in trust fund cash to "Pierre Laval," a "French Canadian oil promoter." The "loan" happened to come at the time of the supreme court decision in favor of Selected. Because Carroll was vague about the loan, said it was not repaid and would not pinpoint the whereabouts of "Pierre," the Laval story set off speculation of bribery, which led to the scandal.

Carroll, his wife and three associates were indicted by a federal grand jury and charged with thirty-one counts of mail fraud and conspiracy. They were convicted and sentenced to five years in federal prison.

In 1964 Carroll specifically repudiated his Laval story when testifying at the trial of Welch and Corn. He said that in return for the favorable supreme court ruling of 1957 he paid Justice Corn $150,000 in cash, mostly $100 bills, that was delivered in an armored car. (Presumably they didn't want some crook to steal it.) He said the money was to help him and "other members of the supreme court in meeting reelection expenses."

Justice Corn pleaded no contest to the charge of income tax evasion; he was fined $11,250 and sentenced to eighteen months at the United States Medical Facility due to his age (eighty) and bad health.

On December 9, 1964, Corn was visited in his prison-room hospital by state and federal officials. He gave them an eighty-four-page sworn statement confirming Carroll's story and adding that he had paid Welch and Johnson $7,500 each from the $150,000. Nine days later he was paroled after serving less than one-third of his sentence.

Nelson Corn had first been elected to the supreme court in 1934 and served continuously until January of 1959, at which time he assumed semiretirement status, presiding on special assignment and drawing three-quarters pay.

According to his statement, the bribery arrangement began one Saturday afternoon in 1936 or 1938 (he was uncertain of the year), during his first term of office, at a meeting with attorney O. A. Cargill to discuss "justice." Cargill told Corn that he liked "to be friendly with all the judges, and would like to have [Justice Corn] friendly enough to go along as a sixth man on opinions, because he liked to win by a fair majority; he always liked to have some extra votes on an opinion." In return, the attorney created a campaign fund for Corn and gave him money from time to time after Corn had voted as he was directed. The opinions on which he so voted were cases in which Cargill was the attorney of record and many cases where he was indirectly involved.

In 1955 apparently the agreement was modified. Justice Corn would now accept money only in specific cases in return for a favorable vote. In *Marshall* v. *Amos* (1955) the attorney split $25,000 six ways to insure a favorable opinion. Corn received $4,000 for his vote.

Oklahoma Company v. *O'Neil,* which involved Cargill's daughter and son-in-law, was another such case. Cargill told Corn that there was a criminal action to be brought in Florida, and the outcome of the case in Florida would depend on the outcome of the one in the Oklahoma court. Corn paid two justices, now no longer on the bench, $2,500 each for their favorable votes.

Justice Corn said that Cargill called him on so many cases, he couldn't remember any of them: "I don't know how many cases. You can check all the cases he has had up there since that time. He'd call them to my attention. I am quite sure he didn't let any slip."

By actual count, there were 1,548 decisions of 5-4 in which Justice Corn voted with the majority during the period from 1937 to 1958. If the votes of the justices to whom he personally paid bribes were also considered, an additional 330 cases must be added, raising the total to 1,878 final opinions of the Oklahoma Supreme Court peddled in exchange for bribes.

In addition, there were 140 more opinions written by Justices Corn, Welch or Johnson only, which do not indicate whether any other members of the court concurred or dissented. Many of the cases decided during this period involved issues that had never before been settled in Oklahoma. All these opinions were relied upon by all the lower courts and by the Oklahoma bar in its daily handling of many issues which never reached the courts. The cost to the people of Oklahoma, both morally and financially, can never be computed.

Attorney O. A. Cargill was convicted of perjury on June 17, 1965.

Former Justice Earl Welch began the practice of law in 1911 in Antlers, Oklahoma. He served as district judge from 1927 to 1932 and was first elected to the state supreme court in 1932.

At the age of seventy-two, Welch was indicted, together with Justice Corn, by a federal grand jury on five counts of income tax evasion. He was charged with evading $13,364 in taxes from 1957 through 1961.

The trial was originally set in the U.S. District Court for the Western District of Oklahoma. Due to the extensive publicity the trial was receiving, it was transferred to the Eastern District.

It seems that the justice had found it necessary to supplement his $16,500 annual salary with bribes in order to support two households. In the course of the trial, through testimony regarding Justice Welch's financial situation, it became known that he had purchased a home in 1949 for a lady acquaintance of his, a Mrs. Ruby Myers.

The purchase was made through Mrs. Myers' sister and brother-in-law at the same time that Welch made substantial withdrawals from his savings account.

Welch married his wife Fern in 1953. He married Mrs. Myers on June 27, 1959, and moved into the house himself.

After two weeks of trial, and testimony from fifty-four witnesses, Justice Welch was convicted on all five counts of tax evasion. The jury had only deliberated for one hour and forty-seven minutes. On November 13, 1964, he was sentenced to three years in federal prison and fined $13,500. He appealed.

When questioned by reporters, Welch made the following statements: "The word *bribery* is about the ugliest word you can say about a judge. I have written several thousand court cases and voted on many, and in not one was there any influence of money. I never took a bribe. I never sold justice."

Noting that the supreme court was then under investigation, he said he was sure no evidence of bribery would be found. But if there were, he said, "I hope they prosecute. I might have been wrong, but I have been honest. This conviction is bad enough, but it is not as horrible as bribery."

On December 10, 1964, the supreme court voted to disbar Justice Welch. But the action was useless, as several years before Welch had written a majority opinion in which the court held that a lawyer ceased to be a member of the bar when he went on the bench.

The state house of representatives recommended impeachment of both Welch and Johnson on charges of accepting bribes. Welch resigned on March 22, 1965, thereby putting himself beyond impeachment. His tax conviction was upheld on appeal.

Seventy-four-year-old Justice Napoleon Bonaparte Johnson, a member of the supreme court since 1948, decided to stick out his impeachment trial, in the traditional spirit of his namesake.

Both Welch (a Chickasaw) and Johnson were Indians. Johnson served as president of the National Congress of American Indians for several years. At the impeachment trial Justice Johnson's defense counsel called Justice Corn "an evil old man" and said that Corn was prejudiced against Johnson because he was an Indian.

"I am an Indian. Welch is an Indian. The wife of the man Corn had a fight with [referring to a slapping match Corn once had in chambers with another justice, Ben Arnold, now deceased] is an Indian. There could have been a deep-seated prejudice there."

Johnson admitted he had received about $3,600 in campaign contributions when he last ran for reelection in 1960. He did not use the money in his campaign because he was unopposed. Instead he used the money for his own purposes and did not report it as income.

He tried to account for his money by saying that he habitually kept about $2,000 in cash behind a curtain in a window of his bedroom.

All such explanations were to no avail, and Justice Napoleon Bonaparte Johnson met his Waterloo on May 11, 1965, when he was found guilty on two counts of bribery by the state senate by a vote of 32-15.

The fourth former justice of the Oklahoma Supreme Court to be linked with court bribery, Wayne W. Bayless, resigned from the Oklahoma bar February 17, 1966, under charges of conspiring to bribe fellow justices. He had served on the supreme court for sixteen years, from 1933 to 1949.

Former Justice Earl Welch died after suffering a heart attack on November 12, 1969.

Former Justice Nelson S. Corn died in 1967 shortly after his parole from the U.S. Medical Facility.

JUSTICE JOSEPH P. PFINGST (NEW YORK)

New York Supreme Court Justice Joseph P. Pfingst was linked with charges of corruption in 1972. Pfingst was elected to a fourteen-year term on the state supreme court on Long Island after practicing law for two decades. Much of his law practice had involved two dairies that were later declared bankrupt: The W. M. Evans Dairy Company, Inc., and Evans Amityville Dairy, Inc.; they provided the justice with considerable income when he was practicing law.

An alleged conspiracy and transfer had begun on November 18, 1965, when Mr. D'Onofrio, a former officer, director and stockholder, was elected president of Evans Amityville, succeeding the late Sam Marcus. In accordance with a plan devised by Pfingst, D'Onofrio acquired sole control of the business of both dairies on February 28, 1966, in a formal agreement with the estate of Mr. Marcus and his son Bernard.

Fifteen days later, D'Onofrio and Pfingst negotiated the sale of customer goodwill and other assets of the businesses to Beers, Inc., and Queens Farm Creameries, Inc., for $229,000. On March twenty-first the two men then issued corporate checks to themselves totaling $10,000 each and separate checks of $10,600 on the next day as purported dividends.

In April 1966, in a series of transactions that involved the help of Mr. Feeney, the business sales manager, the three divided $66,000 in cash received as the proceeds of another sale to Queens Farms.

As a result of these activities, the companies had virtually no assets left to satisfy the claims of creditors. The trustee in bankruptcy collected only $15,500 from D'Onofrio and Pfingst in the course of the bankruptcy proceedings. W. M. Evans Dairy Company was adjudicated bankrupt on June 22, 1966, and Evans Amityville on October 28, 1966.

Justices Pfingst and Feeney both pleaded not guilty, their trial being scheduled for October 15, 1971. D'Onofrio pleaded guilty to one count of the indictment on July twenty-second of the following year. If convicted, the judge faced up to five years in prison and a $10,000 fine on the conspiracy count and five years and $5,000 on each fraud count.

As if Justice Pfingst weren't in enough trouble already, he was indicted by a federal grand jury on September 3, 1971, on charges of having bought his nomination to the post of supreme court justice for $50,000 from the then Republican leader in the town of Babylon, New York, Frederick R. Fellman. (Fellman, at the time of the indictment, was serving a three-year jail term for grand larceny. He had pleaded guilty to charges of having stolen $4,074 from Nassau-Suffolk Mobile Homes over a period of almost two years.)

By obtaining the Republican nomination to the supreme court, Justice Pfingst was virtually assured the election, since the judicial district in which he was running embraced predominantly Republican Suffolk and Nassau counties. He was elected by a margin of about 3,600 votes over his closest opponent.

Pfingst's two-count indictment stemmed from evidence developed in October 1970 by the Federal Bureau of Investigation, which charged both Pfingst and Fellman with conspiracy to travel and use the facilities of foreign commerce to accomplish the payment.

After allegedly having paid the first half of the $50,000 to Fellman on September 6, 1968, the judge went to Zurich, Switzerland, on October fourteenth and withdrew "in excess of $100,000" from a bank account he maintained under the code name of "Egypt." Five days later he paid $25,000 to Fellman "as the balance due on the $50,000 bribe."

The first count of Pfingst's indictment related to the conspiracy, and the second to the withdrawal of the bribe money from the Swiss account.

ALMOST-JUSTICE SEYMOUR R. THALER (NEW YORK)

To preface his distinguished career as lawyer, legislator, and almost-judge, Seymour R. Thaler was valedictorian of his class at Brooklyn Law School. He served as deputy assistant state attorney general and as deputy commissioner in New York City's Department of Investigation before he was elected state senator in 1958.

In thirteen years as a Democratic state senator from the

New York borough of Queens, Thaler gained a reputation for his oratory on the floor of the senate and for his persistent questioning during investigations. His tireless, highly publicized, one-man expose of city hospitals in 1966 found him engaged in finger-jabbing grilling of doctors. The investigation led to the naming of the city's Health and Hospitals Corporation as a new state authority over municipal hospitals.

Thaler lost a special congressional election in Queens in 1962, when he ran as an independent against Benjamin Rosenthal, a Democrat-Liberal. He also tried unsuccessfully for the city controller's nomination in the Democratic primary in 1969.

In 1971 Thaler resigned as state senator to run for a state supreme court judgeship, one of five created for Queens by the New York legislature.

His election was assured months ahead of time as a result of one of the most sweeping bipartisan political deals in the city's history. The agreement whereby Thaler received the endorsement of both parties was worked out by Queens Republican leader Sidney Hein and Councilman Matthew Troy, then newly elected Queens Democratic leader. Thaler won as expected.

But Justice-elect Thaler did not take office on January 1, 1972, as scheduled. Instead, he was indicted with three others on December 21, 1971, and charged with the receipt of $800,000 in stolen United States Treasury bills. Thaler immediately requested that he not be assigned any judicial duties pending the outcome of the case against him. His noble request was granted.

His codefendants were David Altschul, a lawyer with whom he shared office space; Herbert Jacobs, a textile executive; and Michael LaVelle, a printing company owner. Each defendant was charged in the three-count indictment with conspiracy, knowingly receiving stolen securities and transporting them in interstate commerce. They faced, if convicted, maximum prison sentences of five years on the conspiracy count and ten years on each of the other two counts, as well as fines of up to $10,000 on each count.

Treasury bills are highly negotiable, short-term obligations of the U.S. Treasury, issued for three-month, six-month, nine-month and twelve-month periods to finance a portion of the national debt. They are sold through banks, brokers or bond houses, are not registered, and are therefore as negotiable as cash. The bills cannot be repaid until their maturity date, but an investor in a rush to get cash can sell them readily without penalty. They are sold in denominations of $10,000, $15,000, $50,000, $100,000, $500,000 and $1 million.

The $800,000 cited in the indictment represented part of almost $1.5 million in Treasury bills that were found missing in July 1970 from the Wall Street banking concern of Brown Brothers, Harriman & Company. The bills were traced to Thaler as the result of an extensive investigation by the Federal Bureau of Investigation.

Judge Thaler was arraigned in federal court on December 23, 1971; he pleaded not guilty. The following February four counts of perjury were added to his case: he was charged with lying about his part in the transactions when he appeared before the grand jury four times in the fall of 1971. The trial began March 1, 1972.

Edward M. Shaw, the prosecutor, said in his opening statement to the jury that the defendants had "sold their souls and their reputations for a quarter of a million dollars. Their crime was not stealing the Treasury bills, but illegally getting rid of them for cash," he said, adding that they obtained the highly negotiable securities for only 25 percent of their face value. "That's the central fact in this case demonstrating the guilt of these defendants. Anyone, not just a state senator, would have known those Treasury bills were as hot as Mrs. Murphy's stove."

Milton Gould, Thaler's lawyer, told the jury in his opening statement that his client was an innocent victim who later paid back an insurance company for its losses when he discovered that the Treasury bills were stolen. "The indispensable ingredient of criminality in this case is guilty knowledge," Gould said, stressing that "guilt in this case depends on knowledge that these notes were stolen. If he knew these notes were stolen," Gould said, pointing his finger dramatically at Thaler, "then I will concede to the government that he belongs in the penitentiary."

It looks as if Mr. Gould will have to concede. The government's chief witness was David Altschul, the lawyer who rented office space in Thaler's law offices and who participated in the securities deal.

According to Altschul's testimony, the whole affair began when Mr. LaVelle obtained six Treasury bills (how they were obtained was not established) in $100,000 denominations and four in $50,000 denominations, all of which were later shown to bear the serial numbers of those stolen from the Wall Street bank. LaVelle went to his long-time friend Mr. Jacobs, who was a client of Altschul. Altschul said that Jacobs came to his office on September 15, 1970, and told him that his friend LaVelle wanted to sell some Treasury bills at a "substantial discount," and asked if he knew anyone who would want to buy. Altschul then took the matter to Thaler.

Altschul further testified that he met with all the defendants in the law offices several times to draft a written agreement concerning sale of the securities. The agreement was entered in evidence over the objection of Thaler, who claimed it was a forgery.

The bills were given to Thaler, who was to arrange for them to be cashed at a bank, with LaVelle receiving 25 percent and three others sharing a "finder's fee." Thaler then arranged for Fred H. Hill, a Manhattan real estate man, to deposit $500,000 of the bills in the Chemical Bank at Fifth Avenue and Forty-second Street, but Hill subsequently refused to complete the collection.

Next Thaler arranged for a client, Jules Brassner, a Manhattan art dealer, to deposit $250,000 of the stolen bills for collection at the Second National Bank of New Haven in Connecticut.

According to Brassner's testimony, "Mr. Thaler came up to the gallery, as he did often because he loved paintings," and explained that he shared a law office with a lawyer who had a wealthy client who was selling Treasury bills at a large discount of about 50 percent. When Brassner asked Thaler why anyone would want to sell such highly negotiable bills so far below their true value, Thaler replied that the owner of the securities might be doing it for tax reasons of some sort.

Brassner said he subsequently agreed that he would buy the $250,000 in Treasury bills for $117,000 and would divide the $133,000 in profits with Thaler. He deposited the three bills in November 1970 and paid Thaler's $66,500 share of the profits in checks, including $22,500 to the purchase a Corot painting for Thaler at his request.

Thaler ultimately received $93,333; Brassner, $66,500; LaVelle, $62,500; Altschul, $19,333; and Jacobs, $8,334.

There was no indication why the money was divided in that way.

The remaining $550,000 in Treasury bills was returned to Jacobs and LaVelle because it proved difficult to explain to the bank why these bills had not been cashed as soon as they had matured.

Thaler's lawyer introduced in evidence a memorandum written by a representative of Brown Brothers, Harriman & Company's insurance company after a meeting with Thaler in the summer of 1971. When told that the securities sale was being investigated for the insurance company, the memo said "Senator Thaler stated that he is most anxious to cooperate, that there is nothing to conceal. He said that he was shocked and that he never had anything to do with any other Treasury bills. He offered to return every penny of the profit he made."

When asked why he had received the largest share of the proceeds, Thaler is quoted in the memorandum as replying, "I have no excuse. I was just greedy." That might also serve as the only possible explanation for his involvement in the transaction in the first place.

On March 23, 1972, Thaler was found guilty both of selling the bills and transporting them in interstate commerce. For good measure, the jury also found him guilty of perjury. His codefendants Jacobs and LaVelle were convicted on similar counts and, in addition, found guilty of conspiracy. When the verdict was announced, Justice-elect Thaler "shuddered violently and his hands clapped his face in stunned anguish."

On August 8, 1972, the would-be jurist was sentenced to a year and a day in the state prison. Ninety days later he was dismissed from the court and disbarred. The sentencing judge disregarded a dramatic twenty minutes in which Thaler proclaimed his innocence. "I have a feeling I'm in a nightmare," he exclaimed in an emotion-strained voice on the brink of tears. "I am not guilty. It's incredible that anyone would believe I would participate if I knew they were stolen." He begged the mercy of the court not to shatter his boyhood dream of being a judge.

Chapter Three
Bargains

"We used to fix traffic tickets . . . now we fix anything."
—A NEW YORK STATE LAWYER

One of the wisest men of corruption once said, "If you are going to steal . . . steal big." By some distorted sense of propriety, these select judges seemed to radiate toward petty corruption. Whether their motivation was the misbelief that such instances would go undetected, or, if detected, unpunished, is not provable. But the triviality of their extrajudicial activities does not detract from the corrosive effect on their respective communities and the entire judicial system.

First a Missouri judge whose family represented the leadership politically and legally in their Clay County community. Despite an indictment following an investigation of his court records, the magistrate sought office again only to be miserably defeated. He was subsequently indicted for income tax evasion and sentenced to eight years in prison. And, as a reminder that abuse of judicial office is not new, witness the distinguished federal judge from Florida who, after being impeached by the United States Senate, had to be forceably evicted from his office by U.S. marshals. He had forgotten to stop practicing law while judging cases affecting his clients.

Notwithstanding the higher rank of those other accused judges in Oklahoma, a county judge was impeached by that state's legislature a few years ago for his prolific waiver of rules concerning marriage licenses, blood tests and waiting periods. The Oklahoma Bar Association also frowned on the money he received from the waivers.

A more serious incident involved a trial judge from Virginia convicted recently of forgery and larceny. From New Jersey, the bastion of juridical intrigue, comes the judge whose "oversight" in filing tax returns for five years resulted in his conviction by a federal court.

A more imaginative and less tactful judge in Georgia organized a protection racket for those appearing before him. And, determined not to be outclassed by her neighboring state of New Jersey, New York has for several decades devoted herself to the production, elevation, and ultimate conviction of a large array of jurists from throughout the state. When Judge Rudich was removed from the bench, he claimed he was vindicated because the charge had been delinquency and not corruption. His lawyer announced a "clear-cut victory."

The involvement of judges with bail bonds is nothing new. A successful bondsman can always be counted on to guide large campaign contributions, legal and otherwise, each time a judge offers himself to the public. The common fraternization of bondsmen and judges has been a sore point with bar associations in most states for several years. Recently in Illinois a particularly blatant case was discovered, and Judge Louis Kizas climaxed the issue by pleading guilty to fifteen counts of official misconduct so that the bribery and conspiracy charges against him would be dismissed.

Payoffs from litigants, petty bribes, unauthorized loans from estates and, in one case, shoplifting, make up the list of comparatively trivial offenses that destroyed several judges who offered bargain prices for their friendship, counsel and favors.

JUDGE HALSTED L. RITTER (FLORIDA)

U.S. District Judge Halsted L. Ritter of Florida was impeached by the House of Representatives and tried by the Senate. He had been a very successful lawyer in Denver and had moved to Florida for reasons of family health. Four years later President Coolidge appointed him to a lifetime federal judgeship. The appointment was opposed locally by both Republicans and Democrats. This opposition turned out to be quite justified.

Judge Ritter continued to practice law while on the bench. On April 4, 1929, he accepted $2,000 from a client, Mulford Realty Corporation, who held and owned large interests located within his jurisdiction. He also accepted a large amount of securities from Olympia improvement Corporation, another real estate client, to develop property within his jurisdiction. It was also discovered that on April 19, 1929, he had received $47,500 from J. R. Francis, who personally owned large and diverse property interests in the area.

Ritter conspired with his former law partner, A. L. Rankin, and others to continue a certain parcel of property in litigation. He promoted the conspiracy by retaining jurisdiction of the foreclosure proceedings contrary to a motion made in person by the plaintiff. Ritter appointed a person involved in the conspiracy as receiver. Rankin received the exorbitant fee of $75,000, several thousand dollars of which went to the judge.

Ritter was also found to have bartered his judicial authority in exchange for "loans" in a case involving the Florida Power & Light Company and the city of Miami.

Not only did the judge find it necessary to supplement his $17,300 salary with these fees, but he also failed to report such fees as income. He was charged with income tax evasion by the federal court for 1929 and 1930.

Ritter was impeached by the House of Representatives in 1936 on seven charges. The Senate acquitted him on some of the charges but found him guilty on one by a vote of 56 to 28. That charge claimed general misbehavior and contained the ingredients of all the other articles. By so voting, the Senate sanctioned the proposition that to justify removal of a judge, it is not necessary that he be guilty of a violation of the law. It is sufficient to show that his conduct was such as to bring his office into disrepute.

Ritter had to be evicted from his office by a U.S. marshal because he disregarded the impeachment order of the Senate.

JUDGE GLENN J. SHARPE (OKLAHOMA)

Glenn J. Sharpe became county judge of Bryan County, Oklahoma, in January 1965. He was elected to a second term five years later.

On May 17, 1968, the Oklahoma Bar Association filed a petition with the Court on the Judiciary (created as a result of the recent Oklahoma Supreme Court scandals) charging that, among other things, Judge Sharpe had improperly received fees for issuing waiver orders which authorized the issuance of marriage licenses during the period from January 11, 1965, to July 26, 1967. The period covered both his first term and a part of his second term.

Sharpe had received over $13,000 for issuing waiver orders dispensing with blood-test documents, the three-day waiting period and the state's age requirements for marriage. These "fees" were now being called bribes.

Judge Sharpe contended he was merely accepting gifts for extra services rather than charging fees. But the trial court failed to see the difference and found that he had collected and received monies not authorized by law and that such activity amounted to corruption in office. Accordingly, Sharpe was impeached and removed from office by the legislature and disqualified to hold any public office of honor, trust or profit in the state of Oklahoma for a period of three years.

JUDGE J. CEDRIC CONOVER (NEBRASKA)

For some reason that has never been explained satisfactorily, urban areas seem to produce a greater percentage of judicial polluters than their rural counterparts. But good examples of corruption in sparsely populated areas aren't too hard to find; one is Judge J. Cedric Conover of Morrill County, Nebraska.

Conover became a lawyer in 1934 and began serving as county judge three years later in an area with a total population of 16,000. In 1954 he became county attorney. Four years later the former judge's colleagues instigated charges against him, and the Nebraska State Bar accused him of the unlawful and unethical conduct of practicing law in the court of which he was judge.

The record of the proceedings shows that from June 1947 to May 1950 Judge Conover had accepted employment as an attorney by persons interested in the estates of four deceased persons. The cases were all heard in his court with him presiding. He simply got another lawyer to permit his name to appear as the attorney of record.

The costs of the estates' administration proceedings were paid to Conover in his capacity as judge of the county court. He made no report of the receipt of these funds during his term of office. After he had notice of the investigation of his conduct and the charges being brought against him, he paid the costs in one of the estate cases to the county. He didn't pay the costs in the other three until after the hearing concerning his conduct was completed, more than six years after he had received them.

In 1954 and 1956, in his capacity as county attorney, he received various sums of money from the district court as attorney's fees for Morrill County in the prosecution of three tax lien foreclosure cases. He deposited these in his personal checking account. The money was not paid to the county treasurer until after Conover had received notice of the complaint against him.

Judge Conover, unlike other exposed public officials, didn't deny the charges brought against him. Instead, he claimed his actions were the result of ignorance of the law, mistake and error. But the state of Nebraska disagreed, and Conover was permanently disbarred by the supreme court for his actions.

JUDGE WILLIAM M. A. ROMANS (VIRGINIA)

Judge William M. A. Romans of Lexington, Virginia, was convicted in 1968 of seventeen counts of forgery and obtaining money under false pretenses. He was just recently released from the Virginia State Penitentiary.

In a hand-printed statement signed by him and filed in the trial court at Lexington, Judge Romans said he "does not desire to offer, and in fact does not have any, defense" to disbarment proceedings against him by the state bar association. Neither the state nor the public seemed surprised.

The demoralizing impact of the judge's conviction four years ago is still felt in Virginia. At first there were jokes about perverted justice and dilapidated democracy in the state that nurtured more than its share of our founding fathers.

But levity was soon replaced with depression and mistrust of an already suspected political system. An analysis of the chronicles of Virginia judicial life indicate that the Romans affair was genuinely unique. As in all the states, Virginia has been wrestling with the most effective method of judicial selection and the recruitment of honorable talent to the bench. Judge Romans notwithstanding, Virginia has done well.

JUDGE MAYNARD B. CLINKSCALES (GEORGIA)

Judge Maynard B. Clinkscales was a member of the distinguished Superior Court of Jackson County, Georgia. In 1960 the state brought disbarment proceedings against him.

It was alleged that Clinkscales was the secret leader of a protection racket. Supposedly, the judge offered protection to businesses in exchange for $10,000 cash and a $500 per month retainer.

He had also given his approval for one Marvin Pierce, an attorney, to use the name of the county prosecutor without the latter's knowledge. Mr. Pierce, with the judge as a witness, issued a criminal accusation, accepted a plea of guilty by the accused and imposed a suspended sentence—all in the name of the prosecutor. Needless to say, Pierce had a rather extensive criminal practice.

Judge Clinkscales was found lacking in the moral character necessary to continue as a member of the legal profession and was, therefore, disbarred.

As a superior court judge, Clinkscales was the developer and applier of rules of law. Trial judges, indeed, shape the outcome of pending litigation.

Even after their exposure, the degree of contamination from a judge's machinations cannot always be determined. It is impossible to sift through courtroom battles over which the tainted judge presided and focus on specific acts of impropriety.

JUDGE STANLEY J. POLACK (NEW JERSEY)

In April of each year income tax returns are filed by Americans in every walk of life, but according to the U.S. government, Judge Stanley J. Polack neglected to file his returns in 1963, 1964, 1965, 1966, and 1967. An oversight, no doubt. The judge was accused and arraigned in the federal court in Newark, New Jersey, on April 25, 1969. At his trial Polack contended that he had been "negligent" and perhaps "stupid," but that he had no criminal intent. He said, "While it is true that I failed to file the returns when due, I deny most earnestly that such failure was designed with any criminal intent."

Polack was convicted on October 24, 1969, and fined $10,000. He requested time to make the payment, and the court gave him six months. Since that time the Supreme Court of the United States has handed down some interesting decisions as to what happens if a person fails to pay a fine and has jail as an alternative.

83

The Polack case was another conviction symptomatic of the nation's most judicially deteriorated state—New Jersey. Even as you read of these cases, federal investigators publicly tout there are "more indictments to come."

MAGISTRATE ALFRED F. ORSINI (NEW JERSEY)

In 1962 Magistrate Alfred F. Orsini was charged with contempt of the New Jersey Supreme Court and with unprofessional conduct committed while he was sitting on the Municipal Court of Monroe Township, Middlesex County. The charges arose out of evidence of the judge's compulsion for "fixing" traffic tickets.

Shortly after the start of an investigation by the county prosecutor, Orsini resigned as magistrate, confessed his guilt and cooperated in the investigation and prosecution of others who had been involved.

However, the former judge still faced diciplinary action due to his status as a practicing attorney. Since he admitted guilt, the only question to be decided by the New Jersey Supreme Court was the degree of discipline to be imposed.

Judge Orsini had been appointed solely because of political considerations, and the high court found him "ill-equipped for judicial office." The court concluded that Judge Orsini was "economically dependent upon the political generosity of the local machine and therefore had easily become a pawn of others."

The court added that "his wrongs occurred at a time when,

as we now know, too many failed, incomprehensibly, to understand the corrupt quality of such misbehavior." For these reasons, together with what was termed "some extenuating considerations of a personal nature," Judge Orsini was suspended from the practice of law for a period of six months beginning June 4, 1962.

MAGISTRATE MARK RUDICH (NEW YORK)

Brooklyn Magistrate Mark Rudich was first appointed to the bench on December 31, 1927, to finish two years of an unexpired term. He was accused of misconduct three different times before being removed from office in 1939.

In 1930 he was investigated by a committee of the Brooklyn Bar Association on charges of improperly handling cases against two shoplifters, involving an automobile accident and the shooting of a policeman. The judge was exonerated, and on the basis of an investigatory report clearing him, New York Mayor Jimmy Walker reappointed him for a full ten-year term, declaring, "I hope this will be a lesson to you—you are a good judge."

In 1931 Magistrate Rudich was censured by the appellate division of the court in Brooklyn for violating a city magistrate's rule by improperly sentencing two pickpockets without taking into account their fingerprint records already on file with the court.

The accusation that ultimately led to his removal resulted from a three-month study by a Brooklyn grand jury into the local bail-bond racket. The judge was charged with bribery, attempting to corrupt another judge in the disposition of a court case and accepting money as part of a fraudulent bail-bond scheme.

On February 16, 1939, less than twenty-four hours after the appellate division of the supreme court in Brooklyn received the grand jury charges, Rudich was suspended from office pending the outcome of removal proceedings.

His chief accuser was Louis Kassman, a professional bondsman, who had earlier pleaded guilty to perjury in bail-bond matters. Kassman claimed that he had an arrangement with Rudich whereby the judge, in exchange for cash payments, would sign bail releases for Kassman's clients upon a showing of only nominal security or of phony security offered by Kassman's common-law wife (acting under an assumed name) and others. The bondsman said he had handled "hundreds" of such cases with Rudich since their first meeting in 1929.

Magistrate Rudich denied all charges and denounced Kassman as "a wife-beater," an "opium fiend" and a person of such unsavory connections "that had I known any part of them, he could not have come within a mile of me or my doorstep." But, as the facts of the men's relationship became known, the judge's statement lost stature.

Despite dramatic denials and various legal maneuvers, removal proceedings began on March 21, 1939. Newspaper reports of the proceedings were headline material for many weeks to come.

Kassman testified that he had decided to "tell the truth" in this case "because I want to be a man and face everyone with a clear conscience." He said that before, "my life has been a pack of lies, but now I'm telling the truth, no matter who it hurts."

He swore he met Rudich in 1929 through an attorney who

was a close friend of the magistrate. "In those days everything was good, people were running speak-easies, and you
could make money on pre-arraignment bonds to make sure
the defendant appeared in federal court the day after his
arrest," said Kassman. "Judge Rudich charged ten dollars a
bond."

Kassman explained that he could neither read nor write
English and that he had an office boy who looked up telephone numbers for him. He then referred to his "little red
address book" and said that it was upon Rudich's advice that
he had listed the magistrate's telephone numbers with the
names "Rudolph" and "Spiegel" opposite them. "Judge
Rudich suggested that when I called him on the telephone,"
said Kassman, "that I call him Dr. Kane, and he called me
Kane, and later he would call and say, 'Kane, this is Kane
calling,' and I knew it was Rudich."

In March 1937 Ida Unterford (alias Rose Cohen and Fanny
Goldberg), a prostitute, called Kassman at his office and
asked him to provide bail for her. She had been found guilty
of loitering by Magistrate Anthony Burke in the magistrate's
court in Manhattan and was being held without bail pending
the imposition of a sentence. Her attorney was Jacob P.
Nathanson, a former Brooklyn assemblyman who later
pleaded guilty to perjury together with Kassman.

Kassman received $175 to handle the case, and told
Nathanson that he would call Magistrate Rudich and see what
he could do to help them. He then got in touch with the
judge "and explained the whole thing to him. I said, 'Burke is
going to give her a sentence.' He said, 'What can I clear for
myself if I see Judge Burke?' and I said, 'What do you want?'
and we agreed on $100. I said all right and the bargain was
made."

Rudich and Kassman agreed to have a man named Doodle

Rosenthal, who "hung around" Kassman's office, pose as Miss Unterford's husband and say he was a "hard-working waiter." All three men then met in the judge's courtroom and drove in separate cars to the Manhattan courthouse where Rudich and Rosenthal approached Magistrate Burke's bench, while Kassman sat in the back of the room.

The two magistrates talked for ten or fifteen minutes. Rudich asked Judge Burke to be lenient in the case, to suspend sentence or to credit Miss Unterford for the three days she had already spent in jail awaiting sentence. He said he knew her husband and that some other friends had spoken to him about her. He said she had a nineteen-year-old daughter going to college and that it would be a terrible thing to send her to jail because her daughter would then know about her mother. At the close of the conversation, Burke indicated he would probably suspend sentence "as it was the kind of case for that."

Rudich and Kassman left the courtroom by different exits and met outside on Second Avenue where the judge was given $100 cash for his "services." (Ida Unterford was later sentenced to ten days in jail, instead of receiving her expected suspended sentence.)

On November 13, 1936, a Harry Schwartz was arrested and charged with unlawful possession of narcotics and was confined in the Raymond Street jail. Immediately after his arrest, he called his wife and instructed her to get in touch with Kassman. In the meantime, bail was set at $5,000.

Kassman informed Schwartz's wife that he could get her husband out in return for payment of $300. She agreed, and Kassman reached Judge Rudich at a midtown Manhattan hotel where the judge was attending a dinner party. They arranged to meet in the hotel lobby.

Kassman arrived accompanied by Arcangela Battista, a

bondsman whom Rudich knew to be on the list of unacceptable bondsmen. The judge agreed to a deal whereby he would receive $100 in exchange for accepting a bond executed by Battista.

A few days later Rudich, fearing the court clerk might discover Battista was on the undesirable list if the bond was submitted to him for filing, delivered the bond to Kassman and instructed him on how to sneak the papers into the case file. Kassman and another bondsman, Louis Finkelstein, a close friend of Rudich, went to the courthouse in Brooklyn. While Kassman kept the attention of the clerk who had brought out the papers in the case at their request, Finkelstein inserted the bail-bond papers with the regular court papers. Schwartz was released and the fraud went undiscovered.

On March 3, 1938, Harry Lowenthal was arrested and confined in the Seventy-eighth Precinct of New York City on a charge of extortion. He was arraigned in the felony court and bail was set at $2,500.

His wife, Bertha Lowenthal, owned property in Brooklyn, but her equity was not sufficient to cover the bail. After unsuccessful efforts to secure bail by legitimate means, she called Kassman, who, in turn, called Magistrate Rudich. The judge agreed to accept Mrs. Lowenthal and Mrs. Kassman as sureties on the bond for a $50 fee.

At midnight on the following night, they met at the judge's apartment. The bond was executed with Mrs. Lowenthal and Mrs. Kassman, signing as "Jennie Genett," as sureties. Within an hour, Lowenthal was released.

In July 1938 Dr. Robert Kahn was taken into custody and charged with manslaughter as a result of an illegal abortion he performed. Bail was fixed at $5,000. After a week of failing to secure property bail, Kahn's relatives hired Kassman to procure the doctor's release.

Kassman called Judge Rudich at his summer home in Rockaway. The judge and the bondsman worked out an agreement for an insufficient and inadequate security to be accepted and a fee of $50 to be paid the judge. Kassman's wife, under her regular assumed name of "Jennie Genett," was again the principal surety as the purported owner of property to which she had no title.

The magistrate was particularly sympathetic to prostitutes in distress. On October 22, 1938, Mary Kelly was arrested on morals charges and held in the Women's House of Detention. No magistrate in the borough of Manhattan, where the charge was pending, would accept the property offered as security for bail, since it was located outside their jurisdiction.

But the dynamic duo of Kassman/Rudich came to the rescue. For a mere $35 the judge accepted the property bond, and Miss Kelly was released one day after her arrest, minimizing her "business losses."

In another case involving three prostitutes, Kassman arranged for Rudich to take the release bonds in his home in Brooklyn and paid him a total of $60. The rate was $15 a bond, but one of the girls had two charges against her. The judge was cheaper than the prostitutes.

Kassman said that in such matters he would often call the judge two weeks in advance to find out what court he would be sitting in, and that he then went to various bondsmen in the courts and said, "If you've got anything, I can get it thrown out."

On March 25, 1939, Magistrate Rudich was removed from office by a unanimous vote of the appellate division of the supreme court in Brooklyn on the grounds of "delinquency affecting his general character and fitness for office."

Rudich immediately announced he would return to practicing law. He felt he had been cleared because he was removed for "delinquency" and not "corruption." His lawyer said, "The decision of the learned justices of the appellate division completely absolves Judge Rudich of any charge of corruption. The judge and I feel it to be a clean-cut victory. The court by its decision, found that Judge Rudich had not accepted any bribes as charged in the specifications filed by the grand jury. It will be noted the removal is based solely on the ground of delinquency."

The bar association was not so convinced that the judge was "clear." After the county prosecutor announced he would not try Rudich on criminal charges, the Brooklyn Bar Association instituted disbarment proceedings, which came before the same court that had decided the removal case.

In addition to the charges brought in the removal proceedings, Rudich was charged with accepting money for releasing three men who had been arrested for bookmaking. He had held their trial on a Sunday morning when he knew there would be no assistant district attorney present and then dismissed the charges.

Despite the evidence, the appellate division decided to "reserve decision" in the matter since Rudich had already been removed from the bench, and had not yet actually started practicing law. Besides, rehashing the case could only hurt our judicial system.

JUDGE LOUIS W. KIZAS (ILLINOIS)

Louis W. Kizas holds the rather dubious distinction of having been the primary reason for the first convening of the Illinois Courts Commission, the disciplinary board of the

Illinois Supreme Court. In May 1967 the sixty-four-year-old judge's unusual bail-bond practices became the subject of an exhaustive study by investigators from the office of the Illinois attorney general.

The judge's prolific bond approvals came to light after a priest complained to the chief judge of the circuit court that Kizas had released on their own recognizance two men charged with armed robbery of a Catholic church. Release on a recognizance (no-cash) bond for a criminal suspect charged with a felony involving the use of a weapon (the robbers shot at a nun) was most unprecedented even in Chicago, and the two defendants failed to appear in court on the designated date. The chief judge decided to investigate further.

The investigation revealed that in the seventeen-month period beginning January 1, 1966, Judge Kizas had issued nine hundred and forty-four bonds, while the average number written by other circuit court judges was not more than seventy. In addition, records from bond books in 105 police stations in the Chicago suburbs showed that Kizas had signed bonds in more than seventy-five cases in suburban Cook County. He had frequently approved low-cash or no-cash bonds in serious felony cases. On occasion he had substantially reduced bonds set by other judges; and, in response to calls from select lawyers, he would write bonds at police stations throughout the city and suburbs at all hours of the day or night. There was also evidence that the judge had accepted monetary "gifts" in exchange for setting certain bails.

On the basis of these findings, the chief judge, on May 11, 1967, directed the state's attorney general to prepare formal charges against Judge Kizas. He also requested the supreme court to convene the Illinois Courts Commission to pass on the charges and ordered Kizas suspended from the bench with pay ($26,500 annually), pending the outcome.

The complaint filed by the attorney general charged the judge had "illegally taken and received sums of money for and in consideration of his performance of official duties," and that he had "displayed total disregard" for circuit court rules regarding bonds.

Two preliminary hearings were held in August, and October second was set as the date for the commission to hear the evidence. But on September 14, 1967, Judge Kizas resigned from the bench "due to poor health." Since the only issue to be decided was whether or not to remove Judge Kizas, the commission's proceedings became moot and the state's complaint was dismissed.

Despite his resignation, Kizas was punished. On October 27, 1967, the Cook County grand jury indicted him on charges of official misconduct, bribery, and conspiracy to commit bribery on the basis of evidence that he had sold presigned, blank, no-cash bonds and accepted money to set bail. In companion indictments, four lawyers the three bondsmen were charged with bribery or conspiracy to commit bribery. In April 1969, at Kizas' first trial, the jury was hung nine to three. Shortly before the jury was impaneled at the second trial, in August 1969, Judge Kizas pleaded guilty to fifteen counts of official misconduct and was fined $15,000. The prosecution then dismissed the bribery and conspiracy charges. On November 25, 1969, on his own motion, his name was stricken from the state's list of attorneys.

JUDGE JAMES E. MURPHY (ILLINOIS)

While the investigation of Judge Kizas and his instant bond projects was in progress, the chief judge extended the inquiry to include all bonds written by all judges in Cook County for two years prior to 1967. It was discovered that Judge James E. Murphy had also written an unusually high number of bonds. He, too, was suspended from the bench pending a hearing, and the supreme court was again requested to convene the courts commission.

Murphy, only forty-two years old, was an associate judge in the county division of the circuit court. He was a former Chicago policeman and former attorney for the Board of Elections Commissioners.

The charges against Judge Murphy, set forth in the attorney general's complaint, were that he set 702 bonds in a twenty-one-month period; that he set bonds at places other than his assigned place of duty, and at times when bonds would normally have been issued by specifically designated courts (e.g., night bond court, weekend bond court); and that he set bonds in amounts higher than those prescribed by court rules. An amended complaint alleged that the judge "went out of his way to sign bonds for various persons reliably reputed to be racketeers." Finally Murphy was accused of setting a "very substantial number" of unrealistic bonds for persons charged with violations of the laws relating to gambling, prostitution, and narcotics, "which may be classified as crimes of an organized nature."

The Illinois Courts Commission finally began hearings on the evidence on June 3, 1968. A week later it announced the decision that Judge Murphy was not guilty of misconduct and dismissed the complaint. The opinion stated that, if anything, the judge "was indiscreet and unwise and mistaken

94

in judgment in attending to these activities of setting bail at police stations in all parts of Chicago and at all times of night to accommodate persons charged with crime."

For much of the month following the May 1967 church robbery that led to the exposition of Judge Kizas' misconduct and later to charges against Judge Murphy, the cases were front-page news in Chicago's daily newspapers. In early July, while the cases were still fresh in memory, a group of about eighty leading trial lawyers and judges from throughout Illinois met at a two-day conference on civil procedure. Naturally, much of the talk centered around the bond scandal. The consensus was that the Illinois Courts Commission was ineffective as a tool for ridding the judicial system of corrupt or incompetent judges. Even though there were many judges whose conduct had been seriously questioned by members of the organized bar, the commission had been convened only twice (in the Kizas and Murphy cases), and then only because of the extreme pressure from the press.

As an outgrowth of that conference and the committee it established, one year and seven meetings later the Illinois Supreme Court ordered the Courts Commission convened on a permanent basis, thus eliminating some of the delay and political considerations involved in requesting a convening of the commission each time a judge was to be investigated.

JUSTICE MICHAEL M. D'AURIA (NEW YORK)

Justice Michael M. D'Auria of the state supreme court in Nassau County tried to be a good neighbor, but, unfortunately, the cost of his favors was about $2,500 too high.

Justice D'Auria had graduated from St. John's Law School in 1951 and quietly practiced law and politics until 1964, when he was appointed by New York Governor Nelson Rockefeller to fill out an unexpired term as a Nassau County judge. The following fall D'Auria suffered an unusual and unexpected setback in his career. He was defeated in the election for county judge although he was the incumbent with the governor's blessing.

Determined to be a judge, D'Auria decided to start over. What better place to begin than the most popular prebench position in New York—a local party leader? In 1966 he was voted Oyster Bay Town Republican leader. Two years later he was elected with bipartisan support to a fourteen-year term on the New York State Supreme Court.

All went well for more than a year. But on March 31, 1970, Justice D'Auria suffered another setback, this time more serious and more permanent. He was suspended from his office by Marcus J. Christ, presiding justice of the appellate division of the supreme court, who announced that a full inquiry would be conducted into D'Auria's activities. Justice Christ said he was acting in response to two copyrighted newspaper articles that appeared in Long Island's *Newsday,* accusing D'Auria of continuing for more than thirteen months to demand legal fees for his services to a client of his former law firm. Both New York State law and the Canons of Judicial Ethics prohibit a judge to engage in private practice of law.

The articles charged that the judge had demanded legal fees from a couple who were his neighbors for using his influence to assure property rezoning. Charles Orlando, a real estate broker, and his wife Elizabeth, swore that in addition to the legal fees, Justice D'Auria demanded "secret cash

96

payments" totaling $2,500, saying it was "for Councilman Edmund A. Ocker, the majority leader of the Republican-controlled Oyster Bay Town Board, and other unspecified town officials."

Justice D'Auria strenuously denied practicing law or demanding legal fees. He "never heard of secret cash payments" after he went on the bench. He also denied holding three private meetings which the Orlandos said they had with him in 1969.

Following a report on the preliminary investigation of the charges against Justice D'Auria, the Court on the Judiciary was convened to hear and investigate official charges of misconduct in office. But the judge saved the state the expense and himself the embarrassment of highly publicized proceedings. On July 28, 1970, he suddenly submitted his resignation to Governor Rockefeller, who did not hesitate to accept.

Perhaps the moral is: If you're going to do a judicial favor for your neighbors, don't charge them for it—or at least be careful not to charge too much. Most people don't mind buying justice, as long as the price is right.

JUDGE HENDERSON GRAHAM (MICHIGAN)

In 1962 Henderson Graham was the duly elected probate judge of Tuscola County, serving his second four-year term. Following an investigation initiated by the Michigan attorney general, proceedings were begun before the Supreme Court of

Michigan on charges of the judge's misconduct in office and the proper disciplinary measures to be taken. It seems that the judge was in the habit of tapping the estates being handled in his court for personal loans.

The court found that on and prior to February 11, 1961, Judge Graham tried, though unsuccessfully, to secretly negotiate a $20,000 personal loan to himself from an estate subject to his court's control.

That loan involved the estate of a minor, Edwina Green. Judge Graham had appointed Edwina's older sister, Sylvia Goszkowski, as guardian of the estate on September 21, 1959. On October 3, 1960, Mrs. Goszkowski filed with the probate court an inventory of the ward's estate. The inventory disclosed that the parents of the two sisters had been killed in an automobile accident, and that the sum of $16,666.67, representing Edwina's share of the proceeds recovered in the subsequent wrongful death actions, had been distributed to Mrs. Goszkowski as Edwina's guardian. These proceeds, added to the amount previously received, made a net total of $20,294.18 in liquid assets in the hands of the guardian.

In early February 1961 the judge telephoned Mrs. Goszkowski in Detroit for the purpose of negotiating a personal loan from the ward's estate in the sum of $20,000. Mrs. Goszkowski told him she would discuss the proposal with her sister, who was then a student at Michigan State University, and that she would return his call. Since the proposal seemed rather unusual, she called her attorney for advice. The attorney called a member of the attorney general's staff.

Mrs. Goszkowski was directed to call Judge Graham, as she had agreed, in the presence of two officers of the state police. The call was made, in the course of which Mrs. Goszkowski accepted the judge's offer to come to her home in Detroit to discuss the proposal. On February 8, 1961, the judge showed up as arranged with several documents about his real estate and his insurance policies. The conversation was secretly recorded by the officers.

The judge offered as security for the loan a promissory note signed by him and his wife. He said that the sisters could hold a mortgage on his home or his property, but that he would rather they didn't, and that "it wouldn't be necessary to register it."

The conference of February eighth was concluded with no decision made. Mrs. Goszkowski agreed to get in touch with the judge later. Two days later, by appointment, she went to the Detroit office of the attorney general where she placed a call to the judge. She told him that they could not go through with the loan. Later that day, Judge Graham called Mrs. Goszkowski again, and asked to discuss the loan personally with her ward.

A meeting was arranged and held on February eleventh at the guardian's home. The two sisters were present, along with the judge and two police officers who were in the next room recording the entire conversation. The same proposal was presented and discussed for approximately one hour. The two sisters finally told the judge that their decision was "No," whereupon he threatened, to no avail, to raise the amount of the guardian's bond.

In the course of the hearing before the Michigan Supreme Court it was also established that Judge Graham had actually taken over and comingled with his own funds certain cash which belonged in the hands of a duly appointed judiciary of another estate under his jurisdiction, that of John Prief, deceased.

A few days after Mr. Prief's death, a Mr. Montague brought into the Tuscola County Probate Court certain amounts of cash belonging to the decedent. The first amount was $2,990. It was brought in on November 25, 1959, and receipted as estate funds by the probate register. The next amount, $661.51, was brought in by Mr. Montague on November twenty-seventh and receipted as estate funds by the judge himself. No special administrator was appointed, and it was not until October 31, 1960, that a Mr. Claude Sirdan was appointed executor of Mr. Prief's will upon the order of Judge Graham.

Mr. Sirdan promptly asked the judge for the money belonging to the estate and, shortly after the request, received $2,990. The first time Mr. Sirdan asked for the balance, the judge said, "I'll have a check in the mail shortly." No check was sent. The second time Sirdan asked for the money, the judge replied, "You don't need the money too badly right now, and I'll have it to you shortly." It was not until the estate was ready for final distribution that the judge paid the balance and, being in doubt as to the amount owing, did so by his personal "blank check" sent to the attorney for the estate.

The only explanation offered by Judge Graham for retention of the remaining six hundred-odd dollars was that, "It apparently got into a compartment where I kept some of my personal money at times."

The court did not accept his excuse. On April 4, 1962, it found that Graham's judicial misconduct warranted a recommendation to the legislature to adopt concurrent resolutions for his permanent removal from office. Both sides quickly accommodated.

JUDGE FRANK O. ALONZO (ALABAMA)

Judge Frank O. Alonzo began his law career in Alabama in 1961. In the general election five years later he was elected judge of the Court of General Sessions of Mobile County. He was sworn in during an impressive ceremony attended by the Mobile elite on January 16, 1967.

A few months later the Grievance Committee of the Alabama State Bar began disbarment proceedings. The Alabama state legislature simultaneously began the impeachment process.

The primary charges involved Alonzo's dealings with Mobile Adjustment Service, Inc., a collection agency, the bulk of whose collection business consisted of past-due accounts owed to physicians and hospitals in the greater Mobile area.

From January 1, 1966, through January 16, 1967, Adjustment Service, Inc., had mailed delinquent debtors a so-called lawyer's letter, threatening court action if they failed to receive immediate payment. The letter was written on the stationery of Alonzo & Alonzo and signed by Reynolds R. Alonzo, the judge's brother and partner. The Mobile Adjustment Service paid $100 per month for the use of the firm name, and for at least a part of the time the letters were prepared and mailed from the company's office.

Ben F. Stokes, a close friend of Judge Alonzo, was the attorney for Mobile Adjustment Service. Stokes had been most active in Alonzo's campaign for the judgeship, and his client had been a liberal contributor to the campaign fund.

On January 12, 1967, four days before the judge was to take office, Stokes and Alonzo talked by telephone. Alonzo told Stokes that the $100 per month retainer paid to Reynolds Alonzo would have to be increased to $350 per month, or the judge would "hurt" the company in court. Stokes told Alonzo he would have to check with the company directly.

Stokes made a written memorandum of this conversation and the next day purchased a tape recording device and attached it to his telephone.

There were numerous tape-recorded telephone conversations between Stokes and Alonzo in the following days. On January 13, 1967, Stokes called Alonzo and asked him if he was going to hurt him. Alonzo assured him he would "suffer no loss." Stokes then asked whether or not the judge-elect had discussed the money with Mobile Adjustment Service. Alonzo replied "No," that actions speak louder than words. He said he would hold the assignments of the debts the adjustment service was trying to collect invalid and would require every doctor to testify in person concerning the reasonableness of the charges represented by the bills assigned to the service.

Ten days after Alonzo was sworn in as presiding judge of the court of general sessions and ex officio judge of the Inferior Civil Court of Mobile County, Stokes again called him and inquired if he had discussed the increase fee with "Jerry" or "Gordon," and Alonzo again replied "No." He also threatened to deny judgment in all of the company's cases. Alonzo insisted the help he would give was worth the increased fee to the firm. Alonzo also told Stokes he was going to request a newspaper reporter to do an article on the activities of the Mobile Adjustment Service.

Stokes talked next with the judge in the courthouse on January 30, 1967. In the course of this conversation, Stokes advised Alonzo that the company was not going to increase the retainer. Alonzo then told Stokes that he was going to dismiss all cases filed under assignments of the debts starting on February first in the inferior court.

On February first, Stokes again called Judge Alonzo, at which time the judge asked Stokes what cases he handled besides those of Mobile Adjustment Service. He repeated the threat to require all the doctors and hospitals having suits in his court to testify to the reasonableness of their charges. Alonzo stated, "I'm not going to do anything outside the law, but I'm gonna make life miserable for them for a little while."

On February twenty-first Stokes called Alonzo and discussed the possibility of filing a mandamus action against him. Near the end of this conversation, Stokes asked the judge if the increase in the retainer would help, to which Alonzo replied, "Things are gonna be so sweet and nice, you just can go back to filing joint suits and just doing all sorts of things to make life easy and nice and wonderful."

On February 26, 1967, Stokes called the judge and informed him that the Mobile Adjustment Service was going to increase the retainer and would then want what was coming to them. The judge said they would get even better than preferential treatment. He instructed Stokes to have the check made payable to Reynolds Alonzo since his name was on the letterhead.

The first $250 increase check was deposited to the joint account of Alonzo & Alonzo, as was a second check in the amount of $350 dated March 13, 1967. At the same time judgments were awarded by Alonzo to the adjustment company in several cases.

The Board of Commissioners of the Alabama State Bar conducted extensive hearings on Alonzo's conduct. On

December 16, 1967, they announced that the judge was guilty of official misconduct and extortion and ordered his permanent disbarment.

The legislature had impeached the judge the previous June and all appeals failed, and the collection agency and their lawyer lived happily ever after.

JUDGE JOHN LODWICK, JR. (MISSOURI)

In 1966 Lodwick was a prestigious family name in legal and political circles in Clay County. Judge John Lodwick's father was a former mayor of Excelsior Springs and one of three lawyers in the town, where he had practiced since 1936. The judge's brother David was the county prosecuting attorney. The judge's mother was a member of the Clay County Democratic Central Committee. The judge was vice-president of the Clay County Bar Association, former president of the county Young Democrats, and a former Democratic state committeeman.

Lodwick graduated from the University of Michigan Law School, where he was president of his senior class. After two years in the family firm he ran for and won a four-year term as city magistrate in 1954. He won a second term in 1958, and then, in 1962, he defeated an incumbent to win the local probate judgeship.

But in the spring of 1966, the last year of his probate term, a two-week grand jury investigation of Judge Lodwick's magistrate court records for 1961 resulted in an indictment charging him with seven counts of embezzlement. The indictment claimed he had pocketed court fines received when he was town magistrate. The family name was further damaged when local papers reported, a month after the indictment, that the judge had once appointed his father as inheritance tax appraiser of a $935,000 estate.

Due to the judge's high social standing, the indictment set off a major scandal. For the remainder of the spring and summer the case appeared regularly in the local and state newspapers. The judge's lawyer said he would seek an immediate trial date, and it was scheduled for June sixth, only three months after the indictment had been returned. Lodwick contended that local prejudice in Clay County would prevent him from getting a fair trial, and he was given a change of venue.

During the months following the embezzlement indictment the judge publicly appeared unconcerned about his predicament. On April 28, 1966, he again filed his name as a Democratic candidate for probate judge in the August primary election. In Clay County, victory in the Democratic primary meant victory in the general election. His paid political advertisements emphasized his involvement with the Methodist Church, Elks Club, United Fund, Junior Chamber of Commerce, Rotary Club, Shrine Club, Eastern Star, Boy Scouts, Red Cross, Clay County Bar Association and the Missouri Historical Society. The ads ended with a statement of the judge's view that Clay County needed a probate judge who was "experienced, efficient, progressive and acquainted with the people's problems."

Some candidates apparently didn't share Judge Lodwick's confidence that he would win the nomination. Two others had already filed in the primary for the probate judgeship, including the former judge defeated by Lodwick in 1962.

Two Democrats seeking seats in the state legislature publicly rejected the support of local labor groups to avoid having their names appear with the judge's on labor's political literature. As the campaign progressed, the papers kept the controversy alive with front-page headlines and editorials.

Judge Lodwick lost in the primary election. He received 3,151 out of the 18,000 votes cast and carried only 8 of 115 precincts. In the general election in November, as a result of the Lodwick scandal, three Democratic county officeholders were ousted by Republicans, in a county where the GOP had not held any public office in over 140 years.

About a month following the general elections the Internal Revenue Service announced an investigation of Judge Lodwick's magistrate court records in order to determine whether he had received any taxable but unreported income through alleged embezzlement. The IRS investigation continued for a year. Meanwhile, Lodwick completed his term as probate judge, which expired January 1, 1967, and his term as vice-president of the county bar association, which expired in July 1967.

The investigation was completed and evidence submitted to the federal grand jury in Kansas City in January 1968. The following month Judge Lodwick was indicted for income tax evasion. He was charged with having received $6,750 that he did not report and with failing to pay the additional $2,526 in taxes. He was also charged with filing a false return in 1961. At the close of the five-day trial in May 1968, the judge was found guilty and sentenced to the maximum prison term on each charge, a total of eight years.

JUSTICE AARON G. WINDHEIM &
JUSTICE ROBERT MAIDMAN (NEW YORK)

Aaron G. Windheim's salary as police justice in Nyack village, New York, was apparently not sufficient to cover the costs of his leisure-time activities. On January 15, 1972, Justice Windheim received a summons from the Clarkstown police after a security officer at the Korvette department store in Nanuet charged that the judge had left the store with a $31.99 ski jacket and a $4.99 ski hat without making the customary stop at the cashier's counter.

As a Rockland County police justice, Windheim handled traffic cases, family disputes and such criminal matters as shoplifting. The judge refused to discuss the summons and the irony of the fact that he was now the one being charged with a crime of which he had previously found others guilty. He did, however, step down from the bench pending disposition of the charges against him.

Justice Windheim's colleague, Police Justice Robert Maidman, who had just taken office on January first, intervened to have the charges dropped against his colleague, and Maidman was likewise ordered to step down until it could be determined whether he should face charges of official misconduct.

The issue was whether Justice Maidman had abused his power when he held a meeting with the Korvette store officials on January eighteenth, after which the store withdrew its shoplifting charge against Justice Windheim.

The administrative head of the courts said on February seventh that he had asked Maidman to step down until the controversial issue was resolved. But the justice, who had not sat on the bench since earlier that month, said that ill health had prompted him to step down. His court clerk notified the Clarkstown police, the state and Interstate Park Commission that Justice Maidman would not be available to handle legal matters until further notice. She said he had asked her to inform the agencies because he was in poor health and very busy.

The Korvette management later reinstated the charges against Justice Windheim, and he was indicted on February 11, 1972, for petty larceny.

No further action could be taken against Justice Maidman until a grand jury had an opportunity to examine the case. District Attorney Robert Meehan said that in any event, "the jury's findings would be sealed, and it could be months before the decision is opened." In the meantime, perhaps the two judges would have some time to do a little skiing.

Charges were presented to the grand jury on February 11, 1972, concerning Judge Windheim, but they were subsequently dismissed when Windheim stepped down from the bench.

According to the *Journal News* in Nyack village, the county brand jury received a sealed presentment and began an investigation directed at determining the propriety of Judge Maidman's conduct and recommending what disciplinary action, if any, should be taken. In the meantime, the judicial district's court administrator suspended him from the bench until completion of the study. The matter was unresolved for over a year. No one replaced the judge and the court was inoperative; a staggering backlog of cases piled up.

On June 26, 1973, Rockland County Police Justice Robert W. Maidman was censured by the New York Appellate Division for having interfered in a criminal case (involving his law partner). The appellate court said that while Maidman had definitely violated judicial ethics, his misconduct "stemmed from a desire to help and no venality was involved." Windheim had previously resigned as town justice when the district attorney dropped shoplifting charges against him.

Chapter Four
The Sensuous Judge

"I'm going to screw you every way I can, short of reversible error."

—JUDGE FLOYD SARISOHN

The ethical code that guides the lives of judges is rather strict. At least there is no provision or authorization for the "handling" of female employees or for any involvement with women appearing before the court in complicated divorce suits.

Needless to say, the charges against the distinguished criminal judge in Louisiana who presided over the Kennedy conspiracy trial were even more serious. The most liberal community will not condone pimping, procuring pornographic films or staging stag parties as an act of judicial service. Perhaps the most common category of "the sensuous judge" is that which includes the "patters" and "grabbers." Recently one imaginative jurist has taken to lifting the skirts of his employees and autographing their underwear.

The morals of the nation may have changed, but these robed gentlemen represent an illustrative conglomeration who in their own way demonstrate the need for change in judicial selection and supervision.

JUDGE EDWARD A. HAGGERTY, SR. (LOUISIANA)

Criminal Court Judge Edward A. Haggerty presided at the Kennedy conspiracy trial of Clay L. Shaw in New Orleans in 1969. Controversial District Attorney Jim Garrison (who has since faced his own problems) had brought Shaw to trial on charges of conspiring to murder the president. On March 1, 1969, Shaw was fully acquitted.

Nine months later Judge Haggerty was arrested, along with thirteen others, in a motel vice raid. Among the others charged was Malcolm Munday, Jr., who was at one time Garrison's assistant district attorney.

On January 9, 1970, the fifty-six-year-old Haggerty pleaded not guilty to charges of "organizing an assemblage for indecent purposes, procuring lewd films and photographs and procuring prostitutes." The case was heard, without a jury, by Judge Haggerty's fellow judge, Matthew S. Braniff, who ruled that the gathering was a "private" party. He found Haggerty not guilty.

But the Louisiana Judiciary Commission was not satisfied. After a preliminary investigation and a six-day hearing, the commission determined that Judge Haggerty was guilty of charges warranting his removal from the bench. The commission submitted a forty-six-page report in support of its opinion, setting forth its conclusive evidence.

A bachelor party honoring Kenneth Reeves was held at the DeVille Motel on Tulane Avenue in New Orleans on December 17, 1969. The local vice squad, which had been investigating illegal lewd parties, learned of the affair and planned a raid. The detectives never realized who would be there.

The police had tipped newsmen about the raid, and photographers were conveniently on hand to get pictures of Judge Haggerty as he struggled with police in an effort to escape the embarrassing scene.

Haggerty had attended and helped arrange the orgy. He contributed money before the party to assist in its arrangement and more money after the party started. Testimony of those present established that Haggerty knew the party was to be held in the DeVille Motel and that he brought the obscene films to the party. The pornographic films were shown to those attending, including three prostitutes whom Judge Haggerty brought to the party. The "hookers" put on a live show and then sold their wares.

Judge Haggerty admitted inviting the trio of "ladies" to the party and accompanying them across the street from the Rowntowner to the DeVille Motel. He claimed the invitation was a joke and that he did not know the women were "working girls."

During the raid Judge Haggerty's personal behavior was not exactly that of an innocent victim caught up in a raid. As the police arrived, he jogged out of the room in which the stag films were being shown, notwithstanding the fact that a police officer had informed him he was under arrest. He resisted the efforts of two other officers to arrest him in the corridor about forty feet from the door of the room he had just left. After the struggle he was brought back to the room but again tried to break away, this time slugging one of the officers. He was finally subdued on the motel room floor and handcuffed. Unusual conduct for a respectable member of the judiciary.

It was also shown that Judge Haggerty had regularly participated in illegal gambling activities. He associated with Manuel Soto, a known "bookie" with a rather lengthy criminal record. The judge placed bets with Soto in public, on an almost daily basis.

As further evidence of his versatility, Haggerty frequently associated with a Frank Occhipinti, manager and part owner of the Rowntowner Motor Hotel across the street from the DeVille Motel. Occhipinti, who has admitted significant business dealings with certain underworld characters in the New Orleans area, permitted Judge Haggerty to have a bill at the hotel's bar and restaurant in excess of $1,700. No request or demand for payment was ever made.

Occhipinti had a brother Roy who had felony charges pending before the criminal district court. As chance would have it, in February of 1969 brother Roy's matter was assigned to Judge Haggerty, who subsequently heard numerous motions in conjunction with the prosecution of the case. The judge made no attempt whatsoever to reassign the case, nor did he excuse himself. Roy frequently visited his brother Frank at the Rowntowner, where the judge often spent his off-the-bench hours.

It appears that Judge Haggerty was interested in other indoor sports at the DeVille Motel besides lewd sex parties. He was also an avid fan of the games there.

Haggerty was often the big winner and was required to pay the rental on the room used for the game. The usual rate was $12 per night. Between June 24, 1969, and January 15, 1970, forty-two nights' room rental was charged to Haggerty.

Although Judge. Haggerty maintained that all these activities in no way affected his behavior on the bench, on November 23, 1970, the Louisiana Supreme Court, upon the recommendation of the judiciary commission, ruled that he was unfit to be a judge and ordered him removed from office without further delay.

JUDGE FLOYD SARISOHN (NEW YORK)

Floyd S. Sarisohn was admitted to the practice of law in New York State in December 1954. Between January 1, 1960, and December 13, 1963, he served as the duly elected justice of the peace of Smithtown on Long Island. Then he was elected district court judge of Suffolk County for a term of six years beginning January 1, 1964. Judge Sarisohn was a popular young man.

The judge, aged thirty-eight and a veteran of the Korean War, was well respected in his community. He was a vice-president of the Suffolk County Council of the Boy Scouts of America and a director of the Smithtown Young Men's Christian Association.

On August 15, 1966, Judge Sarisohn's career took a nose-dive. The appellate division of the supreme court in Brooklyn announced his suspension from office pending the outcome of an investigation of charges involving moral turpitude in his activities both as a justice of the peace and as a district court judge.

The principal charge against him concerned his relationship

115

with Carmen Sanabria, also known as Elida Peck and Lee Matos, a divorcee and mother of four children. On July 18, 1962, Mrs. Sanabria had pleaded guilty before Justice of the Peace Kane, sitting as a court of special sessions in Suffolk County, to having engaged in prostitution at the Sunshine Valley Motel in Huntington. On October 24, 1962, she was sentenced to three months in jail, with execution of sentence suspended, and placed on probation for three years.

Judge Sarisohn was charged with having offered legal services to Mrs. Sanabria, stating he was a justice of the peace in Smithtown. Sarisohn told the convicted prostitute that he knew Judge Kane and could be of great assistance to her. He was also charged with advising her during August and September 1962 (while awaiting sentence) to mislead the probation department by falsely pretending to have stopped her "professional" activities. Judge Sarisohn was also accused of counseling Mrs. Sanabria as to where she could "work" without getting caught. The YMCA director-jurist assured her she would receive only a suspended sentence if she followed his instructions.

The bulk of the information about the relationship was acquired from recorded telephone conversations between Judge Sarisohn and Mrs. Sanabria. In the course of an investigation of prostitution activities in Suffolk County, detectives, with a court order, had tapped Mrs. Sanabria's telephone. They "accidentally" recorded some conversations between her and a judge.

The following portion of a wiretap made in June 1963 was one of the most embarrassing for the judge, and obviously speaks for itself.

Judge: Well, just be careful and don't get picked up. Don't let them set you up.

Sanabria: What if I go in a room with someone and they break in or something, can they catch me that way?

Judge: No, because, you see, the whole story revolves around you have to prove money passed; that is why, you remember, they used marked bills.

Sanabria: Yeah, they told me to stay away from motels. It looks like I'll have to get me a Rambler with a bed in it.

Judge: Move around a little bit, try to, you know, so you are not settled down in one pattern that they can follow on. For a little while anyway. I wouldn't be too worried about that.

Sanabria: I'm so scared I don't know what I'm going to do.

Judge: There's nothing you can do about it. You have to relax and not be scared. We may be able to get a contact with some people that can help with this. Tempers will cool down. I wouldn't worry too much on the probation angle. Just be careful.

When asked, in 1962, if he could help, the judge said, "I'd be glad to do it. After all, you're a client of the office [this was never explained]. The least I can do is be helpful." Such help even extended to his putting up $100 of his own money to bail her out of jail on October 18, 1962.

Between the time the investigation of Judge Sarisohn's conduct began and the time of his trial, he was also charged with obstructing the investigation itself.

On September 19, 1966, two Suffolk County detectives went to Mrs. Sanabria's home in Corona, Queens, to get a statement from her. She invited them into her kitchen, but as soon as one of them brought out a pad to write on, Judge Sarisohn suddenly rushed in from behind a closed door, shouting, "I've had enough of this. I'll not let you put words into the mouth of this woman!" As a result, the detectives got no statement.

Before it was completed, the investigation uncovered several other incidents of the judge's misbehavior on the bench. While still a justice of the peace, Judge Sarisohn had altered, erased and canceled the record in a case after he had lost jurisdiction of it.

In the case of *Lukon* v. *Sedley,* instituted on February 5, 1962, to recover back rent in excess of $15,000, there were a number of adjournments. The matter was then put over for hearing on September 19, 1962. On that day the landlord appeared, but the tenant did not. Judge Sarisohn ordered that a default judgment be entered. After the clerk of the court had entered the default, the attorney for the tenant telephoned to the judge that he didn't know the case was going to be heard on that day. Without telling anyone, Sarisohn had the judgment eliminated and the case restored to the trial calendar for October 16, 1962. The judge's docket book showed that the entire docket page, including the entry of the default judgment, had been completely erased with ink eradicator.

On March 20, 1964, District Court Judge Sarisohn was presiding in an action entitled *Joy* v. *McClean* in small claims court. Mr. Joy was seeking to recover $107 for property damage to his automobile, which had been struck by an automobile that had emerged from Mrs. McClean's driveway. Mrs. McClean, an elderly woman, had been sued mistakenly since the automobile was of unknown ownership and operation and had evidently been driven by someone else.

Before the trial even started, the judge demanded that Mrs. McClean reveal to him the name of the driver of the automobile. When she refused (probably because she didn't know), he ordered her placed in custody and confined in a detention cell. Although she was not a witness or under oath, he also threatened her with criminal prosecution for contempt. When she finally consented to make payment of $87.50 in settlement of Mr. Joy's claim, she was released from custody.

On January 21, 1966, one Frank Dohman was arraigned before Judge Sarisohn on two counts of third-degree burglary and on one count of second-degree assault. With the avowed purpose of preventing the defendant from getting out on bail, Sarisohn set bail at $500,000 on each count—$1.5 million. Eventually, Dohman was released on bail fixed in another court at $7,500.

On March 22, 1966, Manuel Topol, a newspaperman friend of Judge Sarisohn who had had occasion to write favorable articles concerning the judge, received a traffic ticket for speeding. The ticket called for Topol to appear before the court in Babylon. Since Sarisohn was assigned to hold court in Bay Shore, not in Babylon, the presiding judge of the district court ordered him not to interfere. Nevertheless, he entered the courthouse in Babylon, obtained possession of the "back-up" sheet, endorsed thereon that Topol had been arraigned before him on that day (May 12, 1966) and had pleaded guilty, and that the judge had imposed a fine of $10 and suspended sentence. Evidently the articles Topol had written about his friend's honesty and upright character had not impressed Topol himself.

On July 30, 1966, Judge Sarisohn interceded on behalf of three men who had been charged with disorderly conduct before another judge who had fixed bail. Sarisohn ordered the sheriff to release them without bail, without communicating with the other judge or the district attorney; the judge then removed papers and files from the clerk's office and altered entries to indicate that the men had been legally set free.

On November 12, 1964, and on March 31, 1965, the judge

had used abusive and improper language and been obviously less than impartial in his treatment of the attorney for the defense. Sarisohn tried to compel the attorney in chambers to stipulate to the amount of property damage in a tort case, and when he refused, said, "Look, if you don't stipulate to the property damage and if you don't accomplish something on cross-examining that expert, I'm going to let that jury know that you're the person responsible for delaying this trial," and, "Listen, when we go out there I'm going to screw you every way I can, short of reversible error."

On March 20, 1967, Judge Sarisohn went to trial before a panel of five judges of the appellate division of the supreme court and was found guilty of misconduct in office. After two appeals he was officially removed in 1969. Although held not morally fit to be a judge or ever again hold a position of honor and trust, he returned to the practice of law.

In March 1967 Mrs. Carmen Sanabria was admitted to Creedmore State Hospital, a state mental hospital in Queens.

JUDGE JOHN D. HASLER (MISSOURI)

John D. Hasler, a fifty-six-year-old St. Louis circuit court judge, was indicted by a grand jury on March 21, 1968, on charges of misconduct in office. The problem arose out of the judge's relationship with Mrs. Jean Shelby, a twenty-six-year-old former go-go dancer. Judge Hasler had only been in office for eighteen months.

In October 1967 a divorce proceeding between Delmar Shelby and Jean Shelby came before the judge. After the first hearing in the matter, Hasler and Mrs. Shelby had dinner together. After that they saw each other socially on other occasions, including several times after the judge had heard her testimony and taken the case under advisement. Judge Hasler wrote her several letters with the salutation *Dearest,* and placed several telephone calls to her.

Besides having romantic overtones, the meetings and correspondence involved discussion of the divorce proceedings. Needless to say, the relationship was not known to either Mr. Shelby or his lawyer.

Some months later Mr. Shelby discovered five letters from the judge to Mrs. Shelby. Shelby's lawyer moved that Judge Hasler disqualify himself from the case. The judge granted the motion and transferred the case out of his court on February 7, 1968. Meanwhile, the lawyer had sent copies of the letters to the professional ethics committee of the state bar association.

The story hit the front page of the local newspapers on March 1, 1968, followed by the indictment of Judge Hasler and his trial three months later.

The evidence most heavily relied upon by the prosecution at the judge's trial was the collection of letters. The improper personal involvement was most clearly shown by the judge's letter of January eighteenth, which included the following:

There is still more I want to tell you and discuss carefully about the way I should like to order this decree. You see I not only want but need that extra testimony in the record to help with the order of custody. What I most regret is that G. G. [Granville Gamblin, Mrs. Shelby's lawyer] has not brought up the Motion for Temporary Alimony and Child Support while all this is pending, then I could have ordered it and we wouldn't be in any great hurry, for your parents would then be receiving weekly whatever amount I should have ordered for that purpose that he [Mr. Shelby] be directed to pay from his earnings.

This way, more delay is just pushing off into the future and is not at all helpful to your parents or to you and isn't a bit fair. And good old D. [Delmar, i.e., Mr. Shelby] is just laughing up his sleeve. I am planning to call G.G. into my office and talk to him straight from the shoulder about the way I think he should proceed from this point on. I hope he will. I feel that he most likely will. . . .

Now, for me, read this, re-read it if need be, but you and I know it were best that you destroy this writing now, please. For your own sake (not mine) we cannot suffer comment about the "case" ever to run the risk beforehand, to fall into the wrong hands. It is too, too dangerous. . . .

Here are copies of the very nice letters from Mrs. Pennington [a social worker assigned to the Shelby case]. I showed them to Schecter [Mr. Shelby's lawyer] and he said, "Who are they talking about? I don't recognize the person they're describing here as a good mother, responsible and competent!" I could have hit his sneering face, but I had to hold my temper for I cannot in any way let the slightest thing show that I am interested personally in anything going on for either side. I am certain you understand that this is in your highest interest and that of the children.

Mrs. Shelby testified for the state that she thought she had the judge in her "female clutches." She confessed they had met in motel rooms and that he had once taken pictures of her showing a black eye caused by a beating by her husband, pictures which were later used for evidence in the divorce case before the photographer-judge.

Judge Hasler denied only some of the particulars of Mrs. Shelby's testimony. He contended that his relationship with her was paternalistic and arose from sympathy for her and her children.

He said that the purpose of his first meeting with her was to confront her "eye to eye" about Mr. Shelby's allegations of her adultery and said he was not romantically involved with her.

After five days of trial and two days of deliberation, the jury found the judge guilty. While the maximum penalty was one year in the county jail and/or a $500 fine, Judge Hasler was only fined $1.00.

However, the Missouri House of Representatives conducted its own investigation and, on May 14, 1968, began impeachment proceedings against him. The judge resigned two days before the impeachment trial. On July 27, 1969, he was ordered disbarred by the Supreme Court of Missouri.

JUDGE J. ALLEN O'CONNER (CONNECTICUT)

Circuit Court Judge J. Allen O'Conner, a forty-three-year-old bachelor, lived with his mother in the quiet city of Norwalk, Connecticut. Norwalk has always been a conservative town, and jurists are afforded maximum respect and recognition by the community.

On October 19, 1964, Joseph R. Stasny, Jr., age twenty, was arraigned before O'Conner on the charge of larceny. Stasny had been accused by his employer, General Truck Leasing Company, of stealing four shock absorbers.

The understanding jurist decided to study the problem firsthand. He went to the company's office and discussed the charges with the manager. He asked that Stasny be allowed to make restitution for the theft so that he might return to his

123

family in Pittsburgh. The judge also told the company he would dismiss the charges if the company would accept restitution.

The complaining manager, who was not in a position to turn down the request of an important local jurist, agreed, and the judge and his defendant promptly returned to the court. O'Conner then dismissed the charges on the ground of lack of "criminal intent."

That night, upon the invitation of the seemingly generous and helpful judge, the young man visited O'Conner's summer beach home. In the course of the evening, Stasny discovered that the kindly judge expected a return favor. The next morning Stasny went to the police.

The warrant, requested by State Attorney Otto J. Saur, charged that Judge O'Conner had committed indecent assaults against Stasny at the judge's summer home at Old Mill Beach in Westport.

Another complaint was filed against the judge involving a Richard Spiro, who was also supposedly assaulted.

After posting bail, Judge O'Conner requested the presiding judge to relieve him of his court assignments pending resolution of the charges against him. This request was granted, and the judge committed himself for treatment at Hall-Brooke Sanitarium, a psychiatric hospital in Westport.

His resignation was accepted on November 9, 1964, by Governor John N. Dempsey.

At the trial the judge pleaded nolo contendere to the charge involving Stasny, and the state dropped the charge involving Spiro. He was found guilty on November twenty-fourth and immediately disbarred. On December eighteenth he was given a six-month suspended sentence. The trial judge said he had been "punished enough."

It was also revealed that Judge O'Conner had been arrested

in 1952 on a morals charge while he was in the Air Force in Hawaii. He had resigned his Air Force commission then "for the good of the service," and was discharged on "other than honorable conditions."

Stasny was arrested again and charged with larceny for the theft of a $700 two-way radio from a truck on the same day as the earlier theft.

JUDGE JAMES H. EDGAR & MAGISTRATE JAMES LEE BLODGETT (MICHIGAN)

A Michigan judge and his appointed magistrate last year allowed their "hands of justice" to wander too freely. As a result, the two Don Juans had their wrists slapped on September 6, 1972, for fondling female court employees.

In 1968 James Edgar was elected to his $26,000-a-year judgeship in Lansing, Michigan. Shortly thereafter he appointed James Blodgett to the position of magistrate, which pays $12,700 a year.

The activities of Edgar and Blodgett caused courthouse whispers for months and finally formal complaints. Blodgett spent his spare time unhooking brassieres and forcing women in the building "in good fun" to show their underwear. Judge Edgar was more than looking. When the Supreme Court of Michigan fined the jurist $1,500 and censured him, it was not for handling or mishandling a case but handling or mishandling women in court in a "familiar or suggestive manner." For some reason or another the jurist confused one

125

employee's underwear with an outgoing letter, for he implanted his signature, unrequested, on her panties while she was in them.

Despite the chief justice's stern warning, Edgar's fine and censure was looked upon by many as only token punishment which did little to restore dignity to the courthouse scene. One courthouse regular questioned what would have happened if the ladies had dropped his honor's trousers and implanted their autographs on his judicial Jockeys.

More recently, both have resigned from the bench.

Chapter Five
Court Jesters

"He would wrap his judicial robe about him and steal away from the nightmare into which his dream degenerated."
                    —OHIO SUPREME COURT
                    Discussing Judge David Copland

None of the abuses of judicial discretion and decorum set forth in this book can be taken lightly, but this chapter's conglomeration of court clowns is a little unique. For, although their abuses are as offensive as the more tragic situations, these resemble carnivals more than crises. The cane-wielding federal judge who seeks a companion on the bench from the audience is a classic example. These demonstrations of incompetence and deceit do reveal a somewhat poignant humor.

JUDGE JOHN PICKERING
(FEDERAL—NEW HAMPSHIRE)

One of the most interesting characters ever to judge others was John Pickering of New Hampshire. Although the incidents took place one hundred and seventy years ago, his is a classic case of the blending of judicial incompetence and limitless power, for he had been appointed a federal judge for life.

U.S. District Court Judge John Pickering had the distinction of being the first federal judge subjected to impeachment proceedings before Congress. He was one of New Hampshire's most distinguished citizens, the author of her constitution and a revolutionary patriot. His contemporaries were nearly unanimous in testifying to his intellectual greatness, sobriety and moral integrity.

During the first few years of his judicial service Pickering appeared reasonably competent, but at the beginning of the nineteenth century Pickering began his sixth year judging cases as an incurable hypochondriac with deteriorating faculties. Pressure was brought to bear on him, but the judge refused to resign.

The Judiciary Act of 1801 had provided for cases like Pickering's by giving the circuit court judges the authority to appoint one of their own members to take over the functions of any district judge who became incapacitated. The unfortunate old Pickering had been an insane drunkard for some time and was clearly not capable of performing his duties as a district judge, so Circuit Judge Jeremiah Smith was assigned to take over his duties.

But the 1801 Judiciary Act was repealed, and when the circuit judges were abolished, Pickering returned to the bench.

128

One of the first cases to reach Pickering when he resumed his position in 1802 involved the ship *Eliza,* which had been seized by customs officials for smuggling in October 1802. The validity of the seizure was never tried in a competent court of law. Records suggest the proceeding to have been a farce.

The ship belonged to a prominent merchant, Eliphalet Ladd, who filed suit for its return and applied to Judge Pickering for a release. Ladd got his ship back instantly without bonds or surety.

On the opening day of the trial Pickering arrived at the courtroom drunk. He staggered to the bench and started the trial. Then, apparently feeling lonely, he commanded the deputy marshal to come up and sit beside him on his right. The startled officer objected, whereupon Pickering cursed him roundly and frightened him into hasty compliance. At that moment a young lawyer entered the courtroom, and Pickering demanded his assistance at the bench. The lawyer refused, and the judge started down from the bench to cane him. But then Pickering spotted a former British naval officer among the spectators and accepted him as an advisor on "these nautical matters." Thus fortified against the "Jacobins," Pickering roared, "Now damn them, we will fight them," and ordered the parties to proceed.

U.S. Attorney John Sherburne reminded Pickering that the pleadings had not been read, but the judge replied that he had heard enough about the damned pleadings and would decide the case in four minutes. Ladd's lawyer, seeing that no trial could be held under these conditions, obtained Sherburne's consent to a motion for postponement. Judge Pickering instantly brightened. "My dear, I will give you all eternity," he said, and ordered the trial postponed until the next day, remarking that he would then be sober.

When the court reconvened the next day, Judge Pickering

was in worse shape. After hearing Ladd's case and a few minutes of an argument between the attorneys as to the competence of the government's witnesses, Pickering suddenly ordered that the *Eliza* be returned to his long-time political ally Eliphalet Ladd. "We will not sit here to eternity to decide on such paltry matters," the judge declared.

Sherburne protested that his witnesses had not yet been allowed to testify. "Very well," said Pickering amiably. "We will hear everything—swear every damn scoundrel that can be produced—but if we sit here four thousand years the ship will still be restored." A few minutes later, however, he shut off the witnesses and again ordered the case dismissed.

Sherburne then protested that this decision would injure the revenue. "Damn the revenue," shouted Pickering. "I get but a thousand dollars of it." Sherburne hoped he would be allowed to file a bill of exceptions. "File what you please, and be damned," roared Pickering, and he ordered the court to stand adjourned. When the government sought an appeal order, the judge refused to sign one although the law clearly directed that he do so.

Pickering's courtroom had become a three-ring circus which attracted journalists and sensation seekers from throughout the area. But the government was not amused. Complaints were filed and demands made for Pickering's resignation.

Three months after the *Eliza* fiasco the House of Representatives fought to impeach federal Judge John Pickering.

The articles of impeachment charged the judge with throwing out the rule book as to procedure, improperly enforcing the law and being so drunk that he could not even do these misdeeds properly. The House even threw in a count for profanity on the bench.

Pickering filed no answer and made no appearance in the

proceedings either in person or by attorney. Judge Pickering's son was allowed to give evidence to show that his father was mentally irresponsible. It appeared that if insanity did exist, it was due to habitual drunkenness.

On March 12, 1804, Pickering went on the record books as the first lifetime federal judge to be impeached by the House of Representatives, convicted by the Senate and removed from office. The momentum was started. Within four days impeachment proceedings began against U.S. Supreme Court Justice Samuel Chase (see Chapter IX).

JUDGE JAMES H. PECK (FEDERAL)

James Hawkins Peck was appointed by President James Monroe as the first U.S. district court judge for Missouri at a time of growing antagonism toward the federal courts due to Supreme Court decisions striking down state laws as unconstitutional. Even without his personal problems, Judge Peck was disliked because he imposed federal authority at a time when it was not wanted.

When Peck took office, he was faced with a number of suits by the early settlers of Missouri (the Upper Louisiana Territory) claiming title to large parcels of land under grants from the Spanish crown. The U.S. government resisted these claims and contended that the land was part of the public domain and available for future distribution. A lawyer named Luke Edward Lawless represented many of these settlers, including the heirs of one Antoine Soulard.

The Soulard case was tried first, and Judge Peck ruled in favor of the government. He then wrote a letter to the editor of the Missouri *Republican* explaining the basis for his decision. Attorney Lawless promptly wrote an answering letter to a rival newspaper, the Missouri *Advocate,* in which he challenged the facts and legal conclusions of the judge.

Judge Peck was enraged. He ordered the lawyer to be instantly arrested and brought to court. Without a trial, Judge Peck found Lawless guilty of contempt. Peck's actions suggested that perhaps the defendant had a name that should have been reserved for the judge. He imposed a sentence of twenty-four hours in jail and disbarment from practice before the federal court for a period of eighteen months.

Congressman John Scott of Missouri promptly presented a motion requesting the House of Representatives to investigate the conduct of Judge Peck. On April 21, 1830, the House overwhelmingly voted (123 to 49) to impeach him on one general article containing eighteen specifications, charging abuse of official power and "unjust, oppressive and arbitrary" conduct regarding the contempt order. Since his activities did not technically amount to "Treason, Bribery, or other high Crimes and Misdemeanors," the Senate decided on January 23, 1831, in favor of Judge Peck by a vote of 21 to 22.

This vote did not mean the Senate approved of what Judge Peck had done. Far from it. A few weeks later the Senate passed a special bill denying federal judges the power to punish for contempt except in cases of misbehavior actually committed in the courts.

JUDGE HAROLD L. LOUDERBACK
(FEDERAL—CALIFORNIA)

Judge Harold L. Louderback of the United States District of California believed in paying political debts. He owed his appointment to United States Senator Samuel Shortridge and the judge never forgot it. As a result he appointed Samuel Shortridge, Jr., son of his benefactor, receiver and administrator in major cases.

Louderback felt strongly that he had a right to appoint friends to receiverships even if they were totally inexperienced.

On March 11, 1930, he attempted to force Addison G. Strong, whom he had appointed as receiver, to name a lawyer of the judge's selection to be attorney in the case. When Strong refused, Judge Louderback discharged him as receiver, taking him by the arm, marching him out of his office and remarking as he did so, "You are fired, you are out!" The next day, on recommendation of his friend Sam Leake (a "mental healer"), he appointed as receiver H. B. Hunter, who named Douglas Short, the lawyer whom Strong had refused to appoint, as attorney for the receivership. For their services, Hunter and Short received fees of $40,000 and $50,000 respectively.

Proof of judicial impropriety which may mean impeachment by the House of Representatives does not always mean conviction in the Senate. In 1932 Louderback was impeached by the House, but because of constitutional questions concerning the accusations against him, the U.S. Senate voted to acquit.

JUDGE DAVID COPLAND (OHIO)

Municipal Judge David Copland of Cleveland, Ohio, did not wait until he climbed up on the bench before commencing the practice of public deception.

Copland was trying to earn the endorsement of the Cleveland Bar Association in his campaign for judicial office. He told the association he had attended Columbia University School of Law for three years and had been admitted to practice in New York in 1917. Both claims were false. He had obtained his legal education in a law office.

Once elected to his judgeship, Copland published a court opinion in what turned out to be a fictitious case that had supposedly been heard and decided in his court. If the deception had not been discovered, such a published report would have been relied upon by lawyers and judges alike as a precedent decision.

The Cleveland Bar Association was enraged. They refused to wait for the often cumbersome and long-winded process of impeachment. In its place disbarment proceedings began in 1940.

In the hearings that followed, Judge Copland brazenly admitted the charges against him. The jurist added that he had done nothing improper. He said that he had published his personal views on a hypothetical legal question under the guise of an authentic court finding for the benefit of the legal profession. The judge claimed to be acting not as a judge, but rather as a lawyer writing for the enlightenment of his profession.

Apparently unimpressed, his colleagues ordered his disbarment.

In November 1940 their action was affirmed by the Ohio

Supreme Court, which said of Copland's contention that he was not acting in his official capacity, "He would wrap his judicial robe about him and steal away from the nightmare into which his dream degenerated. He now asks a reviewing court to wash his soiled gown and absolve him of all censure because he bears the title *Judge.*"

JUDGE LOREN M. HULLINGER, JR. (IOWA)

The investigators who began sifting through the records of the municipal court of Cedar Rapids, Iowa, in 1964, focused on the activities of Judge Loren M. Hullinger, Jr.

The first complaint of judicial misconduct concerned Hullinger's "instant" dismissal of select cases filed by the traffic weight department of the Iowa State Highway Commission charging overloading by truckers in Cedar Rapids. These cases were quickly dismissed by Judge Hullinger without proper procedure because he did not believe the law should be applied in his city. He felt that the city of Cedar Rapids could enact its own ordinance if it wanted to, and he refused to allow his court to be part of a state-enforced crusade. Although Iowa law does provide for a judge to dismiss criminal charges on his own motion, it is usually done only after extensive hearings and in the furtherance of justice.

It appeared the judge had dismissed criminal charges without even giving the prosecution an opportunity to present its case. This often led to suggestions that the court was biased toward the defendants. There had also been frequent complaints about Hullinger because of his extensive delays in both criminal and civil cases. Sometimes files had literally disappeared in chambers.

On the basis of the investigation by the Supreme Court of Iowa, Judge Hullinger was found guilty of arbitrary conduct in the discharge of his judicial duties, but the high court decided to give him another chance to correct the objectionable practices under its surveillance.

Unfortunately, the judge's second chance did not work out well. His loose practices came to the attention of the state again in 1971 during a study of court backlog problems in Cedar Rapids.

The investigating statistician concluded that Hullinger was a relatively good judge and generally obeyed administrative rules. After forming this conclusion, the investigator found seventeen cases stuffed in a wire basket in the back of Hullinger's office. They had remained untouched for seven years, and the judge said he knew nothing about them. But it was discovered that a series of rushed and often wrong entries had been made in some of the cases years earlier.

The judge was found to be putting in a work week of approximately twenty-four hours, except when he was occupied in his regular turn in the criminal division. In view of the ever-increasing caseload, this schedule was totally inadequate to permit him to complete his share of the work of the court.

The final disclosure that resulted in the judge's removal was evidence of his excessive drinking just prior to appearing in court. It was determined he had been drunk or suffering from a hangover on too many occasions. When the investigation was completed, Judge Loren H. Hullinger became Mr. Loren H. Hullinger permanently.

JUDGE HOWARD W. McLAUGHLIN (IOWA)

Many of the complaints against Judge Hullinger also applied to Judge Howard W. McLaughlin of the same municipal court of Cedar Rapids.

He had also arbitrarily refused to hear litigants and had improperly criticized them. Trials were delayed, and it was impossible for the parties to learn what had happened to them. McLaughlin seemed to have handled the business of the court according to his own personal whims.

McLaughlin had threatened to use the power of his court oppressively and unjustifiably, through court orders, appointment of dissenting police officers as bailiffs in order to bring them under his control and other methods. He had for several months been engaged in a fight against the city council and city auditor's office. The judge had been trying unsuccessfully to get reimbursement for recent expenses on a trip to New York.

On July 14, 1964, Judge McLaughlin wrote a letter to the city council discussing some of the items of his own claim. He closed with this statement: "You are further advised that my said claim has been determined by *this* court to be a proper court expense and that if this reimbursement claim is not paid forthwith, an appropriate order to effectuate its payment shall be issued."

As justification for this, McLaughlin cited a section of the municipal code which provided that "all other expenses of maintaining said court [the municipal court] not otherwise provided for in this chapter shall be paid from the city treasury." He contended that his trip was a proper expense of the court and that the reasonableness and propriety of his claim were to be determined solely by the court and not to

137

be questioned by the city council. In other words, the judge decided to rule upon his own claim and enforce payment with his own ruling.

It was discovered that the Cedar Rapids telephone directories for 1962 and 1963 contained listings of Judge McLaughlin as a lawyer both in the alphabetical listings and in the yellow pages. The address and telephone number given was that of the judge's former law associate. Both directories were printed after the judge had assumed his judicial duties.

Such listings constituted a violation of Canon 31 of the Canons of Judicial Ethics of the American Bar Association, which had been adopted as rules of McLaughlin's court. But the Supreme Court of Iowa mildly commented that the judge was "subject to criticism for this violation of judicial ethics and of the governing statute."

Like Judge Hullinger, McLaughlin was given an opportunity to correct his practices under the continued surveillance of the supreme court.

JUDGE J. MILES POUND (KENTUCKY)

The incident that finally brought into focus the impropriety of Kentucky's bench involved proceedings against the state's most widely known civil-rights and criminal lawyer, Daniel T. Taylor. Judge J. Miles Pound had brought charges against the lawyer for showing contempt in Pound's Jefferson County courtroom. On March 7, 1969, the Kentucky State Bar Association began closed hearings on the proposed disbarment of Taylor, which was being pushed by Judge Pound.

The Louisville *Courier Journal* had previously commented on the bizarre behavior in Judge Pound's courtroom, but they were not describing Taylor. They had directed their editorial swipes at the judge himself.

In January 1969 James Cortez, a black militant, was in court as a client of Taylor. Judge Pound had carried a pistol with him to the bench. On adjournment, the judge lost his grip on the pistol and juggled it in the air before a gasping courtroom, finally catching it against his chest. The sixty-one-year-old jurist, a former mounted policeman in Louisville, said he had received threats against his life.

In full view and earshot of the jury, Taylor had previously accused Judge Pound of drinking in his chambers, being drunk on the bench and improperly carrying a gun on the bench.

The U.S. Court of Appeals stopped Taylor's disbarment proceedings and held that Judge Pound had improperly brought charges against Taylor merely to intimidate him. It was a desperately embarrassing decision for Pound, particularly since it carried with it the weight of the highest federal appeals court in the area. Many say the judge was never the same after the decision. He is now deceased.

Chapter Six
The Corrupters

"I exercised my judicial discretion in each instance, and my exercise of such discretion cannot be questioned."

—JUDGE FRANK R. FRANKO

In communities where judges are appointed, few people are naive enough to think that loyalty does not occasionally give way to favoritism when the political bosses come before the courts. Even at the highest level of government, when the president of the United States appoints a justice of the Supreme Court, it is no secret that when a situation arises, judicial views align themselves with the man who anointed the judge with perennial majesty.

When judges are elected, another kind of politics comes to play—concern for reelection. It is difficult for a jurist to be totally objective when he knows the community will be going to the polls to determine whether or not he should remain a judge.

Neither method of selection is elaborate enough to prevent

corruption and collusion from slipping through too often. These cases are selected examples.

The distinguished Judge C. Woodrow Laughlin of Texas was indicted by a grand jury, so he rushed home to discharge the grand jury that had indicted him. The judge was removed from the bench, but the political dynasty he represented continued.

New York State's Liquor Authority has had more holes punched in it during the recent decade than most of the Swiss cheese imported by that state. A classic case involved Supreme Court Judge Melvin H. Osterman, who started his career by being declared "not qualified" by the state bar association when the governor recommended him for judgeship. He finished his career convicted of bribery and sentenced to three years in prison. But there is still hope, for he was released early on good behavior.

The political activities of judges in Oklahoma, Pennsylvania, Oregon and Ohio serve as other classic examples of judicial abuse and public corruption. It was as if they were dedicated to a resurrection of the high standards of decency established by the judge to whom our book is dedicated—Sir Francis Bacon, the Lord High Chancellor of England, who, when convicted of bribery, claimed he always took from both sides to insure his impartiality.

JUDGE FRANK R. FRANKO (OHIO)

Youngstown Municipal Court Judge Frank R. Franko was accused of being more interested in exploiting his position for political gain than in the promotion of the efficient administration of justice. When his political antics became the subject of a formal inquiry at disciplinary hearings against him by the bar in 1958, he readily admitted that he had sought judicial office as a means to enhance his political career for prosecuting attorney. He had previously decided to make politics his life after having served four years in the office of city prosecutor.

In order to gain public support for his election as a judge, Franko promised the voters that, if elected, he would make a wholesale reduction of fines for traffic violations and would not mark the backs of violators' driver's licenses as required by law. People adverse to being cited for and found guilty of traffic violations and to having those convictions noted on their licenses elected Franko.

Immediately upon reaching the bench, Judge Franko began the practice of accepting pleas of guilty on traffic matters on Saturday mornings, regardless of the fact that he was not the regularly assigned traffic judge. He continued despite the strenuous objections of the judges who were assigned.

During these self-assigned hearings, he assessed a more or less standard fine of five dollars and costs (suspended) for all traffic violations. The judge refused to mark the backs of licenses and established a policy of voiding parking tickets, on the average of one hundred per month, for no apparent reason.

Shortly before the arraignment of a local citizen on a charge of reckless driving, a major Youngstown newspaper reported that Sergeant Davis of the Youngstown police department was in Florida with his ailing wife when he should have been on duty at home. At the expense of Davis' reputation, Judge Franko issued a subpoena for the policeman and, when he returned to Youngstown, continued the reckless-driving trial from hour to hour and day to day for over two days, allegedly to question Davis on matters of police routine. The sergeant had not witnessed the violation and, in fact, knew nothing of the entire affair. The news coverage of these events kept the judge's name in a prominent place throughout the episode, as he had anticipated.

When it came time for the election of prosecuting attorney in Youngstown, Judge Franko launched an intensive campaign from his headquarters on the municipal court bench. He assembled, published and distributed 85,000 copies of a four-page "newspaper," entitled *The Political News,* in which he referred to himself as "Judge Franko" innumerable times.

He wrote letters to Democrats and Republicans alike requesting support in his campaign, addressing the former as "Dear Fellow Democrat" and the latter as "Dear Fellow Republican." (Franko had been nominated and elected to judicial office as a Republican but had later declared himself a Democrat.) Much like former U.S. Secretary of the Treasury John Connally, Franko was determined to be all things in politics to all men.

To the Democrats he wrote, "How many times, for instance, has the present prosecutor opened his door to Democratic party workers? Isn't it true that, in contrast, you know Judge Franko as a man who has been liberal and humane to the petition of all Democrats."

And to the Republicans Franko wrote, "But it's certainly well-known that as a Republican-elected judge, I have been foremost among constructive critics of the present city administration and have been waging a crusade against the racket-infested . . . gang which now controls a large segment of our county government." That letter was signed, "Your friend and co-worker, Judge Frank R. Franko."

The judge also wrote a letter to those who had appeared

before him in traffic matters, calling their attention to the fact that "I believe today that my policy of not marking driver licenses for trivial traffic offenses and of scaling fines to meet the seriousness of the offense carried out the ideals I promised to uphold."

When the Mahoning County Bar Association finally filed a complaint asking for Franko's disbarment, he answered each of the charges in the same way, saying, "I exercised my judicial discretion in each instance, and my exercise of such discretion cannot be questioned."

The court was not convinced. In its opinion, which confirmed Judge Franko's indefinite suspension from the practice of law, the Ohio Supreme Court said his exercise of judicial discretion was not "so much directed to the administration of impartial justice as it was to 'winning friends and influencing people' in the furtherance of his general political ambitions."

Franko was found guilty of violating the Canons of Judicial Ethics, and a poignant chapter in the history of cleansing the judiciary from political influence and temptation was written.

MAGISTRATE MARTIN L. PAGLIUGHI (NEW JERSEY)

Martin L. Pagliughi started his first term as magistrate of Buena Vista Township in 1952 and was continuously reappointed until his last term's expiration in 1964.

Pagliughi also practiced law in Vineland, New Jersey, and

was Vineland City Solicitor, having been appointed July 1, 1960, for a term of four years.

The judge was a founder of the Vineland Young Men's Republican Club of Cumberland County in 1952 and served as its first president. He was assistant prosecutor of Cumberland County from 1953 to 1957 and served as president of the New Jersey Junior Chamber of Commerce during 1953 and 1954. The people of Vineland, in appreciation of his civic devotion and dedicated leadership, named him their outstanding citizen.

However, these extensive political and community activities brought Judge Pagliughi's conduct into question, especially since such participation in partisan politics is prohibited by Canon 28 of the Canons of Judicial Ethics.

In accordance with an order of the Supreme Court of New Jersey, hearings were begun in February 1962 in a superior court to investigate the following: (1) the judge's activities as a political ward leader and his association with the Vineland Young Men's Republican Club of Cumberland County; (2) whether he had permitted the use of his home for the registration of voters and been involved in voter registration frauds; (3) whether he had signed and notarized petitions of candidates for the Republican Executive Committee; (4) his participation in a political meeting held at Sea Girt, New Jersey, on August 15, 1961, attended by the Republican gubernatorial candidate and other candidates and party leaders from Cumberland County. Days after the investigation began, the judge resigned from his post.

But the New Jersey Supreme Court was not satisfied, and it issued an order to show cause why Judge Pagliughi should not be disbarred or otherwise disciplined, and why he should not be held in contempt of the supreme court for willfully violating Canon 28 of the Canons of Judicial Ethics.

The judge admitted that while a magistrate he had been a ward leader and that he had been associated with the Republican club. But he contended that all those activities were limited geographically to the city of Vineland, which was situated ten miles from the judge's municipal court and in another county. He denied that such activities in any way influenced the operation of his court in Buena Vista Township.

As for the use of his home for voter registration, he contended that this activity did not involve partisan politics on his part. Supposedly no questions were asked concerning partisan party affiliation.

As to the judge's signing and notarizing petitions of candidates for the Republican Executive Committee, he claimed that although this was a political activity, a "fine line of distinction must be drawn between signing and notarizing a petition." He characterized the latter as merely the performance of a perfunctory act, not constituting an endorsement.

Judge Pagliughi maintained that aside from the Sea Girt incident in 1961 and his signing of petitions for candidates, most of his activities were "in gray areas between permissible and forbidden behavior."

The judge claimed he had simply used poor judgment, that he had believed the prohibition of Canon 28 applied only to the locality in which he sat as a magistrate.

But on June 16, 1954, the judge had sent a letter to the administrative director of the courts, in which he asked for a ruling as to whether or not it would be ethical and permissible for him to participate in partisan politics in the county in which he lived since he was a judge in another county. On July 2, 1954, the director replied that he had discussed the matter with the supreme court at its last conference, and that the court was of the opinion, and had requested the director to so advise the judge, "that the Canons of Judicial Ethics prohibit your participating in politics, not only in the county in which your court is located but also in any other county."

Also, at the direction of the supreme court, the director sent a letter to Judge Pagliughi on September 8, 1961, asking him to explain an enclosed newspaper clipping, sent anonymously to the director's office, which referred to the judge's attendance in the Sea Girt meeting. Pagliughi replied that he was not aware his attendance at the "luncheon" was improper. At the time the judge also denied that he was a ward leader or that he held office in any political party.

He claimed he had no recollection of receiving the letter of July 2, 1954, but did admit receiving directives pertaining to the conduct of his office. He also recalled being prohibited from engaging in any political activity while a magistrate of Buena Vista Township "when it was brought to my attention about 1953 or 1954. . . ."

Yet at the conclusion of the hearings, Pagliughi again claimed he believed he was politically restricted only in Buena Vista Township. This position was completely contrary to his earlier view: In a letter of November 14, 1955, the judge had resigned as a member and president of the Vineland Young Men's Republican Club, expressing his regret that he could not be active in the organization "due to a supreme court ruling in which municipal court judges cannot engage in politics."

Although the reviewing court found that Pagliughi had made false and misleading statements and that he had deliberately acted contrary to Canon 28, thereby being guilty of contempt of the supreme court, it was decided that the judge should simply be reprimanded.

The court seemed to recognize the fact that the judge's violations could warrant a greater measure of discipline, but reasoned that a reprimand was more appropriate since "this is the first case involving a violation of Canon 28." And so, the judge's wrists were slapped, and he promised never to do it again.

JUDGE C. WOODROW LAUGHLIN (TEXAS)

The removal of Judge C. Woodrow Laughlin of Texas stemmed from political problems in Duval County, the South Texas dynasty of Boss George Parr, its resident millionaire. By 1954 charges of political payoffs and controlled justice involving Parr, known as the Duke of Duval County, were widespread and generally true. Both federal and state agencies had been conducting investigations into the situation, and public indignation over the blatant corruption in the community was getting out of control.

On the scene appeared Judge C. Woodrow Laughlin. With the political aid and backing of Parr, on November 4, 1952, he was elected judge of the Seventy-ninth Judicial District, composed of Duval, Starr, Brooks, and Jim Wells counties. Even before he took the oath of office on January 1, 1953, charges of upcoming patronage from Boss Parr began to circulate throughout the district.

Soon after, a grand jury was empaneled in Jim Wells County to investigate illegal transactions and the flourishing corruption. Among the public officials investigated were the judge and his brother W. M. Laughlin, who was a member of the commissioners court of the county. Both were sub-

149

poenaed by the grand jury to testify regarding their official conduct and peremptory indulgence of Parr in court matters.

The grand jury filed an interim report highlighting various property transactions. On December 29, 1954, the grand jury indicted Judge Laughlin for the illegal sale to the county of his law library. And other deceptive practices were suggested.

The judge was vacationing in New Mexico at the time the indictments were returned and learned of them by radio four days later. Fearing a maverick grand jury, he drove to Alpine, Texas, and talked by phone with his brother. He decided to discharge the grand jury as soon as he assumed the bench and had already written an order in longhand to that effect. Shortly after midnight on New Year's Eve, he took the oath of office before his father-in-law, and immediately left for his home in Alice, stopping en route at Laredo for a short time to visit friends and have the order discharging the grand jury typewritten.

The judge arrived in Alice at about 1:30 p.m. on January first and after posting bond in the cases against him, went directly to the home of the district clerk (since it was a legal holiday) and filed his oath of office and the order discharging the jury, requesting the clerk to inform the jurors that they had been discharged.

The prosecuting attorney requested the judge not to abuse his authority. Judge Laughlin refused to cancel the order until a proceeding was filed in the Supreme Court of Texas seeking a formal writ to prevent this action.

When the interim report by the grand jury had been released on December second, the judge's brother visited individual members of the grand jury in order to persuade them not to indict him. On December twenty-ninth he had even appeared before the body voluntarily to request that he not be indicted, offering to do "whatever was necessary to prevent the indictment."

Judge Laughlin refused to be swayed by the force of public opinion and two criminal indictments. He continued the blatant partiality of his judicial stewardship. Judicial favors to his political ally, George Parr, lost no momentum. The attorneys practicing before Laughlin's court did not remain unswayed and began seeking a way to remove him from the bench. Their ultimate recourse had never before been tried in the state of Texas.

The state's constitution provided three methods for the removal of district court judges. First was impeachment by the house of representatives and a trial by the senate. Second, the governor could remove a judge on the recommendation of two-thirds of each house of the legislature. Finally, there was authority for the supreme court to initiate removal action upon the oath and petition of at least ten lawyers practicing in the court held by the judge. Since the legislature was not in session, and it was necessary to expedite a solution, a petition signed by eleven lawyers requesting Judge Laughlin's removal was filed with the Texas Supreme Court on July 9, 1953.

The high court appointed a special master to hear evidence in the case and to report his findings to the court. Hearings began on August seventeenth and continued through September eleventh. The judge was present and represented by counsel, and one month later the report of findings was filed with the court.

The master had found justification for five separate charges, each of which was sufficient ground for Laughlin's removal. The first involved the judge's conduct in discharging the Jim Wells County grand jury. The other four charges concerned misconduct by Laughlin in the handling of election ballots in Duval County, improper conduct in effecting an exchange of courts between himself and another judge at the time when an investigation of his own conduct was in progress, improper interference with a grand jury investigation of the slaying of Jacob Floyd, Jr., and, last, his granting of a suspended sentence to a client of one of his friends. The report itself was 64 pages long, and the evidence covered 2,765 pages, with many additional exhibits.

The Supreme Court of Texas then conducted oral hearings on the charges, and on March 17, 1954, ordered Judge Laughlin removed from the bench. But the court did not issue an order preventing him from seeking reelection or from holding positions of trust in the future. This would have required additional expenditure.

Undaunted and belligerent at the Texas court's ruling, Laughlin took an appeal to the U.S. Supreme Court, claiming that the method by which he was removed constituted a denial of due process of law as guaranteed by the Fourteenth Amendment to the Constitution of the United States. But a few months after he filed his appeal, he threw in the towel. On October 25, 1954, the appeal was dismissed at the judge's own request, for which he gave no reason, and Boss Parr's dominion lost one of its leading spokesmen.

JUDGE CHARLES SWAYNE (FEDERAL—FLORIDA)

Judge Charles Swayne of the United States District Court for the Northern District of Florida was impeached and tried in 1904. Swayne had been appointed for life by Republican President Harrison over the protest of all the Democratic members of the U.S. Senate. His primary job was to convict the Florida Democrats who had violated the voting rights of Republicans in the previous election. He was relentless in his task, even extending his normal court sessions in order to bring all offenders before the bar of justice. He might have survived by his zealous bias alone.

Unfortunately, he was equally vigorous in the pursuit of his personal goals. In 1901 a number of suits were filed in Pensacola concerning title to what was then known as the "Rivas Tract." A Miss McGuire was the main plaintiff, and Edgar was the principal defendant.

Just prior to trial, Miss McGuire's lawyers learned that Edgar had sold part of his interest in the land to Judge Swayne; they motioned that the judge disqualify himself in the case. He refused, saying that he had not purchased the land interest, but that a relative of his had done so. Later it turned out that the relative was a very close one indeed—his wife! The plaintiffs, unwilling to try the case before Judge Swayne, filed a new, but identical, suit in the state court in Escambia County against Edgar with Judge Swayne added as a new defendant. They then went into the federal court to have the old case dismissed. Judge Swayne was presiding and quickly expressed his feelings about the new suit against him. After a few opening remarks he held the attorneys guilty of contempt and sentenced them to ten days in jail, a fine of $100 each, and disbarment from practice before the federal district court for a term of two years.

This unconscionable misuse of judicial power fanned the flames of impeachment. In addition, federal law required that federal district court judges be residents of their judicial districts. But Judge Swayne was a native of Delaware and lived there with his family when not holding court in Florida. He also padded his expense account and claimed the maximum per diem expenses whether he spent that much or not.

Swayne had accepted "favors" from litigants before the court in exchange for influencing proceedings against them. On at least two occasions he accepted from a railroad involved in bankruptcy proceedings before him the free use of an entire railroad car and its provisions for a court trip for himself and several relatives. Swayne then had the cost of the trip approved as part of the necessary expenses of operating the railroad.

Judge Swayne was charged in twelve articles of impeachment. His only defense was a legal one—that the offenses were not "impeachable." He argued, in effect, that the particular instances of bribery, expense account padding, and failure to abide by the residence requirements were all relatively minor crimes or misdemeanors. The Democratic House of Representatives wasn't impressed with the defense and impeached Swayne by an almost solid party-line vote. The Republican Senate sensed a political challenge and accepted Swayne's story and, by party-line vote, acquitted him on all charges.

And democracy marched on!

JUDGE LOUIS L. FRIEDMAN (NEW YORK)

Judge Louis L. Friedman, at the age of fifty-six years, achieved the rather dubious distinction of becoming the first

New York judge to be removed by the Court on the Judiciary, which was formed in 1947 to evaluate charges of judicial misconduct.

Friedman had served in the state legislature for fifteen years before being appointed to fill a vacancy on the bench in 1955 by Governor W. Averell Harriman. In November 1956 he was elected justice of the Supreme Court for the Second Judicial District (in Brooklyn) for a term of fourteen years expiring December 31, 1970. But he didn't make it.

On February 22, 1963, the Court on the Judiciary found Friedman guilty of three counts of abuse of office and voted four to one to remove him from the bench.

The judge's problems began a year after his election when the appellate division of the supreme court ordered a judicial inquiry and investigation into ambulance chasing.

Ambulance chasing is the somewhat traditional practice of overeager lawyers hunting cases. It often includes payoffs to ambulance attendants, nurse's aides, doctors, insurance men and investigators who arrange for the sudden appearance of the lawyer and his contact. The practice is widespread and has been the subject of proceedings in most states for many years. Some observers blame the bar association, which does not permit lawyers to advertise, for the ambulance-tracing trend.

As a result of the New York investigation, forty lawyers were disciplined, among whom seventeen were disbarred and several were suspended; others simply resigned their practice. Among those lawyers whose zeal came under scrutiny was Judge Friedman's brother and former law partner, M. Malcolm Friedman.

Before he had assumed the bench, the judge and his brother had established a successful firm specializing in personal-injury cases. Later Malcolm became very well known in that field. After thirty years his techniques were finally uncovered. He was charged with seventeen counts of unprofessional conduct, and found guilty on four: (1) failure to correctly report new income on his tax returns for 1955, 1956 and 1957; (2) serving false bills of particulars; (3) causing the verification of pleadings and other legal documents to be made by clients on blank legal backs or covers, and (4) failure to cooperate with the judicial inquiry into unethical practices of attorneys. As a result, the judge's brother was suspended from the practice of law for two years.

At the time Malcolm was suspended in July of 1962, Judge Friedman was accused of abusing his office. The charges against him primarily involved his conduct in obstructing the investigation of his brother, but he was also linked to two of the four charges against Malcolm. A session of the Court on the Judiciary was convened on August 15, 1962.

It was discovered that the judge maintained in his court chambers exclusive custody, control and management of the moneys, accounts, books and financial records of the law firm of Friedman & Friedman. Control over the financial affairs of his "former" law firm clearly amounted to engaging in the practice of law while serving as a member of the bench.

When told about the pending hearing to inquire into his conduct, Judge Friedman said, "I don't know what it is all about. I don't know what the charges are supposed to be. I've done nothing corrupt. I have done nothing wrong that I know about." Observers and investigators disagreed.

When the law firm's records were sought as an aid to the investigation of his brother, Judge Friedman refused to surrender them. He admitted having destroyed some of the records of particular negligent cases that had been subpoenaed in the investigation.

Then it was learned that the judge had negotiated a personal injury settlement that had come before him, outside of court—violating judicial ethics and court rules. Finally, evidence was uncovered indicating the judge's evasion of state and federal income taxes.

Following his removal from the bench in February 1963, Judge Friedman appealed to the U.S. Supreme Court on the grounds that the New York Court on the Judiciary was both his accuser and trier, thereby depriving him of due process of law as guaranteed by the Fourteenth Amendment. The highest court in the land disagreed and rejected Friedman's appeal.

Undaunted, he sought to reopen the case by bringing an action in the New York Court of Claims to recover $172,000 back pay since the date of his removal. The Court of Appeals had ruled he had a right to bring that action, but the claims court denied the judge back pay on April 23, 1969, almost seven years after accusations had been first lodged against him. Justice had been slow . . . but reasonably efficient.

JUDGE EDWIN L. JENKINS (OREGON)

District Judge Edwin L. Jenkins of Washington County, Oregon, was charged with ten counts of misconduct.

First he was accused of signing a default judgment in favor of his wife. The judgment was for a claim for legal services previously performed by the judge, and assigned by him to his wife. He had acted as her attorney in the claim prior to assuming the bench. After becoming a judge, he ruled on his own case and later admitted that he did sign such a judgment. In his defense the judge stated that he signed many orders and did not remember that particular one.

The judge was an extremely dutiful husband. So much so that the second, third, fourth and fifth charges were that Judge Jenkins appointed his wife as administratrix of four different estates, approved her accountings in the estates and awarded her high fees for extraordinary services. Jenkins also appointed his father-in-law as an appraiser for one of the estates and then allowed him a high fee. The judge again admitted his nepotistic habits, but claimed that he was not aware of the impropriety of his actions.

The sixth charge concerned the judge's appointment of Mrs. Jenkins as the appraiser in a particular estate. The executrix, who was the widow of the deceased, was a close friend of the judge's wife and had requested her appointment.

The seventh charge was that Judge Jenkins appointed his wife as administratrix of the estate of his father-in-law. He admitted the appointment. He had subsequently disqualified himself in the estate when requested to do so by the attorney representing his wife's sister, but did not set aside his appointment of his wife. The judge contended that the appointment was the result of an agreement between his wife and her sister whereby his wife would be administratrix of her father's estate, and her sister would be guardian of her mother's estate. As a result of friction between the wife and her sister, the sister moved to have the judge's wife's appointment set aside. The sisters then agreed that the judge's order appointing his wife would be set aside. (After a hearing before another judge, Jenkins' wife was reappointed.)

The eighth charge was that the judge signed a complaint

charging unlawful trespass against an individual who damaged a door of an apartment house in which the judge owned an interest, and which he operated as landlord. Judge Jenkins arraigned the defendant, accepted his plea of guilty, continued the matter for sentence and ordered the defendant to jail until such time as he paid the amount of the damage. After payment was made, the judge ordered him released from jail and placed on probation for the period of one year. Judge Jenkins admitted the actions, but said he could see nothing wrong with presiding in a case where he was the complainant.

The ninth charge was that Judge Jenkins heard the charge and pronounced sentence in a criminal matter against two defendants who were charged with stealing property belonging to the estate of his father-in-law, for which his wife was administratrix. Again he pleaded lack of awareness of his misconduct.

The final charge concerned the oath taken by the judge when he assumed the bench whereby he swore that he would not seek any nonjudicial office during the term for which he was elected. Despite the oath, Jenkins filed as a candidate for district attorney and made a declaration that if elected to the office he would qualify.

After hearings on all of the charges, the trial committee of the Oregon State Bar recommended a public and private reprimand. But the board of governors of the bar recommended permanent disbarment. The Oregon Supreme Court felt in reviewing the case that those recommendations were unrealistic:

Some of the charges of which the accused is guilty are extremely serious. On the other hand, we believe that the evidence does not indicate venality but rather ignorance and lack of sensitivity for ethical considerations. The accused made no effort to be secretive about his actions in question. They are all of public record. We also believe the evidence indicates that the accused has realized the impropriety of his actions and will in the future be more circumspect concerning ethical considerations.

Judge Jenkins was removed from the bench and suspended from the practice of law for two years. It seems that in Oregon judicial nepotism is permissible, so long as the judge is ignorant and unsecretive and his actions are a matter of public record.

MAGISTRATE E. DAVID KEISER (PENNSYLVANIA)

In November 1965 E. David Keiser was again reelected as magistrate of the city of Philadelphia. He had served in that capacity for twenty-four years. Keiser was a part of what is rapidly becoming an extinct species of the judiciary. Though neither a lawyer nor formally trained in the law, he was one of several laymen who were permitted to serve as a magistrate—exercising important judicial responsibilities in both civil and criminal matters. When the office of magistrate was abolished, Keiser was sworn in as a nonlaw judge of the newly created Philadelphia Municipal Court.

In August of 1966 Judge Keiser was indicted by the Philadelphia grand jury in a twenty-one-count indictment with charges, among others, of conspiracy to obstruct public justice, obstruction and perversion of public justice, bribery

160

and extortion. Shortly after the return of the indictments the judge was no longer assigned any judicial duties. However, he did continue to draw his salary and to earn accrued pension rights for five more years.

Until 1971 Judge Keiser managed to keep the felony charges from being tried by contending he had a serious medical disability that kept him from participating in his trial. Yet he did feel he should be allowed to resume his position on the bench despite his illness.

The same medical contentions were also effective in delaying proceedings before the Pennsylvania Judicial Inquiry and Review Board until June of 1970. Judge Keiser attended portions of these proceedings, but neither testified nor offered any evidence to refute the major charges that he had received money for the purpose of influencing the outcome of two criminal cases in the state courts.

The judge was said to have accepted $2,600 in January 1964 for influencing a judicial decision regarding the sentencing of a defendant in the criminal court of Chester County.

He had also allegedly received $3,000 "on behalf of Edmund J. Mancini" in return for assurances by Keiser that a prosecution pending against Mancini would be disposed of without the imposition of a sentence of imprisonment.

On January 21, 1971, the Supreme Court of Pennsylvania entered an order, effective that date, accepting the recommendation of the judicial board that Judge Keiser be permanently removed as a nonlaw judge of the municipal court of Philadelphia.

On January 26, 1971, Keiser filed a complaint in federal district court contesting his removal on various grounds. The district court held that the order of removal should not be disturbed.

In affirming Keiser's removal, the judge who wrote the opinion included the following quotation from Lord Bacon, who epitomized judicial dishonesty:

> The place of justice is a hallowed place and therefore not only the bench, but the foot pace and precincts and purpose thereof ought to be preserved without scandal and corruption.

Keiser died before being brought to trial on the felony charges.

JUDGE L. D. TALLENT (OKLAHOMA)

On December 6, 1947, the Oklahoma Bar Association filed charges of professional misconduct against Judge L. D. Tallent and recommended that he be disbarred.

In the months of January and February 1945 Tallent collected certain bribes in exchange for the issuance or renewal of beer licenses. In at least one instance he threatened to revoke a license if the demanded amount was not paid. Judge Tallent had instituted a license extortion system.

The Oklahoma Supreme Court (more recently concerned with its own judicial corruption) reviewed the recommendation for disbarment and decided that Tallent should only be suspended for a period of two years. Napoleon Bonaparte Johnson who was subsequently convicted of bribery himself, was the chief justice at the time.

The court believed Tallent was guilty as charged but felt that there were extenuating circumstances. The judge had been a hopeless cripple all his life.

The court noted Tallent's intention and desire to prove himself worthy, saying, "It appears that the respondent appreciates the gravity of his acts and has shown a disposition to rehabilitate himself." This was shown by the fact that he had moved to another state where he was holding a position of trust and confidence. He was now serving his new community as its mayor.

JUDGE MELVIN H. OSTERMAN (NEW YORK)

Melvin H. Osterman was a loyal New York politician. He received his law degree from New York University Law School and a master's degree from Brooklyn Law School. For thirty years he had been the Republican district leader for the Fifth Assembly District on the west side of Manhattan. He was a presidential elector from New York in 1948 and a delegate to the 1952 Republican National Convention. Osterman had been a key campaigner both for former Governor Tom Dewey and General Dwight Eisenhower during their respective presidential races.

As a reward for his loyalty Governor Dewey appointed Osterman to fill an unexpired term on the supreme court bench in 1954. But when the term expired in the fall of that year and Osterman sought election to a full term, the Association of the Bar of the City of New York declared him "not qualified." As a result of the bad recommendation, Osterman was defeated at the polls.

Unmoved by the opinion of the bar and the public, the newly elected Governor Nelson Rockefeller appointed Osterman to the New York Court of Claim on July 11, 1961, during a recess of the state senate. On January 11, 1962, the senate consented to his appointment for a term to expire in eight years. The judge's son Melvin, Jr., was coincidentally serving as a counsel on the governor's personal staff.

The New York Court of Claims is a court of record with statewide jurisdiction and the power to pass on suits against the state and its agencies for the appropriation of property, breach of contract and for torts against its state officers and employees.

The New York State Liquor Authority was one of the state agencies whose orders were reviewable in Judge Osterman's court. In early 1963 a New York County grand jury investigation was launched into crimes committed concerning liquor licensing practices.

The investigation eventually resulted in the exposure of an incredibly blatant system of bribery for liquor licenses and the suspension of penalties for violations of state liquor control laws. Fourteen persons were indicted and convicted.

The bribery technique worked like this: New York State Liquor Authority officials required liquor license applicants and others dealing with the authority to hire designated lawyers and to pay them large sums of money as "legal fees." The money was transmitted by the lawyers to the state officials (after the lawyers took their cut).

Prior to his judgeship (and afterward, as it was later discovered) Osterman had devoted a good deal of his law practice to representing individuals and companies in their dealings with the State Liquor Authority.

On March 26, 1963, Judge Osterman went to the office of Alfred J. Scotti, chief assistant district attorney for New York County, to be questioned about what he knew of a conspiracy to bribe an official of the State Liquor Authority. The district attorney was investigating the Bermuda Sales Corporation, which operated Bermuda Wines & Spirits, and its liquor license. In answer to Scotti's questions, the judge admitted he had practiced law and handled liquor license matters before becoming a judge, but denied that he had continued to do so since. He insisted that in July 1962 he had not discussed with the chairman of the authority, Martin C. Epstein, the difficulties Bermuda was having concerning its license.

On April 15, 1963, the judge appeared before a New York grand jury, and was asked by prosecutor Scotti to sign a general waiver of immunity so that any answers he gave could be used against him in the event of criminal proceedings. Osterman refused to sign a waiver and stated he was only willing to answer questions that involved performance of his judicial duties.

As a lawyer Osterman had represented the Club Paree before the State Liquor Authority. Paree was one of several Times Square area clubs in which Matty Ianniello was a stockholder or sole owner at one time or another. Ianniello, known among club owners as "Matty I.," had for years paid some small fines and won dismissals in court of other cases involving violations of the Alcoholic Beverage Control Law and the city's administrative code. The Club Paree was in trouble more than once with the State Liquor Authority. Records documented that a change of ownership in 1957 listed Philip Simon as sole owner of the club in place of Ianniello. The following year an Anthony Tenneriello was listed as the owner.

Osterman defended the club when the Liquor Authority sought to revoke its license in 1960 on several charges, including failure to obtain proper approval for transference of the license to new owners and misstatements by Ianniello in 1957 as to the source of his money. Club Paree avoided revocation of its liquor license in 1969 by surrendering the certificate before the State Liquor Authority agents could pick it up. The license was formally revoked in 1962. Osterman refused to answer any questions regarding matters he might have handled regarding the Club Paree.

When Governor Rockefeller learned of the judge's refusal to testify and to sign the waiver of immunity, he sent a letter to him demanding his immediate resignation. The judge refused to resign, and Governor Rockefeller asked that the New York Court on the Judiciary be convened specifically to begin removal proceedings.

Judge Osterman was the third high-ranking official to lose public office or face removal as a result of the liquor scandal. Martin Epstein, chairman of the State Liquor Authority, was removed by Governor Rockefeller after Epstein had refused to waive immunity and testify. L. Judson Morhouse resigned as a State Thruway Authority member and chairman of the Lake George Park Commission. He also resigned as Republican party state chairman. Judge Osterman was granted a leave of absence pending the outcome of the proceedings.

The trial before the Court on the Judiciary began on August 6, 1963. Osterman was charged and found guilty of practicing law while sitting as a judge, lying to the assistant district attorney by denying that he had continued to have dealings with the State Liquor Authority after becoming a

166

judge, and failing to cooperate with the grand jury investigation by refusing to sign a waiver of immunity. He was also found guilty of attempting to obstruct the criminal investigation by concealing evidence, including a typewriter being sought in connection with the investigation, in the home of his secretary. The secretary (who was also indicted) had used the typewriter to send the judge's letters dealing with State Liquor Authority matters.

On October 8, 1963, the Court on the Judiciary unanimously voted to remove Judge Osterman from office and to prohibit him from ever again holding any office or position of trust.

But the judge did not leave office in peace. The grand jury probe continued after his removal, and Osterman was indicted for bribery along with Epstein on November 4, 1963. The grand jury had already returned indictments against fourteen others, one of whom committed suicide.

Judge Osterman surrendered himself on November 11, 1963, and was booked and fingerprinted. New York District Attorney Frank Hogan prosecuted him on one count of bribery and five counts of conspiracy to bribe. The bribery charge was a felony which carried a maximum penalty of ten years, and the conspiracy charges carried a year each. The judge pleaded not guilty and was released without bail.

At the trial, evidence clearly established the judge's involvement in the racket. Osterman had conspired with Grace Bodner, the proprietor of the Chateau Lounge in Harlem, to bribe a member of the State Liquor Authority. Miss Bodner had given Osterman $1,500 in cash with the understanding that part would go to the authority official. On January 25, 1962, two days after the money changed hands, a ten-day suspension of the lounge's liquor license for gambling violations was lifted. Subsequent to the exposure of the dealings, the Chateau was again charged with gambling violations and received a fifty-day suspension.

Judge Osterman had also received $2,000 from Lawrence Rossi, owner of the Little Club in Rye, New York, to influence another official regarding a liquor sales violation. After the money had passed, the club got only a letter of warning.

Then the judge conspired with Melvyn Thaler, who had been his law clerk, to ask Fred Flowers and Harold Pront, proprietors of the Valentine Restaurant, for $1,250 to get a suspended sentence on a liquor sales violation. A gambling offense had resulted in a ten-day suspension of their liquor license after a hearing before the State Liquor Authority. On May 23, 1962, the sentence was suspended. Seven days later Thaler received a check from Flowers and Pront for $1,250. Thaler was given immunity from prosecution in exchange for testimony against Osterman and the others.

The judge had also conspired with Ellis Meadows Liquor Store to insure the disapproval of a license application from a competing company, Monroe Wines & Liquors, trying to do business down the street from Ellis.

The most flagrant case that terminated Osterman's judicial career involved the Bermuda Sales Corporation, which was controlled by Huntington Hartford, heir to the A & P grocery-chain fortune. The corporation operated a liquor store whose license had been suspended for selling liquor below the distiller's posted minimum prices. Proprietors of the store failed in their initial efforts to have the suspension lifted.

Eric M. Javits, a thirty-two-year-old attorney who was a candidate for the Republican nomination for state senator and nephew of U.S. Senator Jacob Javits, was the contact man who had put the owners of Bermuda Sales in touch with Osterman's bagman clerk, Thaler.

Javits had obtained Thaler's name at Republican county headquarters when seeking a lawyer for his friend Seymour Alter, manager and stockholder of the store. Javits continued as go-between even after Thaler informed him of the cost to Alter: Javits contacted Vincent Albino, Republican county chairman, who told him to speak with Mrs. Gertrude Parker, secretary to the Republican County Committee. Mrs. Parker got in touch with Osterman, who told her to tell Javits to get in touch with Thaler.

After a meeting with Javits, Thaler gave details of the case to Osterman, who told him to inform Javits that the price would be $25,000. When Thaler gave the news to Javits, the lawyer replied, "We'll let you know." The next day, Javits told Thaler, "Everything's O.K. at this end."

On three more occasions within a week, Osterman met in a Manhattan hospital with Epstein, chairman of the State Liquor Authority. The two men were each to receive $5,000 for their efforts. The deal eventually fell through because "the price was too high," and Bermuda's license was suspended for thirty days.

On April 6, 1964, Judge Osterman brought his trial to an abrupt end by suddenly changing his pleas to guilty to the charges of conspiracy. He also admitted he had offered $5,000 to Epstein. Judge Osterman was sentenced to one year in the New York City penitentiary on Rikers Island for each count and allowed to serve the three years concurrently. He was released on December 24, 1964, for good behavior.

The next prosecution involved Liquor Authority Chairman Martin C. Epstein. The Epstein case was heard by Justice Schweitzer of the supreme court, who was later charged with bribery and retired under fire. And the judicial pollution of New York continued to pyramid.

JUDGE BENJAMIN H. SCHOR (NEW YORK)

Benjamin H. Schor served as committee clerk to the New York City Council from 1948 to 1953. He then became a municipal court justice for two years. Next in his political rise, Schor became deputy commissioner of the State Liquor Authority from 1955 until 1959. As a reward for his dedication, Mayor Robert Wagner appointed Schor to the New York Criminal Court.

Judge Schor was a member of the Brooklyn Criminal Court on November 4, 1966, when he was indicted for two counts of attempted grand larceny, one of extortion, and one of conspiracy to obstruct justice in shakedowns of applicants for liquor licenses.

Jack Brodsky, an owner of race horses and the operator of a Brooklyn used-car lot, was indicted on the same counts. Some months later Brodsky pleaded guilty and was given a suspended sentence. He later became a key prosecution witness in the case against the judge.

But Schor was not so cooperative. He waived immunity and spent an hour and a half in the grand jury room, denying any involvement in the shakedown. When he came out, he said, "I am innocent of the charge that has been made against me today. It is my intention to insist on an immediate trial at which time I shall be vindicated. This indictment cannot and will not stand impartial scrutiny by a court of law."

The judge won a temporary victory in December 1966, when the trial court quashed the indictment and dismissed the charges for lack of sufficient evidence. At the same time, however, the court denounced Schor for his testimony before the Queens grand jury, accusing him of "refusing to answer some questions, dodging and evading answers to others, and when answering, committing transparent perjury."

On January 4, 1967, Judge Schor resigned from the bench because he felt his "usefulness might have been impaired." He resumed the practice of law in Brooklyn.

But on October 3, 1967, Schor was arrested on a new ten-count indictment accusing him of lying to the grand jury the year before. The judge was charged with perjury when he denied that he had ever heard of the Imperial Inn or discussed obtaining a liquor license with either Brodsky or Sidney Balsam of the State Liquor Authority. Both Brodsky and Balsam were called as state witnesses and contradicted Schor's testimony.

The brazen plot was formed in 1966 at the Aqueduct Race Track where Robert L. Landsperg, a prospective owner of the Imperial Inn, spoke to Brodsky about the delay he was experiencing in getting his liquor license approved. Brodsky told Landsperg that he knew a judge who had been a deputy commissioner for the Liquor Authority and who could expedite the license for the right price.

Brodsky swore that he first discussed the delay in licensing with Judge Schor on July twenty-fifth and that the discussions continued for several weeks. He said that Schor "said if the people wanted a license, it would cost them $3,500."

Sidney Balsam, who had since become a schoolteacher, testified that Judge Schor inquired about the license for the tavern and was told that a hearing was pending in the case. Judge Schor took the stand in his own defense and repeated, under oath, the same testimony on which the perjury charges against him were based. He denied that he had ever discussed the Imperial Inn license with either Brodsky or Balsam.

Schor brought nineteen character witnesses, seventeen of

171

whom testified that his "reputation for veracity and honesty" was "excellent," and two of whom said they had never heard anything against him. Among the character witnesses were seven supreme court justices, one retired supreme court justice, the Kings County Surrogate, the niece of another supreme court justice, seven lawyers, a city councilman and two businessmen. If convicted, the judge faced a maximum sentence of thirty years in jail and a possible fine of $27,500.

Undoubtedly impressed by the testimony of the character witnesses, the jury took eleven votes and could not get unanimity. A verdict of not guilty was announced after thirteen hours of deliberation, and the judge was discharged.

Chapter Seven
Current Bench Warmers

"If a man hasn't got guts and personal integrity, I don't want him on my bench."

—Vince Lombardi

There are over 7,000 American judges serving today on federal and state trial and appellate courts. Although the systems and rules vary in each state, and all states differ from the federal judiciary, there is one common denominator for all—an overabundance of incompetent, or corrupt or, at least, easily influenced judges.

The argument that there are just as many crooked television repairmen or auto mechanics and the like doesn't hold up. No repairman or mechanic or anyone but a judge has unlimited control over the freedom and property of each member of his community.

The judges in this chapter are only a small representative grouping. There are several hundred judges judging us who have been accused, and often found guilty, of the wrongs they assess in others. Nevertheless, many of these judges could be most effective; and now, adhering strictly to their ethical and legal responsibilities, perhaps they are not as dangerous to an already sagging democracy as the many yet undiscovered judges who owe allegiance to a few and sell their favors.

It has been extraordinarily difficult to remove judges from the bench for their unwillingness or inability to perform their duties properly. This is true, not only for federal judges with life tenure, but also for judges with set terms of office.

Although a few will fail to win reappointment or reelection, only the most blatant and bizarre cases have resulted in the tortuous processes of impeachment and conviction.

The states have given increased attention to the judicial discipline problem and tried to establish methods for coping with it. But, whatever machinery exists, it is seldom employed. Judges and lawyers are loath to take on other sitting judges. And so we have many bench-warmers who are interesting, to say the least.

JUDGE STEPHEN S. CHANDLER
(FEDERAL—OKLAHOMA)

U.S. District Court Judge Stephen S. Chandler, Chief Judge of the Western District of Oklahoma, was stripped of his entire caseload on December 28, 1965, by order of the Judicial Council of the Tenth Circuit Court of Appeals. The council ruled that Chandler was "presently unable, or unwilling, to discharge efficiently the duties of his office," and they ordered that no cases whatsoever be assigned to him until further notice.

The judge was appointed to the federal bench in 1943 by President Franklin D. Roosevelt and in twenty-two years had earned a reputation as an expert on judicial administration. Chandler had been a leading advocate of plans designed to improve the efficiency of the judicial system. He was a director of the American Judicature Society and spokesman against the backlog of cases in most courts.

But Judge Chandler had become somewhat neurotic in his last few years. He had accused a fellow district court judge of spitting in his face and complained that other federal judges were trying to poison him.

The judge disputed the order, arguing that the Judicial Council did not have the authority to issue it and that he could only be disciplined through impeachment proceedings in the Congress. Chandler contended that the order was an attack on the independence of the judiciary. His appeals were all denied.

The U.S. Circuit Court of Appeals had twice removed him from specific cases involving oil companies (Occidental Petroleum Corporation and Texaco, Incorporated) because of his bias toward one of the parties. In the Occidental case Chandler constantly abused the executives of Occidental Petroleum, calling them "shady characters, pirates, and vultures," and singled out one of them as a "son of a bitch." The judge had also held closed-door hearings in his chambers at which all of the interested parties were not allowed to be present. He even tried to prevent a court officer from performing his official duties in matters relating to a bankruptcy.

But Chandler is still Judge Chandler.

JUDGE MALCOLM V. O'HARA (LOUISIANA)

Malcolm V. O'Hara was elected Judge of Section A of the Criminal District Court for the Parish of Orleans and took office on September 25, 1962. Five years later he was granted a leave of absence by the Louisiana Supreme Court. On October 18, 1967, the attorney general of that state instituted removal proceedings against the judge at the request of more than twenty-five citizens and taxpayers from his election district.

The attorney general based the removal proceedings on the premise that Judge O'Hara was guilty of gross misconduct in his private affairs. Although there were many allegations of misconduct in the petition, the state relied primarily on nine particular charges: (1) practicing law while a judge; (2) associating with a person known by him to be a convicted felon; (3) attempting to gain evidence involving a court proceeding; (4) using his office as judge to influence a wire-tapping case; (5) failing to abide by prior warnings against his association with Zachary A. Strate, a known convicted felon; (6) participating in a meeting to assist a convicted felon in obtaining evidence to be used in a court proceeding; (7) conspiring with

James Gill and Strate to obtain testimony to set aside the Hoffa-Strate conviction; (8) accepting improper gifts and gratuities from a known convicted felon; and (9) refusing to testify before a federal grand jury.

All of the misconduct complaints arose out of the relations between Judge O'Hara and Zachary A. Strate, Jr., which began in 1965. Strate, Jimmy Hoffa, Ben Dranow, S. George Burris, Abe I. Weinblatt, Calvin Kovens and Samuel Hyman were convicted in the U.S. District Court of the Northern District of Illinois of mail and wire fraud and conspiracy to defraud the Teamsters' pension fund. The conviction was affirmed by an appellate court. Judge O'Hara was certainly aware of that conviction before meeting Strate. The two men developed a very intimate and personal relationship. Over a period of approximately two years, Strate and O'Hara constantly discussed Strate's conviction in the federal court.

Strate was desperately trying to reverse the conviction, which was then on appeal. Judge O'Hara was interested in assisting Strate. Grady Partin, an official of the Teamsters Union in Baton Rouge, had been highly instrumental in the conviction of Jimmy Hoffa and three others in a federal district court in Chattanooga, Tennessee, on charges of jury tampering. Several of the attorneys and Hoffa were also involved in the Chicago trial which resulted in Strate's conviction.

In the early months of 1967 Strate was interested in talking with Grady Partin about whether wiretapping had been used in obtaining the conviction of Jimmy Hoffa in Tennessee. He asked Judge O'Hara to arrange a meeting with Partin. O'Hara was a close friend of James "Buddy" Gill, former Commissioner of Conservation of the State of Louisiana, who operated the Baton Rouge Industrial Contractors

Association. Gill and Partin were close, and at Judge O'Hara's request, arrangements were made by Gill for Partin to meet with O'Hara in Baton Rouge.

The day before the scheduled meeting with Partin the judge and his court reporter met Strate at the Fontainebleau Hotel in New Orleans. There they were introduced to Harold Brown, one of the attorneys in the Chattanooga trial. O'Hara was present part of the time while Strate and Brown discussed a document concerning the wiretapping to be prepared for Partin's signature.

On the following day, Saturday, March 3, 1967, the three men went to Baton Rouge in Strate's automobile, which was driven by the judge. Shortly after their arrival at Gill's business, Partin arrived, and O'Hara was called into Gill's office, where he was introduced to Partin as "Judge O'Hara from New Orleans." The judge presented the document to Partin for his signature, but Partin refused to sign it, claiming that the statements in it were not true. O'Hara's attempt to use his judicial position to obtain information was not only improper, but successful.

During the meeting in Baton Rouge, Partin suggested to Gill that it would be helpful to see the district attorney of East Baton Rouge Parish, Sergeant Pitcher, and Judge William Hawk Daniels. The reasons for seeing these two was not clear, but Gill did see Pitcher privately while the others waited at a restaurant. Later he also saw Judge Daniels. It was hoped that from these meetings evidence of wiretapping at the Chattanooga trial would be secured, but these efforts also failed.

The "Sheridan Incident" was Judge O'Hara and his friends' next attempt to secure evidence. Walter J. Sheridan had been a member of the staff of the Senate Committee on Improper Activities in the Labor-Management Field and active in the John F. Kennedy presidential campaign and in Robert Kennedy's senatorial campaign. He was a special assistant to the U.S. Attorney General from 1961 to 1964 and was actively involved in the Chattanooga trial of Hoffa and others.

In the summer of 1967 Sheridan was in New Orleans as a special correspondent for the National Broadcasting Company to investigate and report on the Garrison investigation of the assassination of President Kennedy. Edward Baldwin, Judge O'Hara's former law partner, who was interested in helping Sheridan in this investigation, made arrangements for a meeting between Judge O'Hara and Sheridan, and the judge brought his friend Strate to the meeting. The conversation between Strate and Sheridan centered around Strate's willingness to give information to Sheridan concerning the Garrison probe in exchange for information, to help himself and others, that wiretapping had been used in securing evidence in the Chattanooga trial. Sheridan and Strate did not come to any agreement, and no information was exchanged. What information did Strate have regarding the assassination of President Kennedy? And is there a possible connection between this information and the acquittal of Clay Shaw in the trial before Judge Haggerty? (Remember him from Chapter IV?)

Finally, Judge O'Hara accompanied Strate on at least two trips to Washington, D.C., and one trip to Las Vegas. The expenses of these trips were paid mostly by Strate.

Judge O'Hara finally admitted that he had a close association with Strate, that he acted on his behalf to obtain information in order to set aside a conviction in a federal court, that he ignored warnings given him by members of the state bar concerning this association, and that he accepted Strate's gifts and gratuities.

When all the evidence against the judge had been presented, the Louisiana Supreme Court found that his actions in the relationship with Strate were unacceptable and that he was indeed guilty of misconduct. Nevertheless, on June 4, 1968, the majority of the high court voted to dismiss the suit against O'Hara, saying:

> Although the defendant is guilty of misconduct, we do not find him guilty of that flagrant and extreme misconduct which would warrant his removal under the constitutional provisions. He has compromised his office and the high degree of trust placed in him by the electorate, but the record does not reflect that this conduct has rendered him "utterly unfit" to perform the functions of his office. O'Hara's conduct does not meet the constitutional requirement for removal for "gross misconduct."

Only one justice dissented. Judge O'Hara still sits on the Louisiana bench. Hoffa is free. And Sheridan is rich as a result of his book about how it happened.

JUDGE ERNEST J. SOMERS (MICHIGAN)

On September 23, 1969, the Judicial Tenure Commission of the state of Michigan filed a complaint charging District Court Judge Ernest J. Somers with five counts of misconduct in office. On various days in April and May of that year, the judge was found to have presided on the bench while under the influence of alcohol.

Contrary to statutory authority, Somers had also permitted his court clerk to arraign defendants in criminal cases. The judge also often requested the advice of his clerk in open court as to matters before the court. He indicated that "his" decision was often the clerk's.

On several occasions Judge Somers reduced drunk driving charges without approval of the police department or the prosecuting attorney and without notice to them. Hearings were held on all charges against Judge Somers, and the matter was ultimately submitted for decision to the Supreme Court of Michigan.

The high court found that the judge had been under the influence of alcohol on the occasions charged, and said that he showed "at best, very poor judgment." It did note, however, a general increase in the number of complaints filed with respect to drunken trial judges.

The charges regarding the delegation of authority to the court clerk were dismissed as understandable since the judge had not yet become used to his job on the district court bench.

Since it appeared "that the actions complained of took place for a period of two months in the spring of 1969" and since no additional complaints were made after that time, the supreme court held that the proper discipline should be an Order of Censure. Somers was censured on January 8, 1971, and he, too, still judges!

JUDGE NEVILLE TUCKER (KENTUCKY)

Louisville, Kentucky, Police Court Judge Neville Tucker received a six-month suspended sentence and was fined $500 on November 23, 1970, for failure to file income tax returns in 1964, 1965 and 1966. He pleaded "no contest" to the charge in the U.S. District Court for the District of Kentucky.

Judge Tucker, the son of the African Methodist Espiscopal bishop who gave the invocation at President Nixon's inauguration in 1969, was the first Negro ever elected a Louisville police court judge, where he is still sitting!

JUDGE BERNARD KLIEGER (NEW YORK)

Bernard Klieger of Brooklyn was elected to his civil court judgeship in 1969, after having served as an assistant to Controller Abraham D. Beame for several years. The judge was campaign coordinator for Mr. Beame when he ran for mayor against John V. Lindsay. Klieger was also deeply involved in the campaign of Frank O'Conner for city council president and Mario Procaccino for controller. That campaign reported total expenditures of $1.8 million.

On October 19, 1971, a federal grand jury indicted Judge Klieger on charges of fraudulently scheming to pay for political expenses of the campaign. The indictment accused the judge of having instructed a number of his co-conspirators to prepare and distribute "false bills and invoices with the purpose and intention of disguising corporate political campaign contributions."

Under the scheme, companies that printed material and did other work for the Beame campaign submitted bills for their work to certain corporations. The corporations then paid the bills, as if the work had been done for them in the normal course of their business operations, so that the cost could be tax-deductible. The system was certainly not novel but grew somewhat blatant, even for New York politics.

Several prominent corporations and Martin Tananbaum, the former president of Yonkers Raceway and financial head of the mayoral campaign, were named as coconspirators but not as defendants. Among the corporations were Alexander's Department Stores, David A. Carr Advertising, Leon DeMatteis & Sons Construction Corporation, West Clinton Corporation, Samuel J. Lefrak Agency Disbursement Fund and six companies owned by Jules Miron. Also mentioned were Locals 810 and 1614 of the International Brotherhood of Teamsters.

Two days after the indictment was announced, Judge Klieger issued a statement claiming that "the charges are entirely without substance." That same day he asked to be relieved of his judicial duties pending determination of the charges against him. In the meantime he was to continue receiving his $30,750 annual salary from the public.

In the course of his week-long trial which began in May 1972, three representatives of companies which had done printing and advertising work for the campaign testified that Judge Klieger had personally directed them to send their bills to those corporations.

Klieger, testifying on his own behalf, denied giving the directions and said he was only responsible for ordering day-to-day supplies and services, not for collecting funds or paying bills. He shifted the blame for any such questionable activities to Mr. Tananbaum, who had conveniently died in 1970.

Judge Klieger faced up to five years imprisonment for each

of the three counts and substantial fines and disbarment, if convicted. But on May 9, 1972, he was fully acquitted.

When the jury verdict was announced, the judge said, "I'll be back on the bench tomorrow morning at 10 o'clock, if my doctors allow it. I've been waiting a long time to get back there. I'll be a better judge because of this."

He's still there today.

One of the members of the jury who was interviewed later commented that "there was too much circumstantial evidence and not enough hard facts to convict Judge Klieger." And even a judge is entitled to a presumption of innocence unless and until he is convicted. Klieger was acquitted and Tananbaum was posthumously tarnished.

JUDGE ROSS J. DiLORENZO (NEW YORK)

Another Brooklyn judge, Ross J. DiLorenzo of the New York City civil court, began his political journey to the bench as Democratic leader of New York's Twelfth Assembly District. Neither his trip nor his stay have been entirely smooth.

In 1963 during a period of political infighting between Mayor Robert Wagner and the Brooklyn Democratic machine, the mayor fired DiLorenzo as a member of the city tax commission. But DiLorenzo had the important support of the Kings County Democratic leader, Stanley Steingut, and was elected to a ten-year term as judge the following year.

In 1966 Judge DiLorenzo helped to organize, and became president of, the American-Italian Anti-Defamation League, Inc. (later called Americans of Italian Descent, Inc.), of which Frank Sinatra later became national chairman. An often controversial figure, DiLorenzo has been publicly criticized for his conduct on the bench by lawyers of the Community Action for Legal Services, a group which handles complaints by poor tenants against their landlords.

Judge DiLorenzo was relieved of his judicial duties on October 26, 1971, pending an official inquiry into charges that he had interfered with a Waterfront Commission investigation in 1967. While the charges were being investigated, however, the judge continued to draw his annual salary of $30,000.

The charges concerned the judge's attempts to intercede with the commission on behalf of a fellow member of the Elks and close friend of forty years. DiLorenzo had met and talked with Anthony Piazza, assistant counsel for the commission, regarding his buddy's retention of a license. The judge was also charged with having given false testimony concerning his involvement.

"I did absolutely nothing," Judge DiLorenzo told a reporter. "I gave a hand to an individual. I put in a good word for him. Everybody put in a word, trying to help him keep his license from the Waterfront Commission." At a closed-door hearing in November 1971 the judge admitted he was guilty of an "indiscretion," but contended that he was innocent of any wrongdoing.

On April 3, 1972, Judge DiLorenzo was "slapped on the wrist" and reinstated to the bench. All five justices of the appellate division of the supreme court in Brooklyn ruled that the judge "did not act judiciously or properly," as required by the Canons of Judicial Ethics. Yet they added, "his conduct was not such as to justify removal from office. We conclude, however, that his conduct does warrant censure." Judge DiLorenzo is on the New York bench today.

JUDGE WILLIAM F. SUGLIA (NEW YORK)

William F. Suglia was appointed to a ten-year term as a Criminal Court Judge of New York City by Mayor Lindsay on December 31, 1968. On April 22, 1971, the judge was censured by the appellate division of the New York State Supreme Court for improper behavior involving a woman whose son had appeared before him on a marijuana charge.

The woman was an employee of the court and had informed Judge Suglia on February 22, 1970, that her son was in custody on a charge of possession of marijuana and was scheduled to be arraigned that evening. Judge Suglia and the woman went to his chambers, where there occurred what was called a "personal contact." An effort was made to describe the contact as an "embrace" to soothe the woman, who was upset by her son's arrest.

The son was suddenly released without bail, pending a hearing.

After that the woman made several telephone calls to the judge, ostensibly to discuss her son's case. In the course of the last of such calls, Suglia agreed to meet with her for further discussion and possibly to have a drink. The meeting never took place.

After being "stoodup," the woman lodged a complaint with the City Department of Investigation. This complaint ultimately led to the action taken against Judge Suglia.

After review of the facts the five-member appellate court unanimously agreed to censure Judge Suglia, saying that "whether or not the facts involve wrongdoing, they give all the appearance of wrongdoing and tend to bring the administration of justice into disrepute."

Suglia was on vacation at the time the censure was issued

and was not present before those who voiced disapproval of his conduct. It was suggested that his presence was essential if the censure was to have any effect at all.

Censure as a device to correct misconduct and to enhance the integrity of the administration of justice is frequently used and quickly forgotten. Censure accomplishes nothing. The offender suffers momentary embarrassment. He is neither removed, nor suspended, nor fined. He is simply told he has been a bad boy, and shouldn't do it again. And then judicial business continues as usual.

In the case of Judge Suglia the court did not find that the judge was not guilty of improper behavior. On the contrary, it specifically found that the incident had brought the administration of justice into disrepute. Apparently, it felt that just a little bit of disrepute was tolerable.

JUDGE BERNARD B. GLICKFELD (CALIFORNIA)

Superior Court Judge Bernard B. Glickfeld was also censured. On January 29, 1971, the California Supreme Court issued its order because of the manner in which Glickfeld treated a woman who had complained that he had been too lenient toward defendants who had raped her. The court's action upheld the recommendation of the California Commission on Judicial Qualifications.

The twenty-two-year-old rape victim had been grabbed by three men as she was walking home from a bus stop after her work as a hotel cashier. The men took her money and a ring, raped her six times, and then discussed killing her. Instead, they arranged to have her help them the next day to rob the hotel where she worked. Two of them appeared at the hotel, where the police, warned by the woman, arrested them. The third was arrested later.

The three men were charged with kidnapping, two counts of robbery and six counts of rape. The woman learned from the prosecutor's office that they had each pleaded guilty to one count of rape and one of robbery. She went with a deputy prosecutor to see Judge Glickfeld, who told her that he intended to give light sentences to try to help the men toward rehabilitation. Concerned for her safety, she objected. The judge flew into an absolute rage. He ordered the woman to leave, saying, "Get out of here, you horse's ass."

The woman also appeared in court on the day Judge Glickfeld sentenced the men on the guilty pleas, this time accompanied by a police inspector. She objected when only one of them was given a jail term. Again, the judge got ruffled and proceeded to hurl insults from the bench, displaying his obvious prejudices. "I don't want police inspectors sitting here in court holding some alleged victim's hands, and I am using the term figuratively," was one of his more intelligent remarks of the day. It was strange to call the woman an alleged victim after the men had pleaded guilty to raping her.

On the basis of the pleas of guilty to rape and robbery charges, Judge Glickfeld ordered William Morris to spend fifty-two weekends in jail. Kenneth Beasley was turned over to the California Youth Authority and in effect released on parole. James Jackson, who had a previous conviction, went to jail for violation of parole and on the new charges.

Beasley and Morris were into more trouble even before the censure action against their benevolent judge was completed.

They were arrested in January 1971 as suspects in an attempt to shoot a police sergeant who surprised them as they were in the process of burglarizing a department store. Beasley was arrested at the store, and Morris was picked up after Beasley was questioned.

The officer had been holding Beasley and another suspect at gunpoint when Morris fired five shots at him. They were now charged with attempted murder and burglary.

The district court of appeals reversed Judge Glickfeld's dismissal of five other counts of rape, one of robbery and one of kidnapping against each man, and ordered a trial on the reinstated charges.

The supreme court found that Judge Glickfeld's conduct was "such as to bring his judicial office into disrepute," but that it warranted no more serious punishment than censure.

The judge said in an interview that it was "absolutely ridiculous" to suggest that he consider resigning. He was appointed in 1966 to fill a vacancy on the court and elected to a full term in 1968. His present term of office ends in January 1975.

He is still sitting as a superior court judge in San Francisco. And one woman anxiously awaits his reelection campaign.

JUDGE LELAND W. GEILER (CALIFORNIA)

Some judges are pushy, and that can be tolerated. But when a judge decides to employ the use of a battery-operated dildo to prod people in his courtroom, even the liberal state of California will react. In October 1972 the California Commission on Judicial Qualifications recommended the removal of Los Angeles Municipal Court Judge Leland W. Geiler.

The commission found that Judge Geiler had invited the public defender into his office and thrust a dildo described as a "battery-operated object resembling a penis" into the defender's buttocks. According to witnesses, all thought it a very funny incident at the time. Later that same day in the courtroom the judge grew tired of the public defender's lengthy cross-examination of a witness. The lawyer was representing an indigent on a criminal case, but the judge wanted him to speed things up. Finally the judge ordered his clerk to "get out the machine."

"The battery?" the clerk asked.

"The battery," Geiler answered, and the public defender wisely and immediately concluded, "Your Honor, I have no further questions."

It was also alleged that Judge Geiler once grabbed a Los Angeles traffic court commissioner "by the testicles causing so much pain that he almost passed out." But the commission considered this "friendly horseplay."

The state commission's report also charged that Judge Geiler occasionally asked his married lady clerk, "Did you get any last night?" in front of others. On nine known occasions Geiler used obscene language in his courtroom, and in eight criminal cases he removed public defenders as defense counsel because they refused to plead their clients guilty as Judge Geiler demanded.

The commission's recommendation for removal came after twenty-one days of confidential hearings. It concluded that Judge Geiler was guilty of action prejudicial to the administration of justice, and of willful misconduct. He was disqualified from sitting on the bench until the California Supreme Court acted on the recommendation.

In the fine tradition of all honorable jurists accused of misconduct, Geiler responded to the charges by saying, "I have done nothing to deserve this recommendation by a majority of the commission. I shall oppose it and I am confident I will be vindicated." The matter is yet undecided.

This is only the second time in the eleven-year history of the California Commission on Judicial Qualifications that a recommendation has reached the supreme court. However, after some investigations—which are secret and unpublished—several judges have quietly retired with full benefits.

The other removal recommendation was made ten years ago in the case of Oceanside Municipal Court Judge Charles Stevens. Stevens fought the charge, and the supreme court rejected the commission recommendation. He is still on the bench.

In the case of Geiler, the courts are still probing his prodding!

Chapter Eight
The Chicago Three

*"Otto Kerner had an outstanding reputation. . . . It is ironic
that corruption should reach such a man."*

—JAMES THOMPSON,
United States Attorney

In ancient societies each tribe customarily designated its
wisest member to sit in judgment over the rest of the tribe.
He was called many things, but his function never changed.
He judged the wrongdoers and settled disputes in the village.

After thousands of years of accumulated wisdom, the
primitive practice had been updated and refined so that now
we have a sophisticated chain of command among those who
judge us.

Some cynics claim—and unfortunately there appears to be
periodic justification—that judgeships are reserved for those
who cannot make a living any other way and that judges
progress up the appellate organization in indirect proportion
to their ability and integrity.

Everybody agrees that the quality of trial-level judges in many communities is terrible, but few of us have seen the repeated instances of corruption and inefficiency that seem to plague courthouses of the state of Illinois. Years ago it was said that political judgeships attracted the bottom half of the bar. Although that may not be true generally, it should be noted that many judges are bunglers, some are crooks and several are a little of both.

Recently two members of the Illinois Supreme Court resigned under very accusatory fire. Their $40,000 annual salary apparently had not been enough, according to those who focused on the financial machinations of the distinguished jurists.

In 1972 the American judicial system was rocked with a political earthquake. The conviction of Otto Kerner, former governor of Illinois and one of the most highly respected judges in America, was precedential in an unfortunate way. He became the first sitting federal judge ever criminally convicted when he was sentenced to three years in prison and fined $50,000 in a racetrack-stock bribery scheme. At the close of the trial Kerner told the court that the jury's verdict had "deeply and irreparably tainted the good reputation that I cherished, and years of imprisonment can never compare to the severity of that punishment." Insofar as his remarks apply to the damaged faith in our judiciary, Kerner deserves a Pulitzer Prize for understatement.

JUSTICE ROY J. SOLFISBURG, JR. AND JUSTICE RAY I. KLINGBIEL (ILLINOIS)

Contemporaneously with the Illinois Supreme Court's decision to convene their courts commission on a permanent basis, public accusations of misconduct were made against two members of the Supreme Court itself. On June 11, 1969, Sherman Skolnick, chairman of the Citizens' Committee To Clean Up The Courts, filed a motion in the supreme court asking it to investigate the integrity of its decision in *People v. Isaacs.*

The motion charged Chief Justice Roy J. Solfisburg, Jr., and Justice Ray I. Klingbiel with "undue influence and appearance of impropriety" regarding the decision. Specifically, they were accused of receiving, through a third party, stock in a Chicago bank in the fall of 1966 from the defendant Theodore Isaacs, who helped to organize the bank, while the Isaacs case was pending before the court. Both justices had voted with the 4-2 majority to affirm the trial court's dismissal of an indictment against Isaacs, and Justice Klingbiel had written the opinion.

Isaacs, a former Illinois Director of Revenue and campaign chairman for former Governor Otto Kerner, was a founder of the Civic Center Bank and Trust Company. In 1964 he was indicted on charges of collusion and conspiracy in the manipulation of more than a million dollars in state contracts for the purchase and printing of envelopes to benefit a company in which he held a secret interest. The charges against Isaacs were dismissed by a county court on the technicality that the indictments were improperly worded. Two other defendants in the case (one of whom is now a state senator) pleaded guilty and were fined.

The prosecution appealed the dismissal of the charges to the supreme court. The court's original draft opinion, written by Justice Robert Underwood, recommended that the lower court decision be reversed, and that Isaacs stand trial. This opinion was rejected by a 4-2 vote of the justices. Then Justice Klingbiel—in a departure from the normal rotation of justices—appointed himself (he was serving as chief justice at the time) to write the opinion, which upheld the dismissal of the charges. Neither Justice Underwood nor Justice Walter Schaefer, who had sided with Underwood, filed a formal dissent.

As soon as the charges of misconduct were made public, it became obvious that a serious question existed as to who should investigate the allegations and conduct formal hearings on the evidence. Investigation by the Illinois Courts Commission was viewed with considerable skepticism because the investigating agency for the commission was the administrative director of the courts, who was appointed by and subject to the direction of the supreme court, whose members were the ones being investigated. The supreme court also appoints two circuit court judges who serve on the commission, and the fact that Justice Klingbiel was chairman of the commission at the time did aggravate the extreme awkwardness of the situation.

It was finally decided to appoint a special commission of five senior members of the bar association to gather evidence and file its report by August 1, 1969. The special commission had no trouble developing plenty of material to work with.

Ironically, the first person punished as a result of the investigation was the man who started it. Sherman Skolnick was sentenced to four months in jail for contempt of court for refusing to reveal his sources to the commission. He had repeatedly called the investigation a "whitewash," contending that the commission members were still too close to those being investigated to act impartially. After all, they had been appointed by the supreme court.

After extensive preliminary investigation, the commission held six days of hearings in July, during which it took testimony from twenty-one witnesses, including Chief Justice Solfisburg, Justice Klingbiel, and Theodore Isaacs. The record of investigation included 1,800 pages of transcribed testimony and 133 exhibits.

Chief Justice Roy J. Solfisburg was fifty-three years old and had served on the supreme court since 1960. His name has been mentioned as a possible appointee by President Richard M. Nixon to the U.S. Supreme Court.

The justice, of course, denied any wrongdoing: "No decision of mine and no decision of the Supreme Court of Illinois during my service was tainted with impropriety," he said. The investigation commission did not agree.

It determined that in May and June of 1966 Justice Solfisburg borrowed $14,000 to purchase seven hundred shares of stock in the recently organized Civic Center Bank and Trust Company, of which Isaacs was general counsel and secretary of the board of directors. On September 15, 1966, the supreme court heard oral argument in the case of *People v. Isaacs.* Two months after the oral argument Justice Solfisburg received notice of the annual meeting of the bank's stockholders. The notice was signed by Isaacs. Upon receipt of the notice, the justice authorized five persons, including two associates in Isaacs' law firm, to act as his proxy.

Yet Justice Solfisburg had testified that he was not aware of any connection between Isaacs and the Civic Center Bank.

Robert Perbohner and Robert Dolph, both Illinois Commerce Commissioners, had offered the justice the bank stock at $7 a share less than the market price, saying only that

"there are some prominent Chicagoans in it." Supposedly
with only that information, Solfisburg bought the stock
because he "believed bank stocks were a good investment."

Some of those "prominent Chicagoans" who were stockholders in the bank turned out to be Bailey K. Howard,
president of the newspaper division of Field Enterprises,
which publishes the *Sun-Times* and the *Daily News;* two
ranking executives of the Chicago *Tribune;* eight circuit court
judges; two judges of the U.S. Court of Appeals, one of
whom was former Governor Otto Kerner (since convicted of
felonies); and at least eight reputed members of Chicago's
organized crime syndicate.

After purchasing the stock, Justrice Solfisburg had it
issued in the name of a secret trust he had created. He later
sold it at a profit of $4,300, and there was evidence that
Isaacs had been involved in the resale.

It was also discovered that Isaacs' law firm was employed
by Justice Solfisburg's insurance company and that the
justice had sent his son to Isaacs to be counseled on how to
get into the Illinois National Guard. But Solfisburg denied
any impropriety and any knowledge of Isaacs' connection
with the bank.

Justice Ray I. Klingbiel received a one-hundred-share
"gift" certificate of Civic Center Bank stock in November
1966, two weeks after the court had heard oral arguments in
the Isaacs case and just after he had won reelection to the
bench. He had been a member of the court since 1953.

The same two commerce commissioners who had set up
the purchase by Solfisburg also set up the "gift" to Klingbiel.
The certificate had been issued by the bank, at Isaacs' instruction, in the name of Robert Perbohner, who then
endorsed it and gave it to Robert Dolph. Justice Klingbiel
was taken aside by Dolph at a dinner party and given the

$2,500 worth of stock as a "campaign contribution." The justice was told he could keep it or sell it to pay for his campaign costs. "Then he handed me the certificate and I put it in my pocket," Klingbiel testified. Mr. Perbohner said, "I gave the stock to the judge because I wanted to do something nice for him."

At the time of the gift, Justice Klingbiel had already received about $6,500 in campaign contributions. His campaign expenses were only about $2,000, since he had run unopposed as an incumbent member of the high court. The justice maintained that he didn't ask Dolph anything about the Civic Center Bank, its location in Chicago or who was associated with it. The commission found that if "he did not in fact already know it, Justice Klingbiel could readily have learned that Isaacs was closely associated with, and an important figure in, the Civic Center Bank upon making even a casual inquiry about the bank."

The justice held the stock for almost two years without publicly registering it. He then had it transferred to the names of his two grandchildren. When he did register them, he entered the date January 2, 1968, on the certificate, making it appear that the transfer had come ten months after the Isaacs decision instead of four months before it.

When it was discovered that Justice Klingbiel had not listed the stock on his income tax return, his attorney contended that it was a "clear, unrestricted gift for campaign purposes and had no income tax consequences." But the "gift" did have other consequences.

On September 30, 1969, the special commission issued its seventy-page report, in which it called for the resignation of both justices in order to "restore public confidence in the court." The report stated that they had violated the Canons of Ethics of the Illinois Judicial Conference. It said, "The record in this investigation not only evidences the appearance of impropriety but establishes, by clear and convincing proof, certain positive acts of impropriety on the part of Justice Klingbiel and Justice Solfisburg."

On Saturday, August 2, 1969, two days after the commission submitted its report to the supreme court, Chief Justice Solfisburg and Justice Klingbiel, in separate statements to the press, announced their resignations. The lawyer for the two justices said that they had arrived at their decisions separately and against his advice. The four major daily newspapers in Chicago as well as others throughout Illinois had demanded both resignations.

The high court duo expressed strong disagreement with the commission's findings and reiterated that they had not been guilty of any misconduct. Justice Klingbiel said, "I wish I had the physical stamina to carry this fight to the court commission [of which he was chairman], but I have made the decision for the welfare of my family and for the sake of their health and happiness, as well as my own." The fact that both men could comfortably retire on a pension, which could have been lost had they pushed the issue to the point of defending removal proceedings, may also have contributed to their decisions. Their salary had been $40,000 per year.

JUDGE OTTO KERNER (ILLINOIS)

Otto Kerner graduated from Brown University and then studied in England before attending Northwestern's law school in Chicago. In 1934 he graduated, began practice and married the daughter of the late Chicago mayor, Anton J. Cermak. Cermak had drifted into international headlines when he was shot while attending a political rally with President Roosevelt in Miami.

About the same time, Kerner joined the Blue Ribbon unit of the Illinois National Guard as a private. By 1942 he was a major. During World War II he served with distinction in Africa, Sicily and the Pacific and attained the rank of major general by the time he resigned from the Guard in 1954. At one point he was the executive officer of a battalion headed by General William C. Westmoreland, who was later to testify as a character witness for Kerner at his criminal trial.

After the war Kerner returned to Chicago and, following family tradition, became involved with Mayor Daley's Cook County Democratic machine. He set out to become a legal giant and a judge, and he achieved both goals. Based on the recommendation of the Illinois machine, the late President Harry Truman appointed Kerner U.S. Attorney for Northern Illinois in 1947. For seven years Kerner was a vigorous and aggressive prosecutor. In 1954 he became a county judge, which enabled him to get involved in local politics since he had jurisdiction over the Chicago Board of Election Commissioners. In 1960 Otto Kerner was elected governor of Illinois, and in 1964 the mandate was repeated. Governor Kerner attracted national attention in 1967 when President Johnson named him to head his National Advisory Commission on Civil Disorders.

In his final year of governorship, Kerner resigned to accept an appointment from the President of the United States as a justice to the U.S. Court of Appeals.

Holding office for life, he was now free from the hassle of seeking public approval of his actions through the election process.

On February 19, 1973, Otto Kerner, after a seven-week

trial, earned his place in the almanacs when he became the first federal judge in the 189-year history of the courts to be indicted, tried and convicted while still in office. He has since been asked to vacate but still draws a salary of $42,500 annually. In previous cases when federal judges were accused, they had all resigned immediately after the indictment and before conviction.

The investigation that led to the disclosure of Kerner's financial dealings was begun by federal agents after the death, in October 1970, of Illinois Secretary of State Paul Powell. Powell's personal effects included more than $800,000 in cash and $750,000 worth of racetrack stock holdings. An audit of his stock holdings eventually showed that a number of prominent politicians had been involved in the purchase of racetrack stocks they had been secretly offered at bargain prices. Some shares were purchased for one dollar or less each during the time the officials held influential state offices.

In 1966 Mrs. Marjorie Everett, who operated the Arlington Park and Washington Park racetracks through Chicago Thoroughbred Enterprises, secretly sold Judge Kerner and Theodore Isaacs, his chief financial and political adviser, fifty shares of Chicago Thoroughbred stock at a cost of $25,000 to each man. The stock was then worth about $300,000. Within six months, Kerner and Isaacs traded their stock for 5,000 shares each in Mrs. Everett's Balmoral Jockey Club, another racing association.

These shares were then sold in 1967 to William S. Miller, who a few weeks before had resigned as chairman of the Illinois Racing Board, a position to which he was appointed by Kerner. This transaction netted Judge Kerner and Isaacs a handsome profit of $125,000 each on their original investment of $25,000.

Also in 1966 Kerner, secretly, and Isaacs, publicly, had

bought 14,000 shares each in Chicago Harness Racing, Inc., for forty cents a share. Ten months later they sold this stock for two dollars a share, each netting a profit of $22,400.

The purchase and sale of the stocks were not in themselves illegal transactions. But it was shown that when the deals were being made, the racing interests involved were seeking permits and preferential racing dates in the Chicago area.

The transactions in which Judge Kerner and Isaacs were involved were handled through George J. Schaller, a former law partner of Mayor Daley. Schaller, now a Cook County Circuit Court judge, was then legal adviser to Mrs. Everett. Judge Schaller was also a law partner of William J. Lynch, another former law partner of Daley and now a U.S. district court judge.

Judge Lynch acted as "nominee," or front man, in 1964 for George W. Dunne, the Cook County Board president, who was then a state legislator. Dunne, who has been mentioned as a possible Democratic candidate for governor of Illinois and sometimes as heir to Mayor Daley's Cook County Democratic machine, admitted he bought 5,000 shares of Washington Park Trotting Association stock for one dollar each in 1964 and then sold them for five dollars each two years later, making a profit of $20,000. Dunne had been told about the stock by Secretary of State Powell, whose death originally sparked the investigation.

On December 15, 1971, after a two-and-a-half-year investigation of the Illinois horse-racing industry by a federal grand jury, Judge Kerner and three former state officials were indicted for several felonies.

The judge was charged with accepting bribes—purchasing racetrack stock at virtually giveaway prices in exchange for seeing that certain racetrack owners received favorable treatment in the assignment of racing dates.

Kerner was also accused of lying to a federal grand jury when he testified that he had never discussed the awarding of racing dates with members of the Illinois Racing Commission, he was also accused of making a false statement to Internal Revenue agents when he insisted that an entry in his 1967 income tax return was the name of a Chicago company and not a listing for Chicago Thoroughbred Enterprises stock.

He was further accused of omitting $147,000 from his 1966 tax return, and of lying again to IRS agents when he said he held racing stock only in the Thoroughbred group and the Balmoral Jockey Club. The indictment alleged that he also owned stock in Chicago Harness Racing, Inc.

Named in the indictment with Kerner were Theodore Isaacs; William Miller, the Illinois Racing Board chairman for most of the judge's two terms as governor; Joseph Knight, Director of Illinois Financial Institutions during that period; and Faith McInturf, a business associate of Mr. Miller.

After the indictment was announced, Judge Kerner asked the chief judge of the court of appeals to be immediately relieved of participating in any activity of the court pending the final disposition of the case against him. Chief Judge Swygert granted the request, which did not affect Kerner's salary. Kerner and the others were placed under $10,000 recognizance bonds, and arraigned in January 1972.

Federal lawyers in Chicago subpoenaed the American Bar Association's Committee on the Federal Judiciary, which investigates potential judges for the Justice Department, to determine if the committee's investigation of Kerner prior to his appointment to the bench in 1968 had turned up any evidence of the racetrack dealings. The committee refused to comply with the subpoena, and the government did not press it for compliance.

In April 1972 Kerner's attorneys made a motion for dismissal of the indictments on the ground that unauthorized persons were in the grand jury room in violation of federal law while the jury was hearing evidence in the case. They also filed at least a dozen motions asking that each defendant be tried separately or that certain counts against each defendant be judged in a separate trial.

Both Kerner and his codefendant, Theodore Isaacs, were found guilty on all nineteen counts of the indictment which had included charges of bribery, conspiracy, mail fraud, perjury before a grand jury and income tax evasion. Under the maximum punishment, the judge could be sentenced to prison for eighty-three years and fined $93,000. Isaacs could face up to seventy-three years and a $73,000 fine. Sentencing was delayed, however, to give them thirty days in which to file motions for new trial.

At a press conference immediately after the trial, James Thompson, the U.S. attorney who directed the prosecution, said that he had a "feeling of sadness and tragedy about this case." He said,

> Many people believe all politicians are crooked and all public officials are corrupt. Kerner had the reputation of being different from all that. I voted for him once. He had an outstanding reputation. It is ironic that corruption should reach such a man.
>
> This conviction will change the spirit in this district so that people can expect integrity and fidelity from those who hold public office. This is not the end of the racetrack scandal. More is coming. We are going after corruption in government at all levels so that kids can look to government and politics as the highest in careers.

He promised to pursue political corruption regardless of politics—Republican or Democrat—and regardless of station— high or low. Thompson, considered a likely GOP candidate for mayor of Chicago, denied the indictment was politically motivated.

After the jury returned its verdict, Judge Kerner, his nervous smile intact, quickly exited the courtroom through the judge's chambers to his own chambers in the same building, from which he issued the following statement:

> Despite the verdict of the jurors, at no time that I have held public office have I taken any advantage and I have always made my judgments in consideration of the people I have served.
>
> I have been in many battles in my life where life itself was at stake. This battle is even more important than life itself because it involved my reputation and honor which are dearer than life itself, and I intend to continue this battle.

The conviction of Judge Kerner and his associates was a result of the combined efforts of several investigating agencies. Journalists first rushed in where others feared to tread and the case was assembled by many people combing through court records and other public documents. The Kerner trial served as an illuminating reminder of the fallibility of our federal system of granting lifetime judgeships and of the truth in the poignant observation that America has "the finest judges money can buy."

Chapter Nine
Article I, Section III

Impeachment is . . . a "bungling way, an impractical thing, a mere scarecrow."

—PRESIDENT THOMAS JEFFERSON

It has been said that the greatest president has never achieved the power of the most obscure Supreme Court justice. The degree of accuracy in that comparison is academic. Suffice it to say that a lifetime appointment to the highest court represents in this country the pinnacle of authority over the life and property of all, the actions of the Congress and all the pronouncements of the president.

The impeachment procedure set forth in the Constitution of the United States in Article I, Section III is intentionally demanding, exacting and damn near impossible to implement, perhaps because the political and financial machinations of jurists are supposedly above reproach.

But the cases of the irreverent Samuel Chase, the unfortunate Abe Fortas and the incomparable William O. Douglas bear study as exercises in political futility. In one case, perhaps two, we were just lucky.

JUSTICE SAMUEL CHASE

Samuel Chase, a Baltimore lawyer, was combative and contentious in everything he did. As a young man he opposed the British Stamp Act and led the Sons of Liberty on secret midnight raids to ransack the files, destroy the records, and set fire to the stamps in government offices. His militant opposition to British rule earned him sufficient notoriety to gain election to the First Continental Congress, where he fought for the Declaration of Independence and became one of its signers. He was a leader of the Maryland Convention that ratified the Constitution of the United States, and in 1796 President Washington appointed him an associate justice of the Supreme Court.

The Supreme Court did not have a busy docket in the early days of the Republic. It met for two brief terms a year in Washington, and during the remaining months the six justices "rode circuit," presiding as circuit court judges at the trials of important cases and hearing appeals from district court judges in lesser matters.

Justice Chase was a terror on the bench. He bullied the lawyers, browbeat witnesses, intimidated juries, and with his sarcasms from the bench brought laughter from spectators on hapless defense counsel. Even his friend Chief Justice John

Marshall admitted on cross-examination during the Senate impeachment trial that Chase, as a judge, was "tyrannical, oppressive, and overbearing."

Chase's conduct during the trials under the Alien and Sedition Laws (which made criticizing the president and other public officials a criminal offense), later to be ruled unconstitutional, finally led to impeachment charges against him. He was most obnoxious in his vigorous and overbearing enforcement of these laws during the campaign against President John Adams. He espoused a double standard regarding principles of freedom of speech and association when such principles were applied for the protection of those espousing ideas contrary to his own. It was all right to criticize, and even to sabotage the government as he had done earlier, but it was somehow improper to do so when the government changed from British to American.

He presided at the trial of Thomas Cooper, a newspaper editor in Pennsylvania, and directed the jury to convict him on the premise that any criticism of public officials "effectually saps the foundation of government." He also presided at the trial of a farmer named Fries who had refused, on grounds of principle, to pay certain federal taxes. Chase charged that this was "treason" and sentenced him to be "hanged by the neck until dead." The resulting public uproar resulted in a presidential pardon.

Chase then went to Baltimore where he impaneled a large number of grand jurors and during the impaneling process denounced the Republican proposal for universal suffrage because it would "sink" the country "into a mobocracy, the worst of all popular governments."

Chase then rushed to Richmond to preside at the trial of another noted and outspoken editor named Callender who had published material hostile to President Adams. Chase read the pamphlet prior to trial and announced publicly that "he would certainly punish" the editor and "teach the lawyers of Virginia the difference between the liberty and the licentiousness of the press." When the trial began, Chase refused to excuse a juror who announced that he was morally bound to find the defendant guilty and refused to hear distinguished witnesses offered by the defense. Again the justice was labeled "tyrannical, overbearing and oppressive."

In New Castle, Delaware, Chase refused to dismiss a grand jury until it returned an indictment against a Jeffersonian newspaper publisher. When that grand jury refused to indict, he ordered the U.S. attorney to read all back issues of the paper and report any abusive language to the jury. But the jurors reported that they discovered nothing treasonable except a brief and unpleasant reference to Chase himself. Chase reluctantly let the matter drop.

On March 12, 1804, the House of Representatives issued impeachment charges against Justice Samuel Chase related to these actions and other rulings he made while on the bench. He was impeached on eight articles, charging misconduct in the prejudice of impartial justice in the course of a trial; misconduct in improperly inducing or coercing a grand jury to return an indictment and misconduct in addressing an inflammatory political harangue to a grand jury. Chase offered an elaborate defense, primarily on the ground that the offenses charged did not constitute "high crimes and misdemeanors" justifying impeachment.

The trial before the U.S. Senate resulted in a failure for the impeachment since the prosecution did not get the prerequisite votes of two-thirds of the senators present. But a majority of the votes cast were for conviction on several of the articles.

History balances Chase's revolutionary patriotism with his ignoble actions as a member of the Supreme Court.

JUSTICE ABE FORTAS

Abe Fortas was one of the most brilliant lawyers to graduate Yale Law School, where he was editor-in-chief of their prestigious law journal and ranked first in his class. After graduation, Fortas taught briefly at Yale and then served in various second-echelon administrative positions during the New Deal. He became a lawyer for the Securities and Exchange Commission and at the age of thirty-two was appointed undersecretary of the interior under Harold L. Ickes.

Fortas met Congressman Lyndon Baines Johnson of Texas in the late thirties. They became close friends, and Fortas was at LBJ's side when important events required a trusted advisor and confidant.

In 1948 one such incident proved to be a turning point in both men's careers. Johnson came out eighty-seven votes ahead in the Democratic senatorial primary in Texas, but his opponent had won a court order to keep LBJ's name off the ballot for the general election. Fortas represented Johnson and appealed to U.S. Supreme Court Justice Hugo Black, who granted a reversal of the order. LBJ won the election and later became Senate majority leader. And Fortas won the lifelong appreciation of a future president of the United States.

From Lyndon Johnson's days as a young Texas congressman through his term as president, Fortas was his counsel and closest adviser. In 1964, when top LBJ aide Walter Jenkins ran afoul of the law, it was Fortas (along with Clark Clifford) who tried to get the Washington newspapers to suppress the story.

Fortas practiced law with encylopedic competence and became rich and respected in legal circles in a very short time. He made his fortune by representing wealthy individuals and corporations, his fame by defending the poor in their battles for equal civil rights. It was Abe Fortas who argued the landmark Gideon case before the U.S. Supreme Court, winning the right-to-counsel guarantees of the Sixth Amendment for indigent defendants.

Fortas commanded great respect among lawyers, judges and academicians—even those who disagreed with his legal theories or disliked him personally. In 1965 he was nominated by President Johnson to serve on the Supreme Court as successor to Arthur Goldberg. LBJ's choice was welcomed with great acclaim throughout the legal profession.

Fortas had never aspired to be on the Court. Such a position was not a part of his personal career plan. He was content to continue practicing law as a senior partner in Arnold, Fortas & Porter, one of the super-lawyer factories in Washington, D.C. But as a favor to his old friend the president, he agreed to accept the nomination and began serving on the bench in October 1965.

When Johnson told Fortas to come to the White House for announcement of his nomination LBJ said, "I've just sent 50,000 men to Vietnam and I'm sending you to the Supreme Court." Both decisions turned out to be ill-fated. The decision to send the men to Vietnam ultimately ended LBJ's political career; and the decision to send Fortas to the Court was to all but destroy the latter's legal career. Fortas became the first justice in the history of the Supreme Court to resign under fire after having been accused of misconduct.

Fortas continued to advise and do favors for President Johnson after he took his seat. On June 26, 1968, LBJ nominated him to succeed Earl Warren as Chief Justice of the high court. For the nomination to be approved by the Senate, Justice Fortas had to face the Senate Judiciary Committee. Some senators wanted to hold the job open for possible appointment by the president-elect, who was to take office the following January. Some conservative senators attacked Fortas for his liberal positions on criminal procedure and censorship. But then, delicate considerations relevant to his judicial fitness were raised.

Fortas' relationship with the president bore on the constitutional question of the proper separation of powers between the executive and judicial branches of the federal government. He was accused of acting as a judicial vehicle for presidential wrath against politicians who opposed LBJ's policies. If a person wanted to see the president, Fortas was the man who could arrange it. If the president wished to fend off influential tormentors—including the press—Fortas was frequently sent to do the fending.

He was also accused of trying to obtain a position for former White House press secretary Bill Moyers as undersecretary of state, and of lobbying to secure a federal judgeship for David Bress, U.S. Attorney for the District of Columbia.

The disclosure of the extent of Justice Fortas' participation in White House decision-making was reminiscent of Samuel Chase's adventures. Fortas had assisted LBJ in strategy-planning conferences on the Vietnam war and on the control of urban riots. It was revealed that Fortas had even helped to prepare Johnson's State of the Union Message in 1966, and to draft the message given by the President when he ordered troops into riot-torn Detroit in the summer of 1967.

In the midst of the accusations being made in the Senate hearings on the nomination, the *New York Times* revealed that the justice had accepted $15,000 for conducting a series of lectures at American University's Washington College of Law. The issue was not the fact that he had received such a fee, nor the fact that he had given the lectures, since the Court was recessed for summer at the time. However, the funds to pay Fortas had been solicited as tax-deductible contributions by Paul Porter, Fortas' former law partner, from influential business and financial leaders, several of whom might sometime be involved in litigation before the Supreme Court.

Donations came from Troy Post, a wealthy Texan and Fortas ally whose son had been helped by Porter after an indictment for mail fraud; Maurice Lazarus, who at one time sat with Fortas on the board of directors of Federated Department Stores, Inc.; Gustave Levy, a New York banker and chairman of the Board of Governors of the New York Stock Exchange; John Loeb, a Wall Street banker; and Paul Davis Smith, a New York City lawyer who was also vice-president and general counsel for Philip Morris, Inc.

Critical senators were eager to press questions about this and other matters. Justice Fortas agreed to appear for questioning before the Senate Judiciary Committee, thereby becoming the first nominee for Chief Justice ever to appear before a congressional panel.

But the pressure and possibility of embarrassment became too great. On September 13, 1968, in a letter to the committee's chairman, Fortas reversed himself and declined to appear before the committee.

In a letter to President Johnson on October second, Fortas withdrew as nominee for Chief Justice, in order to end the "destructive and extreme assaults upon the Court." On the Senate floor the day before, his supporters had failed by a wide margin to cut off a filibuster by Fortas' critics which could have delayed approval until after the expiration of Johnson's term of office. The vote was forty-five to forty-three in favor of nomination. But that was fourteen votes short of the two-third's positive margin necessary.

The justice said he would remain on the Court at least for the next term which was to start the following week. He did start the term—but he never finished it.

On May 5, 1969, the late *Life* magazine published an article by Associate Editor William Lambert disclosing Justice Fortas' association with corporate manipulator Louis E. Wolfson.

Wolfson began his rise in financial circles in the 1930s when he took over a family junk business his immigrant father had started in Florida. By the early fifties Wolfson was well known at corporate board meetings and on the financial pages. He took over a Washington, D.C., transit company and siphoned off its rich capital reserves; then he nearly succeeded in gaining control of Montgomery Ward but was narrowly beaten in a proxy battle. At one time he became the largest shareholder in American Motors; when he sold his interest, he got into a dispute with the government over making "false and misleading statements." A prominent financial writer called him "the biggest corporate raider of all time."

Fortas' personal association with Wolfson began in 1965, when he told the justice about the Wolfson Family Foundation, a tax-free foundation set up by Wolfson for charitable, educational and civil rights projects. *Life* did not say that Wolfson hired Fortas to fix his case. But the chain of events and conflicting accounts given (or the failure to give any account at all) by those involved certainly raised serious doubts as to the propriety of Justice Fortas' involvement.

On January 3, 1966, three months after Fortas was sworn in as associate justice, a check for $20,000 was paid to him personally by the Wolfson Family Foundation, and signed by Wolfson's partner, Elkin "Buddy" Gerbert, as foundation treasurer. It was endorsed with the justice's name and deposited in his personal bank account. Ostensibly, Fortas was being paid to advise the foundation on ways to use its funds for civil rights programs.

For some fifteen months, the Securities and Exchange Commission had been conducting an investigation into Wolfson's dealings. Alexander Rittmaster, one of his business associates, claimed that in February, in response to a question regarding what Wolfson intended to do about the investigation, Wolfson said it was going to be taken care of "at the top," and that the matter would never get out of Washington. He also mentioned that Fortas was joining the foundation.

In the next few months, however, two reports were forwarded to U.S. Attorney Robert Morganthau in New York recommending prosecution of Wolfson, Gerbert, Rittmaster and two others.

On June fourteenth, the day after the Supreme Court had adjourned for a week's recess, Justice Fortas flew to Jacksonville, Florida, where he was met at the airport by Gerbert and driven to Wolfson's elegant Harbor View Farm near Ocala, where Wolfson runs one of the largest thoroughbred horse-breeding operations in the nation. The next day, while Fortas was a houseguest at Harbor View, the SEC investigation finally came to public attention when a newspaper reported that an SEC attorney had asked a New York judge to hold up settlement of several stockholders' suits against the Wolfson-controlled Merritt-Chapman & Scott Corporation pending the results of the investigation. Fortas returned to Washington two days later.

According to Rittmaster's testimony, he was told by Wolfson that Justice Fortas was "furious" because the SEC had reneged on a pledge to give the Wolfson group another hearing before forwarding a criminal report. Rittmaster said he was further reassured by Gerbert that there was no need to worry, since Fortas had been at the farm to discuss the SEC matter and that it would be taken care of. If Fortas said that, he was wrong.

On September 19, 1966, Wolfson and Gerbert were indicted for conspiracy in the handling of stock in Continental Enterprises, Inc., by failing to publicly register their projected stock sales. (They made $3.5 million from the sale, after which the remaining stockholders found their shares had dropped from $8 to $1.50.) On October eighteenth Wolfson, Gerbert and Rittmaster (who later became a prosecution witness) were indicted on further charges of secretly buying $10 million in Merritt-Chapman stock and selling it back to the company for a $4 million profit and conspiring to obstruct the SEC investigation. They were also formally accused of perjury.

On December 22, 1966, Justice Fortas sent his personal check for $20,000 to the Wolfson Family Foundation, repaying the money he had received over eleven months before. According to the justice's former law partner, Porter, the money was repaid "because Abe had a whole sackful of petitions for writs; the business of the Court took so much of his time he couldn't do the work of the foundation."

Wolfson and others were convicted. In an interview with a reporter from the *Wall Street Journal*, just days before he went to prison, he said that through political connections he could have gotten a pardon from President Johnson in December 1968 if he had asked for it. He told the reporter he had received that assurance "from somebody who is as close as anybody could be" to Johnson. But, said Wolfson, he turned down this offer because he didn't want any favors.

217

The *Life* article raised the question as to what kind of service Justice Fortas could have performed for the foundation that would justify a fee of $20,000 a year.

Whatever services he may or may not have rendered, his name had been dropped in strategic places at significant times by Wolfson and Gerbert in an effort to stay out of prison for violating securities laws. If this were being done without the justice's knowledge, it probably would not change the fact that his acceptance of the money and other actions of his made the name-dropping effective. Coincidentally, the Arnold, Fortas and Porter law firm had represented Wolfson both before and after Fortas was appointed to the Court. The sentiment was that Fortas must have been aware of Wolfson's dealing and should have acted accordingly, to say the least.

Concurrent with the *Life* story, Justice Fortas issued a statement which raised more questions than it answered. The fee from the Wolfson Foundation, he said, had been tendered and returned, but he made no mention of the amount, nor of the lag of over eleven months between receipt and repayment.

Congressional furor mounted as Fortas failed to respond to the allegations, and suggestions of a relationship between Wolfson and the justice became a daily topic.

On May 5, 1969, the same day the *Life* article appeared, subpoenas were issued to Wolfson's attorneys calling for them to hand over documents relating to the Wolfson-Fortas transactions.

Among the subpoenaed documents was an agreement between Fortas and Wolfson stating that Justice Fortas—or his wife, should she survive him—would be paid $20,000 a year *for life* by the Wolfson Family Foundation.

On May seventh, Attorney General John Mitchell, at the direction of President Nixon, met with Chief Justice Warren and related to him what the Justice Department knew about the situation at that time, including the contents of the lifetime "annuity" document. He also told Warren that unless Justice Fortas resigned, the rest of the information about his dealings with Wolfson would be made public. At this time Mitchell was still a shiny knight.

Pressure for impeachment increased rapidly on Capitol Hill. Senators and representatives were flooded with mail from their constituents demanding that something be done quickly in the Fortas affiar. The justice had three courses of action open to him: explain, resign, or explain and resign. He took the third. The articles of impeachment prepared by Representative H. R. Gross (R., Iowa) would not be considered.

On Wednesday evening, May 14, 1969, Fortas sent his letter of resignation to the White House. It arrived at 5:30 p.m. However, the president's Vietnam speech was scheduled for 10 o'clock that night, so if the White House released news of the resignation immediately, it would have had to share front-page billing in the morning papers with Vietnam. The letter was held over, and Nixon accepted the resignation the next day.

When he submitted his letter to the president, Justice Fortas also wrote one to the chief justice. It was four pages long and more detailed than an earlier letter to *Life* regarding the Wolfson association. Fortas made clear his concern "that the Court may not continue to be subjected to extraneous stress which may adversely affect the performance of its important functions."

His letter to the chief justice was a defense brief as well. It confirmed that while on the court, he had entered into an agreement with the Wolfson Family Foundation, under which he would "perform continuing services," for which he "would receive $20,000 per year for my life with arrangements for payment to Mrs. Fortas in the event of my death." Six months later, having learned that the Securities and Exchange Commission had referred Wolfson's file to the Justice Department for consideration as to criminal prosecution, Fortas said he decided to terminate the agreement. But he still failed to clarify what his actual relationship with Wolfson had been and continued to make no mention of the fact that the money was not refunded until six months after he decided to end the agreement. Fortas did say that he had "not interceded or taken part in any legal, administrative or judicial matter affecting Mr. Wolfson or anyone associated with him." He reaffirmed that there had been no wrongdoing on his part.

This resignation ended a spectacular thirty-year run by Abe Fortas as one of the hardest-charging and most effective Washington politicians. A gifted man and an able judge was lost to public service through his own indiscretion.

Now Fortas is back practicing law for big fees and lobbying for groups like Loeb, Rhoades and Company, a New York investment banking combine. When he visited St. Louis recently I asked him if he missed it all. He smiled and said, "A little."

JUSTICE WILLIAM O. DOUGLAS

Periodic attempts to impeach U.S. Supreme Court Justice William O. Douglas have been kindled, but each has burned out. They have been largely political moves by his critics.

Justice Douglas graduated second in his class from Columbia University Law School in 1925. He worked for awhile with a Wall Street law firm and then joined the Yale Law School faculty. Douglas was appointed to the newly formed Securities and Exchange Commission in 1934 and became its chairman in 1936. In 1939, at the age of forty, he was appointed to the Supreme Court of the United States by President Franklin Delano Roosevelt. Thirty-three years later those determined to remove him from power appeared.

Now in his seventies, Douglas is still considered the youngest member of the Court from the standpoint of energy. He is the Court's fastest and most prolific writer. His liberal, outspoken opinions on free speech, the rights of criminal defendants and civil liberties in general are often written with an unusually sharp pen. As a result he has acquired more than his share of enemies among Republicans and conservative Democrats alike.

The first attempt to impeach Justice Douglas came in 1953 after he issued a stay of execution to Julius and Ethel Rosenberg, the convicted atomic-secret spies. A second impeachment attempt was nurtured in 1966 when he married his fourth wife, then twenty-three-year-old Cathleen Hefferman, less than a month after his third wife had divorced him and remarried.

On May 15, 1969, in the wake of Justice Abe Fortas' resignation, Congressman Gross of Iowa (who had prepared articles of impeachment against Fortas) suggested that the House Judiciary Committee look into Justice Douglas' relationship with the Parvin Foundation. Gross charged, on the floor of the House, that Douglas had received a $12,000 annual fee from the foundation, whose "money in part came from the gambling tables in Las Vegas."

The foundation was funded with three million dollars in profits Parvin made when he sold the Las Vegas Flamingo

Hotel and gambling casino. The foundation's energies were directed primarily at providing foreign student scholarships. Justice Douglas had served on the foundation's board of directors, along with Parvin, for several years and, for a time, as its president. (Parvin had at one time been named as a coconspirator with financier Louis Wolfson but was never tried.)

On May 21, 1969, Douglas resigned from the organization's board. The foundation claimed the resignation had been expected at least a month before the Fortas scandal broke earlier in May. "Justice Douglas indicated to the board in early April that he had been anxious for some time to be relieved of his post as the foundation's sole officer since its expanded activities now involve too heavy a work load," the statement from the foundation said. This same statement was later shown to be recorded in the minutes of the April board meeting.

When he learned that the Internal Revenue Service had instituted an extensive investigation of the Parvin Foundation that same month, Douglas issued a statement in which he called the inquiry a "manufactured case" and another attempt to get him off the Court. The following month the United States Senate approved President Nixon's appointment of Warren Burger as the new chief justice.

On April 13, 1970, Representative Gerald Ford, the Republican leader in the House, called for a congressional inquiry of Justice Douglas in which he said he would document "many charges and allegations in support of impeachment." Ford's move came after the Senate turned down the president's nomination of Harold Carswell to the Supreme Court. Liberals claimed the move was a devious maneuver of President Nixon's to influence votes on the new Supreme Court.

Ford said his decision was actually prompted by an article written by Justice Douglas for the April 1970 issue of *Evergreen Review.* The magazine had also contained erotic photos of nude women and advertisements for sex books and pictures.

The Douglas article, entitled "Redress and Revolution" was an excerpt from his book, *Points of Rebellion.* Ford charged that the book condoned or, at least, predicted violent revolution against the American establishment.

On December 16, 1970, the special House subcommittee assigned to investigate the impeachment charges declared by a vote of three to one that it had found no evidence to support any of the charges. As a step toward impeachment of Justice Douglas, Representative Ford's move was a flop.

At the same time, Harry Blackmun, the best man at Chief Justice Burger's wedding, was confirmed as a justice of the Supreme Court.

Harry Blackmun was a lifelong friend of Chief Justice Burger. The two had attended kindergarten and grade school together in St. Paul, Minnesota, and then had both taught at William Mitchell College of Law, Burger's alma mater. It was Burger, then a circuit court judge, who suggested Blackmun for a seat on the United States Court of Appeals for the Eighth Circuit in 1959. President Eisenhower appointed him.

It is no political secret that Chief Justice Burger strongly urged President Nixon to nominate Blackmun to the Supreme Court. An examination of the early opinions of the two justices reveals an incredible similarity in decisions and judicial philosophy and the expected duplication of votes. One cynic suggested it would be cheaper to have only eight justices and give Chief Justice Burger two votes. Douglas' allies were convinced the impeachment move had been a GOP

223

ploy to divert attention from the two rejected Nixon nominations and Blackmun's ultimate appointment. But Justice Blackmun's recent assertions of judicial independence have encouraged the cynics. And Justice Douglas is still opinionating and frustrating the conservative majority by insisting the high court is underworked.

Chapter Ten
Playing Musical Judges –
The Selection of Our Judiciary

"It seems we are sometimes more concerned with keeping our best players in the major leagues than keeping our best citizens as public officials."

—JOHN F. KENNEDY

THE FEDERAL JUDGES

During recent years even the federal judiciary has been the subject of renewed criticism from lawyers, academicians and lay observers. A belief is being perpetuated, mostly by judges themselves and attorneys who are close to them, that lifetime federal appointments insure an administration of justice clear of politics. Yet most lawyers are fearful of the awesome authority of a federal judge, and will not speak out against him even if absolutely justified. For while they are criticizing or boldly suggesting changes in the archaic selection system, the same judges are presiding in cases that determine the lawyers' livelihood.

The nomination by President Lyndon B. Johnson of Francis X. Morrissey to the Federal District Court of Massachusetts in the fall of 1965 is a classic example. In the face of a "not qualified" rating from the American Bar Association's Standing Committee on the federal judiciary and strong opposition from several of the most distinguished Massachusetts judges and lawyers, LBJ pushed his nominee to the United States Senate for approval. Public dissatisfaction with the Morrissey nomination and the patronage system of appointments came out into the open.

Morrissey was a long-time friend of the political patriarch, Joseph P. Kennedy. His principle qualifications for office were his ties with the Kennedy family. His only judicial experience had been while he sat as a municipal court judge in Boston, a low-echelon post to which he had been appointed after his political ties had been established and publicized.

Lawyers practicing before Morrissey's court avoided discussing his legal virtues publicly. But it was reported in the press that a visitor looking for the judge approached two lawyers outside the municipal courthouse. "If he's in, he's probably somewhere up on the third floor," said one of them; "if not, he is probably having lunch in the main dining room of the Parker House." "But he sure as hell is not in the law library," added the other lawyer with a grin. And so it was.

When John F. Kennedy first entered politics in 1946, Morrissey became his personal traveling secretary, confidant and mentor. Later he performed the same services for Edward M. Kennedy in his Massachusetts campaign for the United States Senate. His duties included playing in the Kennedy touch-football games at the summer colony at Hyannis Port and playing golf with the elder Kennedy. John Kennedy publicly bragged about his goal of getting Francis Morrissey a lifetime federal judgeship.

President Kennedy abandoned his family's efforts to appoint the family friend when a rumor that he was about to nominate Judge Morrissey to the bench in 1961 touched off instant objections from the Bar Association because of Morrissey's lack of experience and legal competence. The rumor faded a few weeks before Kennedy was assassinated during his fence-mending visit to Texas.

President Johnson's action came as result of a promise he had made to Robert Kennedy when he was rejected as LBJ's running mate in favor of Hubert Humphrey. But Johnson withdrew the Morrissey nomination on November 5, 1965, at the nominee's request. The outcry had been too much even for a tough-skinned pro like LBJ to handle.

More recently, congressional attacks on the federal judiciary, the fiasco over Justice Abe Fortas' nomination as chief justice and the scandal that led to his resignation further highlighted concern over the system of the presidential appointment of lifetime federal judges on all levels. The U.S. Senate's blatant rejection of the nominations by President Nixon of Clement Haynsworth, Jr., and Harold Carswell to the Supreme Court, served to underscore uneasiness with our procedures for judicial selection.

One United States senator tried to defend the nomination of a "mediocre" judge by declaring there were many "mediocre citizens" who deserved to be represented. A study of the senator's voting record would show mediocrity was already alive and well in Washington D.C. President Nixon next suggested federal appeals judge, Harry Blackmun. After the disasters of his first two suggestions, Blackmun was quickly appointed. And his record has been refreshingly independent.

The Constitution provides that all federal judges be appointed by the president "with the advice and consent of the Senate." The president nominates candidates to fill vacancies as they occur, and these nominations must be approved, in turn, by a two-thirds majority of the Senate. Until recently, approval of nominations was virtually automatic so long as political courtesies were observed.

President Nixon did not invent the concept of appointing to the high court those who share the administration's views on major issues; but the problem is crystallized when presidents come and go, and the Supreme Court justices remain on and on. Serendipity has permitted President Nixon to name four of the current "nine wise men." The age and health of at least two other justices make it likely that President Nixon will have appointed a majority of our last court of appeal if he remains in office until 1976. This is an unfortunate coincidence for our system of justice. Packing is packing whether it be by President Nixon, President Roosevelt or President Lincoln.

The process of selecting a candidate for nomination as a federal judge supposedly involves officials in the Department of Justice (the attorney general, deputy attorney general, and their deputy assistants) whose task it is to advise the president on whom to nominate; United States senators of the president's party who exert influence for the appointment of persons from their states; political leaders of the president's party, including veteran congressmen, state party chairmen, national committee members, governors, and mayors of large cities who expect to be consulted or at least given a respectful hearing regarding political patronage for their local jurisdictions. Finally, there are those who actively seek judgeships through known political supporters.

Since 1952 the American Bar Association's Standing Committee on the Federal Judiciary has played an informal role by rating the leading candidates and presenting a report either way to the justice department. But a president is essentially a politician, and he tries to take care of his friends while trying not to arouse his enemies. If at the same time he appoints a qualified man, so much the better.

For appointments to the many federal district courts, the senators of the president's party from the state in which the appointment is to be made have the greatest influence. Men and women who are proposed are generally the supporters of the senator or those who have access to his chief financial backers. Occasionally, as during the Eisenhower and Kennedy administrations, Department of Justice officials have taken the initiative in promoting candidates for district judgeships. But, Johnson, like most presidents, was sensitive to the patronage prerogatives of the exclusive senatorial club which he used to head. He instructed his people in the Justice Department "to go along with the senators of his party unless the senators urged totally unacceptable appointments." In view of the Morrissey nomination, the definition of "totally unacceptable appointment" was obviously rather loose. President Nixon seems to cater to senators from either party who support him, but he generally requires that nominees share his law-and-order approach to the administration of justice.

For appointments to the United States Court of Appeals, Justice Department officials normally have somewhat more influence than senators due to the fact that each of the courts encompasses several states. The president can often choose from among several more qualified candidates, and can, therefore, take into account such things as: Who (party organizations, politicians, bar associations, newspapers, financiers) will be happy or unhappy? Is the candidate sympathetic to the general policy commitments of the present administration? Is he or she a competent legal scholar? Yet it is safe to say that political considerations take precedence over policy considerations, which, in turn, are still more vital than the appointment of brilliant legal scholars.

Higher federal judicial appointments, including those to the Supreme Court have traditionally been the personal choice of the president. Reasons for appointments may vary, but they tend to include rewarding a close personal friend or legal advisor and, almost always, appointing a person who shares the same policy views. On occasion a major political commitment is fulfilled. That is how Earl Warren, who delivered the California delegation to Ike, became chief justice. President Nixon, however, has not been able to enjoy this personal prerogative unfettered by continued opposition in Congress.

In July 1970, after the Haynsworth and Carswell nominations were rejected by the Senate, procedures were finally agreed to by the then Attorney-General John Mitchell on behalf of the president and the American Bar Association for screening nominees for the Supreme Court. Under the arrangement, the Department of Justice submitted the names of proposed candidates to the American Bar Association's Standing Committee on Federal Judiciary which conducted an investigation into their backgrounds, and issued a report on the persons' qualifications. The report was to be issued to the Justice Department only, and the names of the potential nominees were to be kept confidential unless and until the president actually proferred the name of a nominee to the Senate.

On October 21, 1971, Attorney General Mitchell abruptly ended this arrangement. The reason he gave was that six names that had been submitted to the Bar Association for evaluation reports were leaked to the press. It seems ironic in retrospect that Mitchell was concerned even then with leaks about the government.

In order to understand the unlimited authority given Mitchell by the president with respect to the not-so-gentle art of judicial selection, it is important to remember President Nixon's decree when Mitchell first became a government official. In December 1968, the president-elect said this about the attorney-general-to-be, whose career has since included campaign managership and public disgrace as a key figure in Watergate and related scandals:

> I suppose that in naming John Mitchell as the next Attorney General of the United States it would be suggested that I did so because he was my law partner, or because he was the brilliant manager of my campaign for the Presidency.
>
> These were, of course, considerations that might have motivated me. But John Mitchell is more than just one of the nation's great lawyers. I have learned to know him over the past five years as a man of superb judgment, a man who knows *how to pick people* and to lead them and to inspire them with a quiet confidence and poise and dignity.
>
> Also I know that he is a strong man, a man who is devoted as I am and as I found the American people were in this campaign to waging an effective war against crime in this country.

A more believable reason is that the president and his advisors were not happy with the committee's ratings of his two principle selections, Mildred L. Lillie of Los Angeles, California, and Hershel H. Friday of Little Rock, Arkansas, neither of whom were rated as "qualified." The names of the two men announced by President Nixon on the same day— Lewis Powell and William Rehnquist—were not on the list. Neither had been even submitted to the Bar Association for consideration.

The ABA claimed that it was not responsible for the leak, and the Department of Justice did not formally claim the lawyer's group was to blame. It now appears clear that the leak came from the Justice Department itself (which had already made three of the names public earlier) in its effort to discredit the committee's ratings and minimize the embarrassment to President Nixon resulting from public disclosure of the "unqualified" judges he was recommending for the Supreme Court.

It must not be assumed, however, that the American Bar Association's ratings are always to be taken as the final word on a judge's merits; for example, strong segregationists, like William Harold Cox and James Coleman, received judicial appointments after having received ratings of "exceptionally well qualified" and "well qualified" respectively. The ratings depend upon the prevailing views of those dominating the bar. More often than not they will be conservatives, and that made Mitchell's dilemma doubly unbearable.

Criticism of this selection process centers around its total involvement in national politics. Many believe it to be improper for the president to use judicial appointments as an extension of his personal policies. The "best" available candidate is frequently by-passed in favor of a politically more acceptable individual of lower quality. Others argue that public opinion, and some judges themselves, indicate dissatisfaction with the politics of judicial selection and that such dissatisfaction decreases public confidence in the judicial process. Only the most naive observer could disregard political influence as an undercurrent of high-court life.

The chief litigant in federal courts is the Department of Justice which plays the major role in advising the president as to who is qualified to serve on the federal bench. If a lower-court judge wants a promotion, he'd better satisfy the government when it comes before the court as a party litigant. Thus, there is a built-in temptation for the court to favor the agency that can benefit the presiding judge's career.

One response to this criticism was a bill introduced in the United States Senate by Republican Senator Hugh Scott of Pennsylvania calling for the establishment of a Judicial Service Commission. The plan would provide a commission of seven members to be appointed by the president with the advice and consent of the Senate for three-year overlapping terms. Three of the members would be lawyers, three laymen, and one a retired federal judge; no more than four of the members could be of the same political party. The commission would examine the qualifications of potential judicial appointees and make recommendations as vacancies would occur. The president would not be required to follow the recommendations, but he would be required to furnish the Senate with a public statement as to why he did not.

If the president has the power to appoint the members of the commission, and is allowed to have a majority from his own political party, it is hard to imagine how politics would be removed from the selection process—no matter who the chief executive might be, or how conscientious.

Politics will always be involved in the process of selecting judges, so long as they are appointed. And there will always be the occasional designation of a totally incompetent or corrupt jurist. Given such a situation, the problem becomes one of how to get rid of the poor selection.

The United States Constitution further provides that all federal judges "shall hold their Offices during Good Behaviour." The grounds for removal are "On Impeachment for, and Conviction of, Treason, Bribery, or other high Crimes and Misdemeanors." If a federal judge is suspected of conduct that amounts to grounds for removal, a complaint is made in the House of Representatives; the House appoints a committee to investigate the charges and, if necessary, draw up articles of impeachment (which are very much like an indictment). The full membership of the House of Representatives then votes on the articles. If the vote is in favor of impeachment, the judge is tried before the Senate which then votes on whether he should be found guilty. The House of Representatives acts as the prosecutor. If found guilty, the judge is removed from office and can be prohibited from ever holding a position of honor and trust again.

Due to the time, expense and political obstacles involved in this constitutionally complex method of removal, a bill was introduced in the Senate in 1969 which would have created a "Commission on Judicial Disabilities and Tenure" to investigate complaints "by any person" against federal judges. The bill would have expanded the grounds for removal to include "wilfull misconduct in office."

Such a ground for removal may be too vague, and would be subject to abuse by those who simply disagree with a judge's opinions regardless of his honesty or competence. The standard of behavior for judges set forth in the Constitution is adequate, if enforced. The only problem with the process of impeachment is that the politicians responsible for its workings are more concerned with their own political careers than with cleaning up the judiciary. In almost every case of impeachment that has arisen since the adoption of the Constitution, the votes in Congress have split closely along party lines. The same would undoubtedly be true even with expansion of the grounds for removal.

The problem is made more complicated by the hesitance of practicing lawyers and congressmen (most of whom are lawyers) to do battle with a federal judge. If the judge survives, he is a lifetime adversary with nearly limitless authority in his jurisdiction.

The answer may have to be the election or rotation of all federal appointed judges. Hopefully, there can be a system avoiding extreme advantages for the incumbents.

STATE JUDGES

There are four primary methods for selecting judges among the fifty states:

Simple appointment with confirmation by a legislative body, partisan election, nonpartisan election, and appointment under some form of merit plan (commonly called the "Missouri Plan," after which it is modeled).

Originally, all state judges in the United States were appointed, not elected. The drafters of our state constitutions provided for the executive appointment of the judiciary, usually by their governors, but subject to some type of check or control by a legislative body. The first twenty-nine states entering the Union did so with an appointive judiciary.

In the 1830s the trend toward universal suffrage as part of popular democracy gave rise to a feeling that the people should also elect their judges. In 1832 Mississippi became the first American state to provide an entirely elective judiciary. It is ironic because some would argue that the Deep South is not a bastion of democracy. Nevertheless, Mississippi took the lead.

New York followed in 1846. By 1860 twenty-two of the thirty-four American states provided for the election of state judges. These elections were partisan in nature, just as the system of appointments had been. The political parties nominated candidates, either by primary election or party convention, in the same manner in which they nominated candidates for other public offices.

From 1846 until the admission of Alaska in 1958, each new state entered with an elective judiciary of sorts.

With the advent of the Progressive movement in the late nineteenth and early twentieth centuries, major political parties were not trusted—and their candidates for judicial office became suspect immediately. Demands were made to take many government offices, particularly judgeships, out of the control of directly elected politicians. And the theory easily developed in this steamy atmosphere that for judges to be neutral and not to take sides they should not really be considered partisan political officers.

Many states accepted this theory and adopted plans calling for the nonpartisan election of judges. But this type of judicial selection is becoming less popular and is beginning to wane in most states. It was not responsive to the existing political machinery, still essential for election.

With the nonpartisan election system failing and judicial corruption and incompetence rising, the Missouri Plan, or some other type of merit selection plan, eventually became the chief recipient of the support formerly given to the nonpartisan ballot by academicians and lawyers.

In 1913 Albert Kales presented a plan in which judges would be elected on a merit basis rather than by popular vote. He proposed that potential appointments of judges be made by the chief justice of the state's highest court from a list submitted by a nominating commission. This proposal has been the basis for most of the subsequent merit-system plans.

During the same year that Kales devised his merit plan, the American Judicature Society was founded for the purpose of encouraging efficiency in the administration of justice. Since then, one of the society's major projects has been to promote the adoption of similar systems for picking judges in all states.

The American Bar Association endorsed a merit selection plan in 1937. A year later its committee on judicial selection and tenure emphasized the need for the plan by reporting that, "with the exception of some of the less populous communities, direct election of judges operates to destroy judicial independence, and in consequence the bench is steadily retrograding, especially in metropolitan areas." Not so, say the advocates of free elections. One cynic has pointed out that when judges are elected, you will at least always find out all the dirt—you can count on a vigorous opponent for that.

It seems ridiculous in a nation that supposedly was founded with a free election concept to say that we are not capable of handling elections when it comes to judges because their jobs are so delicate. If American society cannot effectively select those who will interpret our laws by what rationale can we elect those who make the law or, according to the Constitution, enforce the law?

The establishment bar has continued a concerted campaign for adoption of a selection method which, in the process, institutionalizes bar participation. Its goal is to "eliminate politics" from judicial selection, and to provide "better judges." The antipolitics banner continues to fly—yet the legal profession has still to furnish a definition of the politics

237

it seeks to eliminate, or the criteria by which better judges can be measured. And so long as anyone, chief judge or not, appoints, there will be political overtones.

It is important to remember that a political formula does not always produce an incompetent judicial product. For example, a strong case could have been made against Justice Harry Blackmun when he was nominated to the Supreme Court. His intimate relationship with Chief Justice Burger dates back to their boyhood. But despite having served as the Chief Justice's best man at a wedding and sharing faculty positions at the same school, Blackmun has credibly asserted his judicial views. At least the similarity of their votes on major issues has somewhat waned. It could also be argued that an election need not be won by the glamorous candidate. The public should not be underestimated. They are capable of rejecting the more attractive candidate for the more capable one if they are given the facts.

What is the practical solution to the problem of the high cost of judges that is offered by a merit or Missouri Plan? It has three basic elements: (1) a nominating commission (2) appointment (usually by the governor) from a list submitted by the nominating commission, and (3) review of the appointment by the voters in an election in which the judge runs unopposed. The only question to vote on is whether the judge should be retained in office. It is comparable to a vote of confidence as used in many European nations; a vote that, if presidents, senators, and Supreme Court justices had to face, might result in a new slate every few months.

In the typical plan, the nominating commission is made up equally of lawyers elected by members of the bar, or appointed by the governor, and laymen also appointed by the governor. (The method of selecting the selectors already has political overtones.) The terms of service of the members is

238

staggered and, supposedly, no members are permitted to hold any official position in a political party. The chief justice of the state's highest court is a member and chairman. Members other than the chief justice are limited to one six-year term.

When a vacancy occurs, the governor makes an appointment from a list of three candidates presented to him by the nominating commission. In most states no one is allowed to know who has applied to the commission for appointment or whose names are actually submitted to the governor. Strict secrecy is allegedly maintained. Not only is the public not allowed to know the names of the candidates, but the candidates themselves are also specifically instructed that it is considered a breach of ethics for any candidate, or anyone on his or her behalf, to discuss the candidacy with any member of the commission.

Use of a judicial merit system varies from being mandatory for all courts in the state, to being mandatory for some and voluntary for others, to being voluntary for all. Each of the three styles has enthusiastic proponents critical of the other two.

The system presumably incorporates the best features of both the appointive and elective traditions by giving reasonable assurance that the best candidates available will be selected, since the initial selection is made by a group equipped to determine the fitness of applicants. In theory, the voters are able to unseat weak or incompetent judges by voting against their retention; but the prescribed elections are not designed to capture voter enthusiasm and even greater apathy than usual will no doubt occur.

In 1940, Missouri became the first state to adopt a merit selection system. It is mandatory for all appellate courts and for the trial courts of Jackson County (Kansas City) and the city of St. Louis. One of the major factors which led to its adoption was the one-time control over most judges by political machines, such as that of Boss T. J. ("Tom") Pendergast, when anyone with the right lawyer could get a speedy trial before a sympathetic judge; otherwise, the case might be lost or delayed for several years. Dockets were congested and a campaign for judicial office took a great deal of time and money. At one point, the judges in Kansas City refused to contribute to the Pendergast machine's campaign fund; and in the next session of the legislature, their salaries were abruptly reduced by three times the amount of the requested contribution. The lesson was made clear.

Many combinations of merit systems for finding judges are now operational among the fifty states. In Colorado the nominating commission has a lay majority and is bipartisan, requiring political balance rather than nonpartisanship.

The Kansas nominating commission consists of only one lawyer, elected by the bar, and one nonlawyer appointed by the governor from each congressional district, plus a lawyer, elected from the state at large, who serves as chairman. There are no judges on that commission at all.

In nine other states, the governors have voluntarily instituted merit plans for the judgeships they normally fill by appointment. In Florida a system of judicial polls were started in 1970, in addition to judicial screening by the Bar Association, for judges appointed by the governor.

In advance of a selection, biographies are obtained from the known candidates. The biographies, a photograph of each candidate, and a ballot are mailed to every lawyer in Florida. All attorneys allegedly evaluate candidates for the Supreme Court, while only those practicing in the area served by each district court evaluate the candidates for that particular appellate bench. The lawyers vote on whether they think the candidate is qualified and then mail the ballots back to the bar association. The results are released to the public through the news media.

It is claimed that such a system of polls reduces the influence of politics by allowing highly qualified candidates to seek office in the face of less qualified but politically powerful opponents. Of course, the attorneys passing judgment on the qualifications are themselves engaged in partisan politics, and can easily split along party lines. Many observers do not agree that lawyers should be the major force in the selection of judges. Their interest is vested and less basic than their clients'.

Another argument is that the cost of political campaigns is reduced because this system eliminates the candidate's expenses. However, a candidate less qualified, but with more political power and money, is still in a position to send out campaign material and work to counteract the ill effects of a poor evaluation resulting from the poll.

California has instituted a merit selection system for filling vacancies that occur in trial courts before a judge's term has expired. They also have a merit system for the selection of judges for the district courts of appeal, under which the judges run in a noncompetitive election solely on their record. Positions on the California Supreme Court are filled by the governor with the consent of the senate.

Although New Mexico and Tennessee are among the eight states that have maintained a totally partisan election system, their governors have voluntarily instituted merit systems for filling judicial vacancies.

As of last year, twenty-two states select some or all of their major trial and appellate court judges under some form of the merit selection plan. Among them are: Alabama, Alaska, California, Colorado, Delaware, Florida, Georgia, Idaho, Indiana, Iowa, Kansas, Louisiana, Maryland, Missouri,

Nebraska, New Jersey, New Mexico, New York City, Oklahoma, Tennessee, Utah, and Vermont. Nine states employ gubernatorial appointment with legislative confirmation, while in four (Rhode Island, South Carolina, Vermont and Virginia) the legislature exercises the appointive power. Thirty-five states have formal election of some or all of their judges. (Don't add the numbers expecting 50 because there are overlapping plans in several states.)

Despite the well-meaning efforts for reform and the barrage of propoganda for merit systems, the question of whether they best serve the public interest still remains to be answered. The plans are all theoretically operable and look very impressive and equitable on paper. Some judges and lawyers have greeted merit selection with great acclaim. After all, they were the same people who pushed for its adoption in the first place. An admission that the system didn't do all that it was supposed to would be an admission that their time and effort in developing the system was wasted. How often do advocators of reform condemn the reform once it is established?

But after closer examination, it appears the merit selection system really does not eliminate politics from the judicial selection process. It is not yet established that it benches more competent and honorable judges. Does it really keep corrupt judges off the bench? Can the judges still be held accountable to the people?

Actually, all that has happened is that the politics of the governor and the bar association have replaced the politics of the county party chairman and the electorate. Most bar associations are highly political in nature, and a virtual two- (or more) party system operates in the election of bar representatives to the nominating commission. The lay members of the commission are appointed by the governor and are usually of the "right" political party, since the job is a patronage plum. They are drawn mostly from the business community and tend to reflect the attitudes of the lawyers they know best—those representing their own business interests. A judge is no more nor less obligated to an organization that elected him than are governors and nominating commissions to those same political groups.

The attorneys may be the only members personally acquainted with the candidates and, because of the secrecy involved, information cannot be volunteered to assist the nonlawyer members. Actually, the commission avoids learning even the facts bearing on the candidate's professional or moral competency that any other citizen might possess. The members of the commission are simply presumed to have all the information that the public interest requires.

They receive background data information from the only sources available to them—the state bar, the candidates themselves and, apparently, divine revelation. This secrecy is contrary to the obvious democratic need to have all judges make public a disclosure of their financial status, outside interests, and earnings, and political and other commitments that might influence their future decisions on the bench.

The merit selection system fails to provide for accountability to the people whom the judge serves. It provides for a combination of secrecy and private-group influence which should not be tolerated in a free society, particularly when one considers the nearly limitless power judges gain by donning a robe.

Lawyers may be especially qualified to evaluate a judge's competency in the law, but they also have a special interest in the selection of judges potentially favorable to their clients and thus to themselves. Corrupt or incompetent judges were once practicing lawyers themselves. A governor cannot be held responsible for poor appointments because he shares responsibility with the commission. It must be assumed that the governor will select the best qualified candidate.

Yet, proponents claim there is a benefit in the noncompetitive election for retention of judges in that the electorate is not distracted by such irrelevant matters as the candidate's political affiliations. Because candidates for judicial office generally confine their campaigning to signs, billboards, and an occasional speech about the importance of courts to society, the voters are left to choose the most familiar name or the candidate who spent the most money.

Then, there is the argument that under a merit system the people still choose the judges because they elect the governor who chooses the judicial nominating commission and, later, one of the names on the list. But, in reality, the noncompetitive election for retention of incumbent judges is a meaningless routine, built into a plan for the public relations purpose of reducing voter hostility to the new method. Few lay citizens have any basis upon which to render either a yes or no vote—few are litigants and even fewer are lawyers and most won't bother.

If a nonpartisan selection is better than partisan elections, why not allow a commission to select our legislators, mayors, governors, and even the president of the United States? Supporters of merit selection profess great faith in the people to select qualified candidates for all public offices except one—the judiciary.

The reason seems to be that the other positions are political, but that judges and their functions are or should be nonpolitical. It is decreed that the judicial duties are entirely different from those of the executive and the legislature. Unlike candidates for "policy-making offices" who must take positive positions on controversial public issues, judges cannot campaign on what judgments they would make on the bench because they must remain impartial. This is unrealistic since most decisions have social overtones and judges earn reputations as "lenient" or "strict" in certain fields.

The duties of the executive and the legislature are as different from each other as the judiciary is from both of them. But for political content they are interdependent. Because a judge is supposedly impartial does not mean that he or she need not be opinionated on legal philosophy and the status of the law. To believe that judges make cold decisions completely free of their own political and emotional leanings is totally absurd.

Judges do not only decide particular cases, they also establish precedents on which future decisions will be based. This is especially true on the appellate levels. And their partisan political views and political obligations are always relevant. A judge's party affiliation is a general guide as to his political and social views; and, knowing a judge's political views lends some degree of predictability as to his or her position in a particular case.

For many years Democratic judges were more prone to liberal interpretation of the Constitution and laws to achieve what they regard as beneficial social goals. Republican judges tended to advocate strict construction and practice judicial restraint. The fact that a judge is a Democrat does not mean that he can always be expected to decide in favor of the debtor whenever a consumer credit matter comes before his court; it's simply an indication of his personal philosophy and may come into play. The old guidelines are giving way to more interparty political lines based on either conservative law-and-order supporters or more tolerant civil-rights-oriented viewers.

Judges are partisan political officers whether we think they should be or not; and no matter what method of selection is employed, they will remain so. They are vested with political authority whose use is affected by partisan dispositions. Because of this great authority it must be accepted that they formulate public policy. Once this premise is accepted we can seek the most efficient process of electing those who will serve in the third political branch of our government.

It is only logical that judicially determined policies must ultimately conform to the will of the community. Under a nonpartisan judicial selection system, control over the judiciary does not rest with the people in any way, shape or form. It is exercised by an anonymous and politically nonresponsible group controlled by vested interests within the state bar associations. The people, at least with respect to the judicial third of their government, have ceased to govern themselves, having resigned the judiciary into the hands of an "all-knowing" commission.

The nonpartisan selection system still provides for some partisan appointments. During the first year the system was operating in Utah, four district court judges were appointed. All four, like the appointing governor, were Democrats. The only change in the selection process is that people no longer made the choice.

Based on the assumption that the judiciary's function is not political, supporters of the merit system further assume that a better judiciary will somehow result. But to date there has been no documented correlation found between the level of competence of judges and any new method of selection.

The key question is, what method of selection will provide the maximum accountability of a judge's actions to the people he serves? Which means of selection has the greatest potential for keeping corrupt and incompetent judges off the bench?

Popular election still seems the most credible method for selecting state-court judges. The public's ability to choose need not be underestimated—even in regard to competent jurists.

In Arizona an interesting compromise was reached between partisan and nonpartisan election systems. Judges are nominated in party primaries and run in the general election without party designation. The plan was adopted when the state entered the union and is still in effect today. Most there say it works.

Although the states using partisan elections generally provide for such systems in their state constitutions, most judges are initially appointed by the governor (or in some large cities such as New York City, by the mayor). Many vacancies occur as a result of death, retirement or resignation. Judges don't plan their deaths to coincide with their term; and judges who retire or resign usually do it during the term of office of a governor of their own political party. A judge will then be appointed to fill the post until the next election. (They learned that from the United States Supreme Court and previous presidents.) The first time the new judge runs for election, he runs as an incumbent. Due to inadequate information and a lack of voter awareness, an incumbent is seldom defeated at the polls.

In Georgia, the state constitution provides for the election of its state court judges (except in the city of Atlanta which now uses merit selection). But since 1938, 95 percent of the appellate judges were originally appointed rather than elected. The last nineteen members of the court of appeals were originally appointed, and so became incumbent candidates for reelection. Approximately one half of the present trial court judges went to the bench by appointment. There have been very few instances in which appellate court judges

247

have met any opposition at the polls, and in the past forty-five years no appellate judge has been defeated. In the past four years, 72 percent of the superior court judges had no opposition, and 96 percent were reelected. Georgia observers will admit fighting "the courthouse" is tougher than the perennial fight against city hall.

Now there is nothing wrong with the governor filling vacancies with members of his own political party. The fact that a gubernatorial candidate from a particular party was elected demonstrates that the public sentiment is in favor of his policies. But, the appointive power is subject to severe abuse, and provides for only indirect accountability of the judges to the public. It is used as a way to avoid the method provided by the constitution, the highest law of each state and the first mandate of the people. Such a deception is a travesty of justice and should not be tolerated. Special elections can be held on an annual or other regular basis.

Periodically, the reaction to an unpopular court decision is a movement to change the court's composition and methods for selecting judges. Such an episode has occurred very recently in California. In a state in which unmatched political influence invades most courthouses, the Supreme Court of California is universally recognized as the most effective high court in the nation.

An organization called the Committee to Restore Justice was formed to promote a constitutional amendment which critics of the committee claim would expose supreme court justices to political favor.

The Los Angeles Times blasted the so-called court reformers and called their committee:

> . . . another of those backlashes to justice that so often have
> followed controversial decisions and that, in themselves, illustrate

the overwhelming importance of insulating the court from the pressures of emotion, politics and special interests. In their reactions to individual decisions, these critics ignore the essential role that the courts have played over the years in protecting the fundamental rights of American society.

There are genuinely impressive arguments in favor of exposing state and federal judges to public critique through a ballot box. There are equally moving considerations in support of a sophisticated selection method which minimizes political influence but still provides for the appointment of judges.

The American Bar Association is determined that high-level judges should not be exposed to the heat of a political campaign and they favor the "selection of judges should not be made through election contests between competing candidates."

The debate contrasting methods of selection is conducted in a factual vacuum; both reformers and defenders of the status quo operate primarily on speculation. The basic problem with the quality of judges today is that there is no effective means of selection or reasonable means of control by the public. The success of any system in eliminating corruption and incompetence is dependent on the level of citizen awareness, without which all systems fail.

This book should have shocked you. If you are still saying "judges and politicians are all crooks anyway"—then we failed. You should be adding, "Now we can finally do something about it."

Epilogue
Where Do We Go From Here?

"Thou shalt not wrest judgment; thou shalt not respect persons, neither take a gift; for a gift doth blind the eyes of the wise, and pervert the words of the righteous."
                                        —Deuteronomy 16:19

What do we do about it? Do we begin by discarding the traditional means for selecting and retaining even our Supreme Court and other federal judges? I think so. Philosophically, a lifetime of unlimited power vested in any citizen is a little frightening. The contemporary history of the United States Supreme Court is the best argument for immediate reform of its structure. If you were an ardent conservative and terribly critical of the Warren court, then you would have marched for change in the 60s. If you are concerned with today's shift to the right in high-court temperament, then you now favor the same restrictions on judges in the 70s that your political opponents favored a decade ago.

When Attorney-General John N. Mitchell reviewed Harrold

251

Carswell's judicial and personal record and said, "He's almost too good to be true," he inadvertently prophesied a seventy-eight-day political war which proved Harrold Carswell was the wrong man in the wrong place at the wrong time. The incident helped to illuminate a shady area of political infighting that infects fundamental processes in the selection of judges for the Supreme Court.

President Nixon made it very clear from the beginning that he considered his right to appoint justices to the highest court an absolute prerogative. Accordingly, he designated only those men who shared his political philosophy and would help judicially enforce his campaign promises. He didn't invent the concept. Abraham Lincoln and Franklin Roosevelt felt the same way. Chief Justice Warren Burger publicly shared Nixon's "law-and-order views" and felt that the Warren Court had gone too far on constitutional guarantees in criminal cases. The abortive attempts by Nixon and the now discredited John Mitchell to have Judge Haynsworth or Judge Carswell join Burger further proved the president's commitment to onesidedness on the high court.

After his embarrassment over the Haynsworth exposé, the president complained that the Senate would never accept a Southern judge no matter how qualified he was. At the time, several outstanding jurists were suggested, including the very distinguished Judge John Wisdom of the Fifth Circuit Court of Appeals, California Appellate Judge Shirley Hufstedler, Second Circuit Court of Appeals Judge Henry Friendly and California Supreme Court Justice Louis Burke.

While the selection of local judges and revelations of their questionable personal activities gives rise to minor political problems, the approval of a vulnerable candidate for the high court creates a threat to our system itself. At worst, it could lead to harrassment of a racial or political minority. In this case, it could have created another "Dred Scott" atmosphere. It was Chief Justice Roger Taney who concluded that the Constitution would not allow slavery to be kept out of the newly settled West.

Politically, the Dred Scott case had the earmarks of a commitment to the South—much the same as Nixon's commitment to Senator Strom Thurmond and other Southerners in Miami to secure his nomination in 1968. Was it constitutional principle or political expediency that nurtured the Dred Scott decision? Would it be constitutional principle or similar expediency for "Supreme Court Justice Carswell" to adjudicate the views that earned him the reputation as "the most openly and blatantly segregationist federal district judge"?

One leading Republican senator, who finally cast a crucial vote against Carswell, called the choice an attempt to rub the United States Senate's nose in the mess it had made of the Haynsworth nomination. The Justice Department had rated Carswell well below Haynsworth and a few other candidates. This seemed to confirm the view that the choice of Carswell was vengeance—to make the Senate sorry it hadn't accepted Haynsworth. To others it was an attempt to downgrade the Supreme Court of the United States and implement the Southern Strategy.

The National Association for the Advancement of Colored People took a position against the nomination on the ground that it was "clearly designed to compromise the Negroes' future judicial protection far beyond the life of any single administration"; and the *New York Times* ran an editorial calling the nomination "a shock," adding that it "almost suggests an intention to reduce the significance of the Court by lowering the caliber of its membership."

The real drama of the defeat of the Carswell nomination is

in its relevancy to the rapidly changing attitudes of the public toward the judiciary. Although he was accused of being a racist with a record of discrimination from golf courses to fraternities, and held the unique distinction of a 50 percent reversal record, compared to some other judges Carswell was still a minor leaguer. There have been too many judges whose incompetence or corruption have been overwhelming.

The feeling of unease about the quality of our Supreme Court judges was crystallized with the Abe Fortas incident and the Haynsworth and Carswell nominations, but the disquietude has its source in the notoriety afforded more blatant acts of impropriety on the bench and it isn't only in the much publicized judicial pollutors like Judge Kerner or the Oklahoma Supreme Court justices who were imprisoned.

In 1969 the chief justice and an associate justice of the Supreme Court of Illinois resigned in the middle of a special investigation concerned with their business relations with a criminal defendant while an appeal on his case was pending before their court. This situation was somewhat unique since it involved two members of a large state's highest court. It parallels problems occurring throughout the country, such as the case of the Georgia trial judge who was disbarred for offering "protection" to a local businessman for a retainer of $10,000 and a fee of $500 a month; the two judges in Iowa, admonished by the state's supreme court for handling court business "according to their personal whims and predilections"; the Michigan judge, found guilty of secretly borrowing money from an estate being probated in his court; the Missouri judge who resigned when impeachment proceedings were pending based on his personal involvement with a woman divorcee defendant in his court; the New Jersey judge suspended from membership in the bar for six months for his involvement in a complex traffic-ticket-fixing racket; the

New York judge removed on charges of advising a convicted prostitute placed on probation on how to continue her business without getting caught; the Oklahoma judge removed for accepting $13,000 in fees as payment for court orders waiving certain statutory requirements for the issuance of marriage licenses; the Oregon probate judge who sought unsuccessfully to thwart disciplinary proceedings against him based on the appointment of his wife as an appraiser of an estate before his court; and the Virginia judge convicted of seventeen counts of forgery and obtaining money under false pretenses. The list of the finest judges money can buy continues to grow.

But, in addition to these more dramatic incidents of judicial abuse, there are voluminous cases of less dramatic misconduct involving tardiness, absurdly long vacations and daily rudeness to lawyers, litigants and witnesses.

The twentieth century has witnessed great changes in our system of law—the decline of precedent and the use of litigation for social rather than, as traditionally, private purposes. The courts are now the combat zone for revolution. Appointments to the high bench now have significance far beyond judicial stature and prognosis as to philosophical alignment.

In his Holmes Lecture at Harvard a decade ago, Professor Herbert Wechsler suggested that the Supreme Court should not use political methods but, rather, develop a series of neutral principles of constitutional law. "It is true," he said, "that the approach to politics by most is essentially instrumental, but however tolerant we might be of such an approach to politics, we expect something different, a new strata, if you will, from the Supreme Court."

In a more recent lecture at Harvard, Professor Alexander Bickel of Yale suggested that the dominant theme of constitutional interpretation by the Earl Warren Court was the idea of progress. In his lecture, Bickel chronicles the (to him) disappointing effects of the Warren Court's efforts to achieve social progress through the process of constitutional interpretation. A comparable case for "progress" is argued by conservative academicians saluting the Burger court.

In 1896, while still a justice on the Supreme Judicial Court of Massachusetts, Oliver Wendell Holmes expressed his skepticism: "The true grounds of decision are considerations of social advantage and it is vain to suppose that solutions can be obtained merely by logic and the general propositions of law which nobody disputes." Holmes is revered by those who have watched, with some anxiety, the Court's assent to a position as a major force for social change. He was the judicial spirit admired by such diverse men as Mr. Justice Frankfurter and President Richard Nixon. However, Holmes had the ability to separate what may have been his personal viewpoint and his responsibility on the bench. This was the same intangible judicial temperament found by so many senators to be lacking in the nomination from Florida—Mr. Carswell.

When Justice Fortas was forced to resign from the high court in May 1969, Nixon went hunting for strict constructionists. He needed another to join in the Nixon-Burger high-court philosophy. After his second defeat in the traditionally routine game of placing high court justices, Nixon allegedly capitulated. Proclaiming the Senate would never accept a Southern judge, he reached out for his new chief justice's best friend, Harry Andrew Blackmun of Minnesota.

Justice Blackmun had a reputable background, but one wonders whether the first two appointments to the Supreme Court by one president should indeed be men (Burger and Blackmun) who: grew up and went through elementary school together, sharing classes and a paper route; taught together as part of the same law-school faculty for six years; were both appointed by President Dwight D. Eisenhower to the Circuit Court of Appeals; and enjoyed such intimate personal and political relationships as to raise serious questions about any real independence of each other on the Supreme Court.

Harry Blackmun had been best man at Warren Burger's wedding. Yet, despite fifty-two years of intimate friendship, when Justice Blackmun was asked on April 15, 1970, by a *New York Times* reporter, if his friendship with Burger had anything to do with the nomination, he replied, "I wouldn't know anything about that." That is as politically naive (or misleading) as responding to a similar question as to whether sharing Nixon's views had anything to do with his appointment by, "I wouldn't know anything about that."

Carswell announced that he would resign from the bench to run for the United States Senate in Florida. This led some of his defenders finally to agree that his enemies had been right in charging he was a political animal and lacked judicial temperament. His sponsor was the white supremacist governor of Florida, Claude Kirk. The senators who had blackballed the would-be justice were not called upon by the Florida electorate to welcome him back to Washington and Governor Kirk was relieved of his official duties as well.

Kirk was succeeded by Reuben Askew, a Bible toting, honest man who has brought a breath of fresh air into Florida politics on every level. Askew has initiated much needed reforms in all branches of government and has come down hard on judicial corruption. As a result, he is respected in the state and thought of as a potential candidate for the vice presidency in '76.

The Carswell-Haynsworth-Fortas-Blackmun era (or error)

is not unique. It is just the most recent and, perhaps, the most vivid demonstration of the inability of the Supreme Court to remain totally aloof from the American political scene.

When Congressman Emanuel Celler's special subcommittee studied efforts to impeach Justice Douglas, it became a comic opera. The conservatives were dedicated to avenging their humiliation in failing to get either Haynsworth or Carswell on the high court. The liberals were anxious to release steam over the Abe Fortas incident. But the Republicans who started the move to oust Justice Douglas lost out to the Democrats. In this case, Congressman Celler out-maneuvered his opponents in the House of Representatives and Attorney-General John Mitchell, who was then adding fuel to the fire.

The "prosecutor" was Gerald Ford, the House Republican leader. Former Attorney General Ramsey Clark, Mitchell's predecessor and an avowed enemy of the Nixon Administration, was helping the defense. The justice was represented personally by the prestigious New York law firm of Paul, Weiss, Goldberg, Rifkind, Wharton & Garrison. Ramsey Clark was a member of that firm in charge of its Washington office.

Douglas had written some twenty-seven books while sitting on the high court. Although that may have been some kind of a record, it was not an impeachable offense. The Douglas book *Points of Rebellion* came under particular attack when Congressman Ford said the justice's writings were evidence of his "espousal of hippie-yippie-style revolution." But, actually, the Douglas affair was merely an outlet for the philosophical differences between conservatives and liberals which were peaking in an era of pornography and promiscuity. One idiot actually suggested that Douglas should be impeached because he had married a very young law student. No such statement was made when Senator Thurmond married an equally young lady. Douglas has been around a long time—ever since Franklin D. Roosevelt turned around the majority on the high court.

Impeachment is the only way in which an obstinate justice can be removed from the Supreme Court. President Thomas Jefferson called our impeachment procedures a "bungling way, an impractical thing, a mere scarecrow." President Nixon would, undoubtedly, agree since efforts to impeach Justice William O. Douglas have collapsed again.

Many are convinced that there is no true value to lifetime judicial appointments. They believe that the great expertise developed by Supreme Court judges should be brought back to the people in trial courts. Top lawyers and academicians in several jurisdictions agree that the proposal which, at first blush, is radical is, in reality, sensible and basically conservative.

The plan is to abolish the lifetime appointment of Supreme Court justices. A high-court judge would be appointed for one term of, perhaps, eight years. After service, he would return as a federal district judge, actually trying cases for the remainder of his judicial career. Give him the pomp and pension but not the lifetime of supreme power.

In effect, we would be rotating our top judicial talent and putting them at the pinnacle of justice in this country for sufficient time to do some good, but not long enough to develop a Godlike ego. Ramsey Clark was politically hatched in Texas cronyism. L.B.J.'s fondness for his father, Supreme Court Justice Tom Clark, was never a secret. His appointment as Attorney General caused little excitement save for his father's voluntary deescalation to the Federal District Court. As a trial judge, Clark was good because he brought with him the knowledge and experience only obtainable on the Supreme Court of the United States.

If this plan were made operational, the great philosophical sweeps which label our courts each decade could be avoided. Each case before the court would be evaluated on its own merit and justice could be reborn.

I have never accepted the logic of a theory which dictates that we elect our favorite citizen president of the United States, but restrict his term of service while, at the same time, we allow that president to appoint justices for life with awesome authority to determine the validity of our laws and, ultimately, to resolve all matters concerning the lives and property of Americans.

In 1906, the famed Dean Roscoe Pound expressed the hope that in the "near future" our courts would become "swift and certain agents of justice, whose decisions will be acquiesced in and respected by all." Unfortunately, we have not come very close to achieving Pound's goal. A current review of Pound's horizons has registered the warning that:

> We are approaching the total bankruptcy of our remedy system. . . . The legal system of the United States simply cannot carry the weight that is on it . . . American civil justice has broken down; the legal system fails to perform the tasks that may be expected of it.

One of the problems is that our higher courts are remote and that remoteness obscures much of their weakness.

Even in a state like California where the judicial system is relatively progressive and efficient, there is great need for reform. The problems of judicial administration can only be solved there by adding more judges to an already bulging state roster. But additional robes and gavels and titles do not automatically eliminate delays or backlogs or create greater community respect for the system. There must be a tightening on the state level in the methods of judicial selection that will utilize the state legislature, much as the United States Senate is utilized in screening federal candidates.

The Watergate seventies is already being chronicled in very harsh terms. But it is a healthy and natural instinct for citizens to be critical of their own times. If, on the contrary, we relax in our own self-satisfaction, we may stagnate, or even retrogade. Blessed are the social prophets, cynics and reformers who paint with a "heavy brush" when focused on the wrongs and injustices around them.

Almost a hundred years ago Matthew Arnold told England that the upper class was materialized, the middle class was vulgarized, and the lower class was brutalized. Anyone who is familiar with the culture of Victorian England would agree that Arnold had used a very heavy and broad social brush, indeed, that he had substituted the "warts for the whole fact." And Arnold was a distinguished and cultivated critic if ever there was one. He proved that it is inevitable that when a social reformer wants to sound the alarm, he will resort to extravagant exaggeration.

It might be argued that this book is such an exaggeration by suggesting that anyone setting foot in a courtroom has cause for concern. If the judge is "not already crooked he may be getting ready to yield to corruption." If filthy lucre has not won his affection then, perhaps, he is merely influenced by those planning his reelection campaign. Or, if the parties are lucky, the judge may simply be closely attentive to the views mentioned earlier by former law partners and other cronies.

Is it all an exaggeration? Are there just a few rotten apples in the barrel of justice or do we have crates full of incompetent and corrupt administrators and interpreters of our laws? Some critics follow the advice of British philosopher F. H.

261

Bradley: "Where all is rotten it is man's work to cry stinking fish."

There are times when it becomes necessary to ask whether everything in fact is rotten. This happens when the impression becomes pervasive that it is no longer necessary to look at specific evils, since one is completely surrounded by them. "There is no point in trying to introduce reforms in hell—one can only try to destroy it," says Professor Milton R. Konvitz of New York University's Law School. He claims there are many persons who have heard so often and so loudly the cry of stinking fish, that they are firmly convinced that everything American is, indeed, nothing but corruption and rottenness.

For them, the attacks on our social institutions and on our traditions have put America beyond the pale of social reform. For them, social criticism no longer pinpoints specific problems or evils that call for correction—no more than they would think of reforming the institutions and practices in hell.

And so it is important specifically to recognize, not only those judges who have risen above the pressures of their position, but also the system in which they survive. That may be another book. The Missouri Plan may not be the right answer but it works better in selecting judges than those plans utilized in many states. A free election in which the people pick their own judges may, occasionally, result in victory by the more personable candidate. Nevertheless, it is better than a system of no election at all. It has been said that halitosis is better than no breath at all. So, too, it may be suggested that a judge elected with a winning personality is better than no judge elected at all.

Louis M. Kohlmeier, Jr. has correctly surmised that the dichotomy of the American spirit and the Constitution is as old as the nation. The Pulitzer Prize-winning author says the Constitution is color-blind, but the American majority is not. The latent prejudices which are in all of us are not limited to race. The most virile strain is discrimination caused wherever double standards are used, in a family, in a community or in a national institution.

It is rare that we have the opportunity to reaffirm the spirit of the Constitution and eliminate inequity and moral rust. The challenge of judicial reform must be met because it may be the last arena for the survival of democracy. Until the public has complete confidence in its courts, it cannot have complete confidence in its country.

Affidavit of Verification

COMES NOW your affiant, having been duly sworn, and declares and verifies that:

1.   At the request of Charles Ashman, author of "The Finest Judges Money Can Buy," your affiant has personally examined each and every case history set forth in the manuscript and compared and verified all contents therein contained with the relevant official records of the named courts and further compared and verified said contents with the appropriate appellate court decisions, administrative records and Bar Association reports concerning the judges named.

Your affiant further verifies that each fact set forth in said manuscript conforms with those sources with respect to accusations against and disposition of all matters mentioned.

2.   Your affiant has personally and directly inquired of the courts in question and verified the current status of the judges therein named and the disposition of all matters therein set forth.

3.   Your affiant has further verified the status of all judges therein named still presiding in their respective courts and due care has been taken to verify the status of past proceedings or those presently pending concerning them.

4.   Your affiant has further verified that the contents of said manuscript have been set forth with due regard to the truth and accuracy of those official court records, Bar Association reports and other applicable documents.

5.   Further, your affiant has researched and reviewed the applicable law and there is nothing in the contents set forth in said manuscript violative of any state or federal laws, including but not limited to libel and slander and privacy in that the facts contained in said manuscript are accurate and truthful and within the realm of fair comment and criticism of public officials.

6.   Your affiant is a member of the California Bar and the original of this affidavit is on hand with the law firm of Belli, Ashe, Ellison & Choulos and copies have been submitted to the respective Attorneys-General of all states where judges herein named are presently presiding.

Further affiant sayeth not.

SIGNATURE ON FILE.

266

Horse sense is what a horse has that keeps him from betting on people.

W. C. Fields

Appendix I
A Quick Reference Guide
to the Finest Judges
Money Can Buy

JUDGE	STATE	DATE*	OFFENSES CHARGED	DISPOSITION
		PROLOGUE		
1. John B. Tally	Alabama	1894	Murder	Impeached and removed by Supreme Court
		CHAPTER 1: BLACK-ROBED MAFIA		
2. Mitchell D. Schweitzer	New York	1972	Bribery	Retired
3. Edward J. DeSaulnier	Massachusetts	1972	Bribery	Resigned, censured, disbarred
4. Vincent R. Brogna	Massachusetts	1972	Bribery	Censured, still sitting
5. Ralph DeVita	New Jersey	1970	Bribery, obstructing justice	Sentenced to two years prison
6. Anthony Guiliano	New Jersey	1970	Bribery	Indicted, suspended, died
7. James DelMauro	New Jersey	1972	Accepting illegal fees, income tax evasion	Resigned, suspended from bar for one year, tax indictment pending
8. John N. Stice	Kansas	1959	Burglary, robbery, conspiracy, receiving stolen property	Removed and disbarred
9. Raulston Schoolfield	Tennessee	1958	Bribery, extortion, profanity	Impeached and removed by legislature

*Date Action

CHAPTER II: THE HIGH COST OF JUSTICE

JUDGE	STATE	DATE*	OFFENSES CHARGED	DISPOSITION
10. Martin T. Manton	Federal (New York)	1939	Bribery, obstructing justice, fraud	Convicted, sentenced to two years prison and $10,000 fine
11. J. Warren Davis	Federal (New Jersey)	1941	Bribery, obstructing justice	Retired, indictment dismissed, resigned
12. Albert W. Johnson	Federal (Pennsylvania)	1945	Bribery	Resigned
13. Robert W. Archibald	Federal (New York)	1912	Used office for personal financial profit	Impeached and removed by Congress
14. Nelson S. Corn	Oklahoma	1965	Bribery, income tax evasion	Convicted on tax charge, sentenced to 18 months prison
15. Earl Welch	Oklahoma	1965	Bribery, income tax evasion	Resigned, convicted, sentenced to three years prison
16. Napoleon Bonaparte Johnson	Oklahoma	1965	Bribery, income tax evasion	Impeached and removed by legislature, convicted on tax charge
17. Wayne W. Bayless	Oklahoma	1966	Conspiracy to bribe fellow justices	Resigned
18. Joseph P. Pfingst	New York	1972	Brankruptcy fraud, conspiracy	Convicted, sentenced to four months in prison and thirty-two months probation

JUDGE	STATE	DATE*	OFFENSES CHARGED	DISPOSITION
19. Seymour R. Thaler	New York	1972	Selling and transporting stolen treasury bills, perjury	Convicted, sentenced to one year and one day prison and fined, disbarred

CHAPTER III: BARGAINS

JUDGE	STATE	DATE*	OFFENSES CHARGED	DISPOSITION
20. Halsted L. Ritter	Federal (Florida)	1936	Bribery, practicing law, income tax evasion	Impeached and removed by Congress
21. Glenn J. Sharpe	Oklahoma	1968	Bribery	Impeached and removed by legislature
22. J. Cedric Conover	Nebraska	1958	Embezzlement, practicing law	Permanently disbarred and removed by supreme court
23. William M.A. Romans	Virginia	1968	Forgery, false pretenses	Convicted, sentenced to three years prison
24. Maynard B. Clinkscales	Georgia	1960	Protection racket	Permanently disbarred and removed by supreme court
25. Stanley J. Polack	New Jersey	1969	Income tax evasion	Convicted, fined $10,000
26. Alfred F. Orsini	New Jersey	1962	Fixing traffic tickets	Suspended from bar for six months
27. Mark Rudich	New York	1939	Bail-bond fraud, bribery	Removed by appellate division of supreme court
28. Louis W. Kizas	Illinois	1967	Bail-bond fraud	Resigned, convicted, fined $15,000

JUDGE	STATE	DATE*	OFFENSES CHARGED	DISPOSITION
29. James E. Murphy	Illinois	1968	Bail-bond fraud	Found not guilty, complaint dismissed, still sitting
30. Michael M. D'Auria	New York	1970	Bribery, practicing law while a judge	Resigned
31. Henderson Graham	Michigan	1962	Exploiting probates for personal loans	Removed by legislature
32. Frank O. Alonzo	Alabama	1967	Collection agency fraud, extortion	Impeached and removed by legislature, permanently disbarred
33. John Lodwick, Jr.	Missouri	1968	Embezzlement, income tax evasion	Convicted on tax charge, sentenced to eight years prison
34. Aaron G. Windheim	New York	1972	Shoplifting	Grand jury investigation, resigned
35. Robert Maidman	New York	1972	Obstructing justice	Grand jury investigation pending, suspended

CHAPTER IV: THE SENSUOUS JUDGE

JUDGE	STATE	DATE*	OFFENSES CHARGED	DISPOSITION
36. Edward A. Haggerty, Sr.	Louisiana	1970	Pimping, procuring porno films, gambling	Found not guilty on criminal charges, removed by supreme court
37. Floyd S. Sarisohn	New York	1967	Moral turpitude, obstructing justice	Removed by appellate division of supreme court

JUDGE	STATE	DATE*	OFFENSES CHARGED	DISPOSITION
38. John D. Hasler	Missouri	1969	Emotional involvement with divorce litigant	Resigned, disbarred by supreme court
39. J. Allen O'Conner	Connecticut	1964	Sexual assault	Convicted, six months suspended sentence, disbarred
40. James H. Edgar	Michigan	1972	"Handling" female court employees	Censured, fined, resigned
41. James Lee Blodgett	Michigan	1972	"Handling" female court employees	Censured, fined, resigned

CHAPTER V: COURT JESTERS

JUDGE	STATE	DATE*	OFFENSES CHARGED	DISPOSITION
42. John Pickering	Federal (New Hampshire)	1804	Drunkenness, arbitrary abuse of authority	Impeached and removed by Congress
43. James H. Peck	Federal (Missouri)	1831	Arbitrary abuse of authority	Impeachment charges dismissed
44. Harold L. Louderback	Federal (California)	1932	Arbitrary abuse of authority, political favoritism	Impeachment charges dismissed
45. David Copland	Ohio	1940	Fraudulently gaining admittance to the bar, filing fabricated legal opinion	Disbarred and removed by supreme court

JUDGE	STATE	DATE*	OFFENSES CHARGED	DISPOSITION
46. Loren H. Hullinger, Jr.	Iowa	1971	Drunkenness, incompetency, arbitrary abuse of authority	Removed by supreme court
47. Howard W. McLaughlin	Iowa	1964	Arbitrary abuse of authority, padding expense account	Reprimanded by supreme court and reinstated
48. J. Miles Pound	Kentucky	1969	Drunkenness, armed while on the bench	No action taken

CHAPTER VI: THE CORRUPTORS

JUDGE	STATE	DATE*	OFFENSES CHARGED	DISPOSITION
49. Frank R. Franko	Ohio	1958	Used judicial position for personal political advancement	Suspended from practice of law indefinitely
50. Martin L. Pagliughi	New Jersey	1962	Voter registration fraud, improper political activity	Resigned, reprimanded
51. C. Woodrow Laughlin	Texas	1954	Obstructing justice	Removed by supreme court
52. Charles Swayne	Federal (Florida)	1904	Bribery, padding expense account	Impeachment charges dismissed

JUDGE	STATE	DATE*	OFFENSES CHARGED	DISPOSITION
53. Louis L. Friedman	New York	1963	Obstructing justice for family member, practicing law	Removed by Court on the Judiciary
54. Edwin L. Jenkins	Oregon	1966	Appointed relatives, sat on family cases	Suspended from bar for two years by supreme court
55. E. David Keiser	Pennsylvania	1971	Bribery, extortion, obstructing justice	Removed by supreme court, indicted by grand jury, died
56. L. D. Tallent	Oklahoma	1948	Liquor license fraud	Suspended from bar for two years
57. Melvin H. Osterman	New York	1964	Liquor license fraud	Removed by Court on Judiciary, convicted, sentenced to one year prison
58. Benjamin H. Schor	New York	1970	Liquor license fraud	Resigned, found not guilty at trial

CHAPTER VII: CURRENT BENCH-WARMERS

JUDGE	STATE	DATE*	OFFENSES CHARGED	DISPOSITION
59. Stephen S. Chandler	(Federal) (Oklahoma)	1965	Bias, incompetency, senility	Deprived of caseload by order of 10th Circuit Judicial Council, order rescinded, still sitting
60. Malcolm V. O'Hara	Louisiana	1968	Influence peddling, obstructing justice, practicing law	Removal charges dismissed

JUDGE	STATE	DATE*	OFFENSES CHARGED	DISPOSITION
61. Ernest J. Somers	Michigan	1971	Drunkenness, delegating authority to court clerk	Censured by supreme court, still sitting
62. Neville Tucker	Kentucky	1970	Income tax evasion	Convicted, six months suspended sentence and fined $500, still sitting
63. Bernard Klieger	New York	1972	Fraudulent political campaign-fund scheme	Found not guilty, still sitting
64. Ross J. DiLorenzo	New York	1972	Influence peddling	Censured by appellate division of supreme court, still sitting
65. William F. Suglia	New York	1971	Improperly influenced by woman whose son was before him on criminal charges	Censured by appellate division of supreme court, still sitting
66. Bernard B. Glickfield	California	1971	Verbal abuse of rape victim	Censored by supreme court, still sitting
67. Leland W. Geiler	California	1973	Prodding public defender with a dildo, foul language in court	Suspended pending action by supreme court on recommendation of removal by Judicial Qualifications Committee

CHAPTER VIII: THE CHICAGO THREE

68. Roy J. Solfisburg	Illinois	1969	Bribery	Resigned

277

JUDGE	STATE	DATE*	OFFENSES CHARGED	DISPOSITION
69. Ray I. Klingbiel	Illinois	1969	Bribery	Resigned
70. Otto Kerner	Illinois	1973	Bribery, conspiracy, mail fraud, perjury, income tax evasion	Convicted, sentence still pending

CHAPTER IX: ARTICLE I, SECTION III

JUDGE	STATE	DATE*	OFFENSES CHARGED	DISPOSITION
71. Samuel Chase	Supreme Court	1804	Arbitrary abuse of authority, political bias	Impeachment charges dismissed
72. Abe Fortas	Supreme Court	1969	Questionable conflict of interest	Resigned
73. William O. Douglas	Supreme Court	1970	Questionable conflict of interest, advocating "revolution"	No evidence to support impeachment charges

CHAPTER X: PLAYING MUSICAL JUDGES

JUDGE	STATE	DATE*	OFFENSES CHARGED	DISPOSITION
74. Francis X. Morrissey	Massachusetts	1965	Ruled "not qualified"	Presidential nomination withdrawn

Appendix II
Canons of Judicial Ethics

Many states have adopted this abbreviated version of the Judicial Canons recommended by the American Bar Association.

Included with the rules are these "ancient precedents" which are used as references. Note the last distinguished source. The Bar Association evidently did not get around to deleting Bacon's *Essays* in light of his political demise, as set forth in the prologue of this book.

And I charged your judges at that time, saying Hear the causes between your brethren, and judge righteously between every man and his brother, and the stranger that is with him.

Ye shall not respect persons in judgment; but ye shall hear the small as well as the great; ye shall not be afraid of the face of man; for the judgment is God's; and the cause that is too hard for you, bring it unto me, and I will hear it.
Deuteronomy 1:16-17

Thou shalt not wrest judgment; thou shalt not respect persons, neither take a gift; for a gift doth blind the eyes of the wise, and pervert the words of the righteous.
Deuteronomy 16:19

We will not make any justiciaries, constables, sheriffs or bailiffs, but from those who understand the law of the realm and are well disposed to observe it.
Magna Charta, XLV.

Judges ought to remember that their office is *jus dicere* not *jus dare;* to interpret law, and not to make law, or give law.

Judges ought to be more learned than witty; more reverend than plausible; and more advised than confident. Above all things, integrity is their portion and proper virtue.

Patience and gravity of hearing is an essential part of justice; and an over speaking judge is no well-tuned cymbal. It is no grace to a judge first to find that which he might have heard in due time from the Bar, or to show quickness of conceit in cutting off evidence or counsel too short; or to present information by questions though pertinent.

The place of justice is a hallowed place; and therefore not only the Bench, but the foot pace and precincts and purpose thereof ought to be preserved without scandal and corruption.
"Of Judicature," Sir Francis Bacon.

RELATIONS OF THE JUDICIARY

The assumption of the office of judge casts upon the incumbent duties in respect to his personal conduct which concern his relation to the state and its inhabitants, the litigants before him, the principles of law, the practitioners of law in his court, and the witnesses, jurors and attendants who aid him in the administration of its functions.

THE PUBLIC INTEREST

Courts exist to promote justice, and thus to serve the public interest. Their administration should be speedy and careful. Every judge should at all times be alert in his rulings and in the conduct of the business of the court, so far as he can, to make it useful to litigants and to the community. He should avoid unconsciously falling into the attitude of mind that the litigants are made for the courts instead of the courts for the litigants.

CONSTITUTIONAL OBLIGATIONS

It is the duty of all judges in the United States to support the federal Constitution and that of the state whose laws they administer; in so doing, they should fearlessly observe and apply fundamental limitations and guarantees.

AVOIDANCE OF IMPROPRIETY

A judge's official conduct should be free from impropriety and the appearance of impropriety; he should avoid infractions of law; and his personal behavior, not only upon the Bench and in the performance of judicial duties, but also in his everyday life, should be beyond reproach.

ESSENTIAL CONDUCT

A judge should be temperate, attentive, patient, impartial, and, since he is to administer the law and apply it to the facts, he should be studious of the principles of the law and diligent in endeavoring to ascertain the facts.

INDUSTRY

A judge should exhibit an industry and application commensurate with the duties imposed upon him.

PROMPTNESS

A judge should be prompt in the performance of his judicial duties, recognizing that the time of litigants, jurors and attorneys is of value and that habitual lack of punctuality on his part justifies dissatisfaction with the administration of the business of the court.

COURT ORGANIZATION

A judge should organize the court with a view to the prompt and convenient dispatch of its business and he should not tolerate abuses and neglect by clerks, and other assistants who are sometimes prone to presume too much upon his good natured acquiescence by reason of friendly association with him.

It is desirable, too, where the judicial system permits, that he should cooperate with other judges of the same court, and in other courts, as members of a single judicial system, to promote the more satisfactory administration of justice.

CONSIDERATION FOR JURORS AND OTHERS

A judge should be considerate of jurors, witnesses and others in attendance upon the court.

COURTESY AND CIVILITY

A judge should be courteous to counsel, especially to those who are young and inexperienced, and also to all others appearing or concerned in the administration of justice in the court.

He should also require, and so far as his power extends, enforce on the part of clerks, court officers and counsel civility and courtesy to the court and to jurors, witnesses, litigants and others having business in the court.

UNPROFESSIONAL CONDUCT OF ATTORNEYS AND COUNSEL

A judge should utilize his opportunities to criticize and correct unprofessional conduct of attorneys and counsellors, brought to his attention; and, if adverse comment is not a sufficient corrective, should send the matter at once to the proper investigating and disciplinary authorities.

APPOINTEES OF THE JUDICIARY AND THEIR COMPENSATION

Trustees, receivers, masters, referees, guardians and other persons appointed by a judge to aid in the administration of justice should have the strictest probity and impartiality and should be selected with a view solely to their character and fitness. The power of making such appointments should not be exercised by him for personal or partisan advantage. He should not permit his appointments to be controlled by others than himself. He should also avoid nepotism and undue favoritism in his appointments.

While not hesitating to fix or approve just amounts, he should be most scrupulous in granting or approving compensation for the services or charges of such appointees to avoid excessive allowances, whether or not excepted to or complained of. He cannot rid himself of this responsibility by the consent of counsel.

KINSHIP OR INFLUENCE

A judge should not act in a controversy where a near relative is a party; he should not suffer his conduct to justify the impression that any person can improperly influence him or unduly enjoy his favor, or that he is affected by the kinship, rank, position or influence of any party or other person.

INDEPENDENCE

A judge should not be swayed by partisan demands, public clamor or considerations of personal popularity or notoriety, nor be apprehensive of unjust criticism.

INTERFERENCE IN CONDUCT OF TRIAL

A judge may properly intervene in a trial of a case to promote expedition, and prevent unnecessary waste of time, or to clear up some obscurity, but he should bear in mind that his undue interference, impatience, or participation in the examination of witnesses, or a severe attitude on his part toward witnesses, especially those who are excited or terrified by the unusual circumstances of a trial, may tend to prevent the proper presentation of the cause, or the ascertainment of the truth in respect thereto.

Conversation between the judge and counsel in court is often necessary, but the judge should be studious to avoid controversies which are apt to obscure the merits of the dispute between litigants and lead to its unjust disposition. In addressing counsel, litigants, or witnesses, he should avoid a controversial manner or tone.

He should avoid interruptions of counsel in their arguments except to clarify his mind as to their positions, and he should not be tempted to the unnecessary display of learning or a premature judgment.

EX PARTE APPLICATIONS

A judge should discourage *ex parte* hearings of applications for injunctions and receiverships where the order may work detriment to absent parties; he should act upon such *ex parte* applications only where the necessity for quick action is clearly shown; if this be demonstrated, then he should endeavor to counteract the effect of the absence of opposing counsel by a scrupulous cross-examination and investigation as to the facts and the principles of law on which the application is based, granting relief only when fully satisfied that the law permits it and the emergency demands it. He should remember that an injunction is a limitation upon the freedom of action of defendants and should not be granted lightly or inadvisedly. One applying for such relief must sustain the burden of showing clearly its necessity and this burden is increased in the absence of the party whose freedom of action is sought to be restrained even though only temporarily.

EX PARTE COMMUNICATIONS

A judge should not permit private interviews, arguments or communications designed to influence his judicial action, where interests to be affected thereby are not represented before him, except in cases where provision is made by law for *ex parte* application.

While the conditions under which briefs of argument are to be received are largely matters of local rule or practice, he should not permit the contents of such brief presented to him to be concealed from opposing counsel. Ordinarily all communications of counsel to the judge intended or calculated to influence action should be made known to opposing counsel.

CONTINUANCES

Delay in the administration of justice is a common cause of complaint; counsel are frequently responsible for this delay. A judge, without being arbitrary or forcing cases unreasonably or unjustly to trial when unprepared, to the detriment of parties, may well endeavor to hold counsel to a proper appreciation of their duties to the public interest, to their own clients, and to the adverse party and his counsel, so as to enforce due diligence in the dispatch of business before the court.

JUDICIAL OPINIONS

In disposing of controverted cases, a judge should indicate the reasons for his action in an opinion showing that he has not disregarded or overlooked serious arguments of counsel. He thus shows his full understanding of the case, avoids the suspicion of arbitrary conclusion, promotes confidence in his intellectual integrity and may contribute useful precedent to the growth of the law.

It is desirable that appellate courts in reversing cases and granting new trials should so indicate their views on questions of law argued before them and necessarily arising in the controversy that upon the new trial counsel may be aided to avoid the repetition of erroneous positions of law and shall not be left in doubt by the failure of the court to decide such questions.

But the volume of reported decisions is such and is so rapidly increasing that in writing opinions which are to be published, judges may well take this fact into consideration, and curtail them accordingly, without substantially departing from the principles stated above.

It is of high importance that judges constituting a court of last resort should use effort and self-restraint to promote solidarity of conclusion and the consequent influence of judicial decision. A judge should not yield to pride of opinion or value more highly his individual reputation than that of the court to which he should be loyal. Except in case of conscientious difference of opinion on fundamental principle, dissenting opinions should be discouraged in courts of last resort.

INFLUENCE OF DECISIONS UPON THE DEVELOPMENT OF THE LAW

A judge should be mindful that his duty is the application

of general law to particular instances, that ours is a government of law and not of men, and that he violates his duty as a minister of justice under such a system if he seeks to do what he may personally consider substantial justice in a particular case and disregards the general law as he knows it to be binding on him. Such action may become a precedent unsettling accepted principles and may have detrimental consequences beyond the immediate controversy. He should administer his office with a due regard to the integrity of the system of the law itself, remembering that he is not a depository of arbitrary power, but a judge under the sanction of law.

IDIOSYNCRASIES AND INCONSISTENCIES

Justice should not be moulded by the individual idiosyncrasies of those who administer it. A judge should adopt the usual and expected method of doing justice, and not seek to be extreme or peculiar in his judgments, or spectacular or sensational in the conduct of the court. Though vested with discretion in the imposition of mild or severe sentences he should not compel persons brought before him to submit to some humiliating act or discipline of his own devision, without authority of law, because he thinks it will have a beneficial corrective influence.

In imposing sentence he should endeavor to conform to a reasonable standard of punishment and should not seek popularity or publicity either by exceptional severity or undue leniency.

REVIEW

In order that a litigant may secure the full benefit of the right of review accorded to him by law, a trial judge should scrupulously grant to the defeated party opportunity to present the questions arising upon the trial exactly as they arose, were presented, and decided, by a full and fair transcript of the record; any failure in this regard on the part of the judge is peculiarly worthy of condemnation because the wrong done may be irremediable.

LEGISLATION AND RULES

A judge has an exceptional opportunity to observe the operation of rules and statutes, especially those relating to practice, and to ascertain whether they tend to impede the just disposition of controversies; and he may contribute substantially to the public interest by communicating the results of his observation and experience to those who have authority to remedy such defects.

INCONSISTENT OBLIGATIONS

A judge should not accept inconsistent duties; nor incur obligations, pecuniary or otherwise, which will in any way interfere or appear to interfere with his devotion to the expeditious and proper administration of his official functions.

BUSINESS PROMOTIONS AND SOLICITATIONS FOR CHARITY

A judge should avoid giving ground for any reasonable suspicion that he is utilizing the power or prestige of his office to persuade or coerce others to patronize or contribute, either to the success of private business ventures, or to charitable enterprises. He should, therefore, not enter into such private business, or pursue such a course of conduct, as would justify such suspicion, nor use the power of his office or the influence of his name to promote the business interests of others; he should not solicit for charities, nor should he enter into any business relation which, in the normal course of events reasonably to be expected, might bring his personal interest into conflict with the impartial performance of his official duties.

PERSONAL INVESTMENTS AND RELATIONS

A judge should abstain from making personal investments in enterprises which are apt to be involved in litigation in the court; and, after his accession to the Bench, he should not retain such investments previously made, longer than a period sufficient to enable him to dispose of them without serious loss. It is desirable that he should, so far as reasonably possible, refrain from all relations which would normally tend to arouse the suspicion that such relations warp or bias his judgment, or prevent his impartial attitude of mind in the administration of his judicial duties.

He should not utilize information coming to him in a judicial capacity for purposes of speculation; and it detracts from the public confidence in his integrity and the soundness of his judicial judgment for him at any time to become a speculative investor upon the hazard of a margin.

EXECUTORSHIPS AND TRUSTEESHIPS

While a judge is not disqualified from holding executorships or trusteeships, he should not accept or continue to hold any fiduciary or other position if the holding of it would interfere or seem to interfere with the proper performance of his judicial duties, or if the business interests of those represented require investments in enterprises that are apt to come before him judicially, or to be involved in questions of law to be determined by him.

PARTISAN POLITICS

While entitled to entertain his personal views of political questions, and while not required to surrender his rights or opinions as a citizen, it is inevitable that suspicion of being warped by political bias will attach to a judge who becomes the active promoter of the interests of one political party as against another. He should avoid making political speeches, making or soliciting payment of assessments or contributions to party funds, the public endorsement of candidates for political office and participation in party conventions.

He should neither accept nor retain a place on any party committee nor act as party leader, nor engage generally in partisan activities.

Where, however, it is necessary for judges to be nominated and elected as candidates of a political party, nothing herein contained shall prevent the judge from attending or speaking at political gatherings, or from making contributions to the campaign funds of the party that has nominated him and seeks his election or re-election.

291

SELF-INTEREST

A judge should abstain from performing or taking part in any judicial act in which his personal interests are involved. If he has personal litigation in the court of which he is judge, he need not resign his judgeship on that account, but he should, of course, refrain from any judicial act in such a controversy.

CANDIDACY FOR OFFICE

A candidate for judicial position should not make or suffer others to make for him, promises of conduct in office which appeal to the cupidity or prejudices of the appointing or electing power; he should not announce in advance his conclusions of law on disputed issues to secure class support, and he should do nothing while a candidate to create the impression that if chosen, he will administer his office with bias, partiality or improper discrimination.

While holding a judicial position he should not become an active candidate either at a party primary or at a general election for any office other than a judicial office. If a judge should decide to become a candidate for any office not judicial, he should resign in order that it cannot be said that he is using the power or prestige of his judicial position to promote his own candidacy or the success of his party.

If a judge becomes a candidate for any judicial office, he should refrain from all conduct which might tend to arouse reasonable suspicion that he is using the power or prestige of his judicial position to promote his candidacy or the success of his party.

He should not permit others to do anything in behalf of his candidacy which would reasonably lead to such suspicion.

PRIVATE LAW PRACTICE

No judge of any court except municipal corporation courts shall receive any compensation for any public service other than his salary as a judge, or practice law or do law business. A judge who is permitted to practice law is in a position of great delicacy and must be scrupulously careful to avoid conduct in his practice whereby he utilizes or seems to utilize his judicial position to further his professional success. He should not practice in the court in which he is a judge, even when presided over by another judge, or appear therein for himself in any controversy.

If forbidden to practice law, a judge should refrain from accepting any professional employment while in office. He may properly lecture upon or instruct in law, or write upon the subject, and accept compensation therefor, if such course does not interfere with the due performance of his judicial duties, and is not forbidden by some positive provision of law.

GIFTS AND FAVORS

A judge should not accept any presents or favors from litigants, or from lawyers practicing before him or from others whose interests are likely to be submitted to him for judgment.

SOCIAL RELATIONS

It is not necessary to the proper performance of judicial duty that a judge should live in retirement or seclusion; it is desirable that, so far as reasonable attention to the comple-tion of his work will permit, he continue to mingle in social intercourse, and that he should not discontinue his interest in or appearance at meetings of members of the Bar. He should, however, in pending or prospective litigation before him be particularly careful to avoid such action as may reasonably tend to awaken the suspicion that his social or business relations or friendships constitute an element in influencing his judicial conduct.

A SUMMARY OF JUDICIAL OBLIGATION

In every particular his conduct should be above reproach. He should be conscientious, studious, thorough, courteous, patient, punctual, just, impartial, fearless of public clamor, regardless of public praise, and indifferent to private, political or partisan influences; he should administer justice according to law, and deal with his appointments as a public trust; he should not allow other affairs or his private interests to interfere with the prompt and proper performance of his judicial duties, nor should he administer the office for the purpose of advancing his personal ambitions or increasing his popularity.

IMPROPER PUBLICIZING OF COURT PROCEEDINGS

Proceedings in court should be conducted with fitting dignity and decorum. The taking of photographs in the courtroom, during sessions of the court or recesses between sessions, and the broadcasting or televising of court proceedings detract from the essential dignity of the proceedings, distract participants and witnesses in giving testimony, and create misconceptions with respect thereto in the mind of the public and should not be permitted.

Provided that this restriction shall not apply to the broadcasting or televising, under the supervision of the court, of such portions of naturalization proceedings (other than the interrogation of applicants) as are designed and carried out exclusively as a ceremony for the purpose of publicly demonstrating in an impressive manner the essential dignity and the serious nature of naturalization.

CONDUCT OF COURT PROCEEDINGS

Proceedings in court should be so conducted as to reflect the importance and seriousness of the inquiry to ascertain the truth.

The oath should be administered to witnesses in a manner calculated to impress them with the importance and solemnity of their promise to adhere to the truth. Each witness should be sworn separately and impressively at the bar or the court, and the clerk should be required to make a formal record of the administration of the oath, including the name of the witness.

GENERAL PURPOSES AND DEFINITIONS

These Canons of Judicial Ethics are adopted in the belief that the character and conduct of a judge is of the utmost importance in the administration of justice and should be a matter of primary concern; and that established ethical standards tend to become habits of life. The enumeration of particular duties should not be construed as a denial of the existence of others equally imperative though not specifically mentioned. The term judge or judges includes commissioners of appellate courts, magistrates and others exercising judicial powers.

Appendix III
Articles of Impeachment
of Sir Francis Bacon, Lord Chancellor

500 pounds 1. In the cause between Sir Rowland Egerton and Edward Egerton, the Lord Chancellor received five hundred pounds on the part of Sir Rowland Egerton, before he decreed the cause.

400 pounds 2. In the same cause he received from Edward Egerton four hundred pounds.

50 pounds   3. In the cause between Hodie and Hodye, he received a dozen of buttons of the value of fifty pounds about a fortnight after the cause was ended.

310 pounds   4. In the cause between the Lady Wharton and the co-heirs of Sir Francis Willoughby, he received of the Lady Wharton three hundred and ten pounds.

110 pounds   5. In Sir Thomas Monk's cause, he received from Sir Thomas Monk, by the hands of Sir Henry Helmes, an hundred and ten pounds; but this was three quarters of a year after the suit was ended.

100 pounds   6. In the cause between Sir John Treavor and Ascue, he received on the part of Sir John Treavor an hundred pounds.

100 pounds   7. In the cause between Holman and Yong, he received of Yong an hundred pounds after the decree made for him.

160 pounds   8. In the cause between Fisher and Wrenham, the Lord Chancellor, after the decree passed, received from Fisher a suit of hangings worth an hundred and sixty pounds and better, which Fisher gave by advice of Mr. Shute.

800 pounds   9. In the cause between Kenneday and Vanlore, he received a rich cabinet from Kenneday, prized at eight hundred pounds.

2,000 pounds   10. He borrowed of Vanlore a thousand pounds upon his own bond at one time, and the like sum at another time, upon his lordship's own bill, subscribed by Mr. Hunt, his man.

200 pounds   11. He received of Richard Scott two hundred pounds after his cause was decreed (but upon a precedent promise), all which was transacted by Mr. Shute.

100 pounds   12. He received in the same cause, on the part of Sir John Lentall, an hundred pounds.

100 pounds   13. He received of Mr. Wroth an hundred pounds in respect of the cause between him and Sir Arthur Mainwaring.

500 pounds   14. He received of Sir Ralph Hansby, having a cause depending before him, five hundred pounds.

900 pounds   15. William Compton being to have an extent for a debt of one thousand and two hundred pounds, the Lord Chancellor stayed it, and wrote his letter, upon which part of the debt was paid presently, and part at a future day. The Lord Chancellor hereupon sends to borrow five hundred pounds; and because Compton was to pay four hundred pounds to one Huxley, his Lordship requires Huxley to forbear it six months, and thereupon obtains the money

from Compton. The money being unpaid, suit grows between Huxley and Compton in Chancery, where his Lordship decrees Compton to pay Huxley the debt, with damages and costs, when it was in his own hands.

100 pounds 16. In the cause between Sir William Bruncker and Awbrey, the Lord Chancellor received from Awbrey an hundred pounds.

700 pounds 17. In the Lord Montague's cause, he received from the Lord Montague six or seven hundred pounds; and more was to be paid at the ending of the cause.

200 pounds 18. In the cause of Mr. Dunch, he received from Mr. Dunch two hundred pounds.

800 pounds 19. In the cause between Reynell and Peacock, he received from Reynell two hundred pounds, and a diamond ring worth five or six hundred pounds.

1,100 pounds 20. He took of Peacock an hundred pounds, and borrowed a thousand pounds, without interest, security, or time of payment.

200 pounds 21. In the cause between Smithwick and Wich, he received from Smithwick two hundred pounds, which was repaid.

300 pounds 22. In the cause of Sir Henry Ruswell, he received money from Ruswell; but it is not certain how much.

700 pounds 23. In the cause of Mr. Barker, the Lord Chancellor received from Barker seven hundred pounds.

800 pounds 24,25,26. The four and twentieth, there being a reference from his Majesty to his Lordship of a business between the grocer and the apothecaries, the Lord Chancellor received of the grocers two hundred pounds. The five and twentieth article: In the same cause, he received of the apothecaries that stood with the grocers, a taster of gold worth between 400 and 500 pounds, and a present of ambergrease. And the six and twentieth article: He received of the new company of the apothecaries that stood against the grocers, an hundred pounds.

1,000 pounds 27. He took of the French merchants a thousand pounds, to constrain the vintners of London to take from them fifteen hundred tons of wine; to accomplish which, he used very indirect means by color of his office and authority, without bill or suit depending; terrifying the vintners by threats and imprisonments of their persons, to buy wines whereof they had no need nor use, at higher rates than they were vendible.

28. The Lord Chancellor hath given way to great exactions by his servants, both in respect of private seals, and otherwise for sealing of injunctions.

12,230 pounds Total

Appendix IV
Retirement
and Removal of State Judges

State	Mandatory Retirement	Removal Procedure
Alabama	No	Impeachment of supreme court justices. All other judges can be removed from office by the supreme court under its regulations.
Alaska	Yes (70)	Impeachment. Commission on Judicial Qualifications.

State	Mandatory Retirement	Removal Procedure
Arizona	No	Impeachment. Recall. Commission on Judicial Qualifications.
Arkansas	Yes (70)	Impeachment and address.
California	Yes (70)	Commission. Impeachment.
Colorado	Yes (72)	Impeachment (except county judges and justices of the peace). Commission on Judicial Qualifications. Supreme court can order removal upon felony or offense of moral turpitude.
Connecticut	Yes (72)	Impeachment. Judicial Review Council recommends impeachment.
Delaware	No	Impeachment. Court on the Judiciary. Removal by governor.
Florida	Yes (70)	Impeachment. Judicial Qualifications Commission.

State	Mandatory Retirement	Removal Procedure
Georgia	No	Impeachment.
Hawaii	Yes (70)	Impeachment. Board of Judicial Removal. Commission for Judicial Qualifications.
Idaho	Yes (70)	Impeachment. Judicial Council Commission
Illinois	Yes (70)	Impeachment. Removal. Courts Commission.
Indiana	No	Impeachment by supreme court.
Iowa	Yes (72)	Impeachment. Special court.
Kansas	Yes (70)	Impeachment. Removal.
Kentucky	No	Impeachment. Address. Removal.
Louisiana	Yes (75)	Impeachment. Address.

State	*Mandatory Retirement*	*Removal Procedure*
		Removal by the supreme court. Judiciary Commission.
Maine	Yes (71)	Impeachment and address.
Maryland	Yes (70)	Removal by governor upon conviction of high crime or upon impeachment. Commission with removal by the state assembly.
Massachusetts	No	Impeachment and address.
Michigan	Yes (70)	Impeachment. Removal by supreme court upon recommendation of Judicial Tenure Commission.
Minnesota	No	Impeachment. Removal by the governor.
Mississippi	No	Impeachment. Removal.
Missouri	No	Impeachment. Commission on Retirement, Removal and Discipline.
Montana	Yes (70)	Impeachment.

State	Mandatory Retirement	Removal Procedure
Nebraska	Yes (70)	Impeachment. Commission.
Nevada	No	Impeachment.
New Hampshire	Yes (70)	Address.
New Jersey	Yes (70)	Removal by supreme court. Impeachment.
New Mexico	No	Impeachment. Judicial Standards Commission.
New York	Yes (70-76)	Impeachment. Court on the Judiciary. Removal by resolution of the legislature.
North Carolina	Yes (70)	Impeachment. Removal. Inferior court judges can be removed by superior court.
North Dakota	No	Impeachment and removal. Removal by impeachment. Removal by judicial proceedings. Removal by governor.

State	Mandatory Retirement	Removal Procedure
Ohio	No	Impeachment.
Oklahoma	No	Court on the Judiciary. Impeachment.
Oregon	Yes (75)	Removal. Commission on Judicial Fitness.
Pennsylvania	No	Impeachment.
Rhode Island	No	Impeachment.
South Carolina	Yes (72)	Impeachment.
South Dakota	No	Impeachment (except county judges who are subject to removal by the governor.
Tennessee	No	Impeachment.
Texas	Yes (75)	Impeachment. Address. Judicial Qualifications Commission. Removal of district judges by supreme court.

State	Mandatory Retirement	Removal Procedure
Utah	No	Impeachment. Commission on Judicial Qualifications. Board of Commissioners of the state bar association.
Vermont	Yes (70)	Impeachment. Committee of the Judiciary (commission).
Virginia	Yes (70-75)	Impeachment. Judicial Inquiry and Review Commission.
Washington	Yes (75)	Impeachment. Removal.
West Virginia	No	Impeachment.
Wisconsin	Yes (70)	Impeachment. Address.
Wyoming	No	Impeachment. Removal.